Also by Giuliano Hazan

Every Night Italian
The Classic Pasta Cookbook

HOW TO
COOK
ITALIAN

Giuliano Hazan

Photographs by Dana Gallagher

Illustrations by Laura Hartman Maestro

SCRIBNER

New York London Toronto Sydney

SCRIBNER
1230 Avenue of the Americas
New York, NY 10020

SCRIBNER and design are trademarks of Macmillan Library Reference USA, Inc.,
used under license by Simon & Schuster, the publisher of this work.

For information about special discounts for bulk purchases,
please contact Simon & Schuster Special Sales:
1-800-456-6798 or business@simonandschuster.com

DESIGNED BY ERICH HOBBING

Text set in Berthold Akzidenz Grotesk

Manufactured in the United States of America

1   3   5   7   9   10   8   6   4   2

Library of Congress Control Number: 2005051567

ISBN-13: 978-0-7432-4436-7
ISBN-10: 0-7432-4436-2

For Gabriella,
la mia piccola buongustaia

CONTENTS

Italy

VALLE D'AOSTA

ALTO ADIGE
Bolzano
TRENTINO
Trento
FRIULI
Trieste

Como
Milan
VENETO
Verona
Padua
Venice
LOMBARDY
Mantua

Turin
Asti
PIEDMONT
Parma
Ferrara
Modena
Bologna
EMILIA-ROMAGNA
LIGURIA
Genoa
Cesenatico

Pisa
Florence
MARCHES
Ancona
Siena
Perugia
TUSCANY
UMBRIA

Adriatic Sea

N
W   E
S

Ligurian Sea

LATIUM
ABRUZZI
MOLISE
Rome
Foggia
Bari
APULIA

Tyrrhenian Sea

Olbia
Caserta
Avellino
Naples
CAMPANIA
BASILICATA
Salerno

SARDINIA

Mediterranean Sea

Palermo
Messina
CALABRIA
Reggio di Calabria

SICILY

Agrigento

Ionian Sea

PREFACE

This book is about how I cook Italian food at home. It's about how I shop, how I organize myself in the kitchen, and what kind of tools and equipment I like to use. The food in this book is inspired by what I grew up eating at home and learned to cook once I left home because I missed the food I was used to. It's also inspired by dishes I have eaten in homes and restaurants while traveling in Italy. Although it may seem odd to find recipes for home cooking in restaurants, eating in restaurants in Italy is often like eating in someone's home. In fact, one of the best compliments a restaurant can receive is that its food is as good as homemade. Some of the best food I've had has been in simple family-run trattorias.

The dishes I brought back from Italy are those with simple, genuine flavors that highlight the ingredients used. Like *Burrida*—pan-roasted fish with garlic, rosemary, and red wine vinegar—a dish that fishermen on Friuli's coast once made with fresh, but damaged fish they could not sell. Or the Ligurian seafood salad with pistachios that a customer taught to her favorite restaurant. And the almost magical restorative powers of the artichoke and potato soup our Sardinian friend Rita welcomed us with when we arrived at her inn late one night totally exhausted. This is the kind of food that characterizes Italian cooking best. It's food whose flavors are direct and genuine, unburdened by overly complex preparations and long ingredient lists. Italian food does not hem and haw; it asserts itself proudly. If it were a painting, it would not be made of varying shades of beige but of the vibrant colors one sees on the houses in so many Italian towns.

Italian food is also incredibly varied and speaks clearly of the region from which it comes, much like its inhabitants' accent. Northern Italy's wealth is expressed in its food, for example, with its use of butter, cream, veal, and white truffles. As you move farther south the land becomes more mountainous and you'll see more dependence on olive oil and sheep and goats rather than cattle and dairy products. Although the south's ingredients may not be as rich, its flavors unquestionably are.

No matter where you are in Italy, meals have a certain rhythm. Instead of an appetizer and main course, a typical Italian meal consists of a first and second course that are equal in portion size. The first course (*il primo*) is more than an appetizer and is a pasta, risotto, or soup. The second course (*il secondo*) is a smaller portion than a main course and is a meat or fish dish, usually accompanied by a vegetable. A special-occasion meal might begin with an antipasto and include a cheese course followed by dessert. A less formal everyday meal might end with fresh fruit, served as is, or perhaps sliced and marinated.

Each time I returned home to Sarasota, Florida, I sifted through all those notes I took and began the task of re-creating the dishes I enjoyed most. Reading my notes I considered how to produce the flavors I remembered with the ingredients I had available from our local supermarket and a few specialty food shops. The process of getting from an idea and taste memory to finished recipe goes something like this: I cook a dish, taking meticulous notes of everything I do, and then my family eats it. We decide if it needs some changes, if it's worth pursuing, or if it's perfect the way it is. If changes are necessary, I retest until we're happy. It is a slow process, with many rejects, but the dishes that made the final cut are the ones that gave us the most pleasure and were the best suited to being cooked an ocean away from their origin.

Some of the recipes here are the result of inspirations that came about at the market or simply staring into the refrigerator wondering what I was going to make for dinner. But they are all dishes that use an Italian approach. Using different ingredients than one finds in Italy does not make a dish less Italian. Tomatoes, after all, were not indigenous to Italy and started being used only after they were brought back from the New World. Yet now we think of tomatoes as being intrinsic to Italian food.

So what is it that makes a dish Italian? Learning a particular cuisine is a little like learning its language. You must learn its syntax and idiomatic expressions before you are able to express yourself fully. You could think of Italian cooking as using some basic building blocks that can be put together in a variety of ways. To begin with you must decide whether the dish will be made with olive oil or butter. Pretty much anything you cook will begin with one or the other. Which one you use will depend on the flavors of the subsequent building blocks. Butter is used when the overall flavors of the dish are delicate and mild. Onions will almost always follow but rarely garlic, because the flavor of butter and garlic is not idiomatic to the Italian palate. Veal is happiest with butter and rarely seen with olive oil, but you'll almost always use olive oil with more boldly flavored meats such as lamb. Garlic and onions are equally well suited to olive oil, and there are certain vegetables, such as eggplant and artichokes, that taste more Italian when they are cooked with olive oil rather than butter. Fish is almost exclusively prepared with olive oil. In part, it is flavor combinations like these that make a dish Italian. In French cuisine, for example, the pairing of butter and fish is very common. What also makes a dish Italian is that sauces enhance the flavor of what they are saucing and never obfuscate it. Last, but certainly not least, Italian cooking is about using what's fresh and locally available whenever possible.

Cooking without eating is a pointless exercise, and Italians love to cook because they love to eat. Because we love to eat we like to take our time doing it, and it's important to do it together with our families. Family mealtimes are sacred in Italy. In America, today's harried lifestyle and busy schedules leave little time for the table. The need to make time to eat together as a family is more important than ever. It allows for conversation and strengthens the family bond. Cooking for one's family is an act of love and nurturing. The food we prepare for our family and the memories connected with it are an important legacy we pass on to the next generation. After all, some of our most powerful childhood memories are connected to food.

Cooking at home on a regular basis need not be a difficult task. With some planning and organization it takes little time. The majority of the recipes in this book take less than an hour to make and many can be prepared in little more than thirty minutes. The key to working quickly and easily in the kitchen is to work efficiently. Over the years I have refined my recipe writing style, giving step-by-step instructions in the sequence that is most efficient. For example, all the ingredients need not be chopped, diced, and peeled before you start cooking: While onions sauté, tomatoes can be peeled. While greens are boiled, garlic can be chopped. While the chicken browns, the vegetables that go with it can be peeled and cut. Some dishes that require longer cooking times but only occasional supervision can be done while you do other things around the house. Many of these dishes will keep well for several days and are ideal for those days when reheating something is all there is time for.

If you are one of those people who shops for food daily that's wonderful, but if you plan your meals for a whole week, this book is for you too. The chapter on how to stock an Italian pantry tells you what to have on hand so you can always whip up a great meal at a moment's notice. You'll learn about the key ingredients of Italian cooking and what to look for when buying them. A chapter on equipping the Italian kitchen describes what pots and pans, knives, and utensils to have on hand and how to use them. I've also included a chapter that describes the basics of Italian cooking techniques, such as sautéing, braising, and pan roasting.

I hope all this will help make cooking great Italian food at home easier and that you will enjoy sharing the food in this book with your family as much as I have with mine. *Buon appetito!*

Giuliano Hazan

Sarasota, Florida

January 2005

HOW TO COOK

ITALIAN

MY KITCHEN

The right tools and equipment make all the difference in cooking just as they do in any other craft. What is "right" or "wrong" can be rather subjective, however, so I will tell you what works for me. I hope you will find some useful ideas to apply to your kitchen as well.

Oven and Cooktop

Up until a few years ago all my oven did was bake or broil, and somehow I managed to get along fine. When I needed to brown something quickly, I used the broiler; the rest of the time I baked. Most of the new ovens give you the choice of using convection baking and pure convection in addition to baking and broiling. I have discovered that convection heat can be quite useful. The difference is that regular baking uses radiant heat, whereas convection cooking uses a fan that circulates the hot air. Circulating heat tends to cook the surface of foods faster, while radiant heat penetrates foods more. Thus regular baking cooks foods through more evenly, while convection baking is great for browning and making things crisp. For example, to roast a chicken I roast it first on the regular bake setting to cook the center, and then I finish it with convection heat to make the skin deliciously crispy. Similarly, cakes are better baked because you don't want them browned, but breads come out better with convection heat. Since circulating hot air intensifies heat, if I cook something in a regular oven that calls for convection heat, I raise the heat by 25° to compensate.

I personally prefer cooking on a gas cooktop instead of electric. The immediacy of turning on or off a gas burner and the ability to actually see how high a flame is makes gas the cooktop of choice for me. Electric cooktops have come a long way from the electric coils that I made do with for many years before I had a gas stove, and some people do prefer cooking on electric. If you use an electric stove, you may find that pans take a little longer to heat, and when a recipe calls for lowering the heat, you may need to move the pan off the burner until its temperature adjusts.

Cookware

Your pots and pans should conduct heat to food evenly throughout the pan. Since Italian cooking is so dependent on stovetop cooking, use pans that allow you to sauté without burning and that do not have hot spots so that a risotto can cook evenly, for example. Aluminum is an excellent conductor of heat, but it is soft and reacts to acidic foods, so the aluminum either must be encased in stainless steel, which is more scratch resistant and nonreactive to acidic foods, or it must be hard anodized. I have found hard-anodized aluminum one of the best surfaces for Italian cooking. The food makes direct contact with the conductive metal, optimizing its ability to sear food and allowing the juices to caramelize on the pan bottom. This also makes it possible to form a sauce by dissolving the "browned bits" with moisture, be it water, wine, broth, or the liquid tomatoes release. This is essential in Italian cooking because sauces are usually made simply from the cooking residues on the bottom of the pan.

Nonstick pans have their place in the Italian kitchen too. The coating on the cooking surface prevents the food from sticking and allows you to use very little oil, which makes it possible to cook eggs easily as well as delicate foods, such as fish, that can tear easily. In nonstick pans food actually first steams or poaches on the coated surface which keeps it from sticking, but this also prevents caramelization. That's why I use nonstick pans only for frittatas, simple tomato sauces that need to cook quickly, and sometimes fish fillets.

Finally, the design of handles and lids is also important. The handle should be heatproof and allow you to lift the pan easily, without tipping to one side. Lids are used extensively in Italian cooking, so they should not be ignored in your choice of cookware. Glass lids can be convenient for getting a glimpse of the contents of the pan without having to remove the lid. Also, a domed lid is best suited to return moisture to the contents of the pan.

braising pan

skillet

The pan I use most is probably the skillet, and I have several in 10- and 12-inch sizes and one 10-inch pan with a nonstick coating. I also have an 8-inch skillet that occasionally comes in handy. My next most essential pan is a braising pan for pan roasting and risotto. Mine measure 12, 10, and 8 inches in diameter and are about 4 inches deep. If you can only have one, get a 10-inch. Of course, no Italian kitchen could be without a pasta pot. I have both 8- and 12-quart stockpots. I use the large one when I make homemade meat broth and when I cook more than a pound of pasta. The rest of my arsenal includes saucepans ranging from 1½ quarts to 4½ quarts, and a bowl-like pan, sometimes referred to as a sauteuse, that I use for cooking clams or mussels.

Knives

I cannot emphasize enough the importance of using the highest-quality knives. Dull knives make any preparation laborious and frustrating, even for the most skilled cook. A good sharp knife not only makes your job easier but also is safer to use, ironically, because you do not need to push as hard and it is less likely to slip. For illustrated instructions on how to hold and cut with a knife, see page 29.

In general, a good-quality knife should have a high-carbon stainless-steel forged blade. It should feel solid and well balanced in your hand. Although there are dozens of styles and sizes, I have found that 99% of the time I use one of four knives: an 8-inch chef's knife, a small paring knife, a serrated bread knife, and a flexible boning knife. The chef's knife is the one I reach for most often. I use it for all my chopping, slicing, and dicing. A chef's knife

paring knife

boning knife

chef's knife

should have a gently curved blade which allows you to rock the knife back and forth as you chop or slice. The paring knife is for detail work, such as deveining shrimp or trimming an artichoke bottom. The serrated knife, in addition to slicing bread, is useful for paring citrus rinds and slicing tomatoes. The flexible boning knife is great for trimming meats and fish.

You can add a slicing knife to your collection for carving fowl and slicing roasts. It's a knife with a long narrow blade, sometimes with shallow pockets along the blade which allow air in to prevent the blade from sticking and possibly tearing tender food. I also have a 10-inch chef's knife that I use for cutting large foods, such as melons, or chopping large amounts of food. Of course, there are many more knives you could add to your collection. But remember it is better to have a few high-quality knives than a large collection of mediocre ones. Keeping your knives sharp is important, because use quickly dulls their edges. For a detailed explanation of how to keep your knives sharp, see pages 27–28.

Cutting Boards

Call me old-fashioned, but I still prefer a wood cutting board. I like the way a knife feels on wood better than any other surface I've tried. Wood also seems to have self-healing properties. Minor cuts which tend to remain on plastic seem to disappear on wood boards. Research has shown that wood is also safer to use than plastic when cutting meats because wood has antibacterial properties. Of course, it is still essential to thoroughly clean wood boards with soap and hot water after cutting meat, but any stray bacteria that remain trapped in the wood board will eventually die, whereas they thrive on plastic boards. One disadvantage of wood is that it tends to retain odors. If you cut fruit on a board that was used for onions or garlic, the fruit takes on those flavors even if the board was thoroughly washed. To avoid this, I keep two sets of boards: one for fruits and salads and another for everything else. To prevent the boards from slipping on the counter, I put a piece of rubber shelf liner underneath.

Miscellaneous Tools and Utensils

The following is a list of tools and utensils that I find particularly useful:

Brushes You should have two types of brushes: one with soft bristles to clean mushrooms and one with firm bristles for scrubbing vegetables, such as zucchini and potatoes.

Cake tester This inexpensive little tool is one of my favorite and most used tools, even though I rarely use it to test cakes. I find this thin metal skewer indispensable for checking the doneness and tenderness of meats and vegetables by piercing them with it.

Food mill Although a food processor easily purées foods, a food mill produces a smoother texture by removing skin, strings, and seeds. I use my food mill to mash potatoes and to purée beans to add to a soup.

Graters For grating hard cheese such as Parmigiano-Reggiano, I use the drum-style grater with the handle. It is fast and efficient, making it possible to grate the cheese at the very last moment, preserving its fragrance and moisture. For grating citrus zest, I have found nothing better than a

narrow, flat rasp. It grates finely and is very sharp, so that you get just the aromatic citrus skin without the bitter white pith underneath.

Kitchen twine You may need twine to tie meats for oven or pan roasting. If you don't buy kitchen twine, make sure the twine you use does not contain synthetic materials that melt or are toxic.

Oven thermometer Check your oven every four to six months with a good oven thermometer to make sure the temperature you set it at is actually the temperature inside the oven. If this is not the case, have your oven serviced to recalibrate it.

Pastry scraper I would never want to be without my pastry scraper, although I rarely use it for baking. I always keep it next to my cutting board for transferring chopped or sliced foods. Many people use a knife, but there is no quicker way to dull a sharp knife than to scrape the blade across a cutting board. The pastry scraper can be made of metal or plastic.

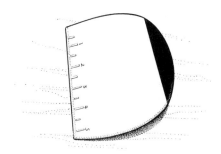

Pastry/pasta wheel I use this crimped cutting wheel to cut pasta sheets into pappardelle or to seal filled pastas such as ravioli.

Peeler My preference is the Y-shaped peelers because they make the back-and-forth sawing motion I describe in Basic Techniques (page 32) much easier. Using the sawing motion rather than pulling straight down keeps the blade sharper longer. For some jobs, such as peeling carrots and potatoes, it's just easier to peel straight down. So I have at least two peelers on hand: one I keep sharp for more delicate jobs, such as tomatoes, peppers, or fruit, and one I use to pull straight down.

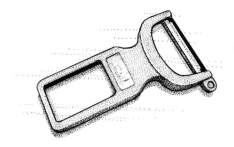

Rubber spatulas Choose a heat-resistant silicone spatula. You'll be able to scrape custard or melted chocolate from a hot pan, as well as stir and scrape food while it's cooking without worrying about melting the rubber.

Bent metal spatula A great tool for spreading frosting or whipped cream over a cake.

Scale Measuring by weight is much more precise than by volume. I have an electronic scale with a tare feature that allows me to subtract the weight of the container or bowl before weighing what I need.

Timer I have never subscribed to the notion that real cooks don't use timers. I find a timer very helpful, especially while doing more than one thing at a time. Of course, I never assume something is done just because the timer goes off, but at least I don't have to worry about over-cooking food because I forget about it. In fact, I have a three-event timer for when I have more than one dish cooking at the same time.

Tongs I love tongs. They are like a heatproof extension of my hand, and I use them all the time to turn and pick up food from the pan. I have several 12-inch tongs, as well as one 16-inch that I use to reach into a tall stockpot or when I grill. I prefer tongs that lock shut because they are easier to store. Tongs should have enough tension not to be floppy but not so much they feel like an exercise tool.

Wooden spoons Wooden spoons are essential. Metal spoons should not be used to stir food because they scratch your pans, especially if you use anodized aluminum pans.

Small Appliances

Espresso maker When Italians make coffee at home, the majority use a stovetop coffee maker called a Moka (see Basic Techniques on page 39 for how to use one). Although the Moka does not produce a classic espresso, it does make very respectable coffee, which can be used to make any of the desserts requiring coffee in this book. If you yearn for that perfect *caffè* with its rich flavor and seductive layer of *crema,* I recommend splurging on a superautomatic espresso machine, which will do everything from grinding the beans to calibrating the precise amount of coffee and water required.

Moka

Food processor I do not use a food processor all that often because for most jobs I find a knife is just as fast if you consider the time it takes to clean the machine. But there is no doubt that for very fine chopping, such as making pesto or grating large amounts of food, the food processor is a godsend.

Ice cream maker If you will make ice cream on a regular basis, consider investing in a machine with a built-in compressor. It allows you to make several batches in a row and easily freezes even the richest of mixtures. Otherwise, an inexpensive ice cream maker, with a cylinder you keep in the freezer and either a hand crank or an electric paddle, should be fine. You may find that some ice cream mixtures rich in egg yolks take a long time to freeze. One solution is to put the cylinder in the freezer for 5 to 10 minutes, take it out and churn for 5 minutes, then repeat until the ice cream is done.

Juicer An electric juicer is useful if you regularly drink freshly squeezed orange juice (or when your five-year-old decides to set up a lemonade stand); otherwise a good hand model should be fine.

Pasta machine The only kind of pasta machine you should use is the one with rollers. Avoid the one where all the ingredients go in at one end and noodles come out the other. Extruding pasta machines are not suited for egg pasta. They're what factories use to make flour-and-water pastas. To make egg pasta at home, make the dough by hand (a very simple process that will take less than 10 minutes, see pages 170–176), then use the rollers of the machine to thin out the dough and the cutters to cut it. The hand-crank model is perfectly adequate, but you can also get the kind that attaches to a stand mixer, which makes the job even easier.

Stand mixer Versatility, power, and convenience make the stand mixer undoubtedly superior to the hand-held.

STOCKING THE ITALIAN PANTRY

Certain items should always be on hand so you can prepare many of the recipes in this book once you've bought the main meat, seafood, or vegetable ingredient. In fact, you can make many pastas, risottos, or soups just with the staples. Of course, this assumes you plan on eating at home more or less on a daily basis. If you only cook once a week or less, you should probably keep mostly nonperishables on hand.

In the Pantry, Nonperishables

Olive oil Olive oil is used in Italian cooking for the flavor it adds to a dish. Therefore it is essential to choose an olive oil that has excellent flavor. Extra virgin olive oil is the highest grade of olive oil and is called for in every recipe in this book where olive oil is used. To be labeled extra virgin, an olive oil must be very low in acidity, less than 0.8% by law, although good extra virgin oils are all less than 0.5%. In addition the oil must be obtained from the first pressing of olives without the use of heat or chemicals, hence the term "cold press" so often seen on labels. Still, not all olive oils that meet these requirements are necessarily very good. The best olive oils are those from carefully maintained olive groves, where the olives are picked by hand. Experienced producers, who often have learned their craft from past generations, do the blending of different varieties of olives. Sometimes when a particular variety of olive is prized for its characteristics, such as *ogliarola* in Apulia, a single varietal olive oil may be produced. Olive oil is produced in almost every region of Italy and varies greatly from region to region. You may find you like the more delicate northern olive oils for certain dishes and more robust and full-flavored oils from central and southern Italy for others. The important thing is that it is just as important to use a high-quality olive oil for cooking as it is for dressing salads and drizzling on a finished dish.

Red wine vinegar The overwhelming popularity of balsamic vinegars has unfortunately almost eclipsed red wine vinegars. Balsamic vinegar is not a substitute for red wine vinegar; it's a completely different product. A well-balanced, rich, full-flavored red wine vinegar is essential in dressing an Italian salad.

Balsamic vinegar The original true balsamic vinegar is not really a viable commercial product. When someone started a new batch, they rarely lived long enough to see it to completion for it took a minimum of fifty years to develop fully, sometimes even seventy-five years or more. It is made by first cooking down the must (partially fermented grapes) of the white Trebbiano grape. After it is allowed to turn into vinegar, it begins its journey through a series of five increasingly smaller barrels made of different kinds of wood, the last always being juniper. The vinegar spends five years in each barrel, becoming more and more concentrated. Finally, it is transferred to the aging barrels, where it remains for twenty-five years or more. Obviously, this is not what you find in half-liter bottles costing less than ten dollars. The closest thing to real balsamic vinegar is sold in perfume-sized bottles whose price is never less than three digits. Only a few drops of that precious liquid is necessary to enhance a salad or finish a dish. Otherwise, look for bottles that are around 8 ounces and sell for twenty-five to forty dollars. Although they could not be mistaken for the real thing, they approximate it well enough and are what I recommend for recipes that call for balsamic vinegar.

Dried pasta Of course, this is one of the essential items of the Italian pantry. As long as you have pasta and a few other basic ingredients described in this chapter, you can always put together a meal. Have several different shapes on hand because different sauces work best with different shapes of dried pasta. The three basic kinds are long pastas, tubular pastas, and special shapes. The basic long pasta is spaghetti to which you might add spaghettini (thin spaghetti), spaghettoni (thick spaghetti), and bucatini (thick, hollow spaghetti). The main tubular shapes are penne, maccheroni, and rigatoni. Special shapes include fusilli (spirals), farfalle (bow ties), orecchiette (little ears), and many others. Of course, you could easily fill an entire cabinet if you were to stock every shape, but I suggest you have at least one from each group plus a small soup pasta. For a discussion on what to look for when choosing brands, read the introduction to Pasta on pages 99–100.

Rice For the recipes in this book, the only rice you need is short-grain rice for risotto. Carnaroli, Vialone Nano, and Arborio are all now available in the United States. Carnaroli is considered by many to be the prince of risotto rices, and Vialone Nano is a specialty of the Veneto. Arborio is the least interesting of the three, although perfectly acceptable. The differences are in flavor, texture, and size. Try all three and decide which appeals to you most.

Salt Salt is essential in coaxing out the flavor of food. Using spices instead of salt only succeeds in adding extraneous flavors that may mask main ingredients instead of enhancing their flavor. Only in rare instances do I give measurements for salt; seasoning with salt is something for which you really need to develop a feeling. I use sea salt exclusively because I find it best at bringing out flavor without adding bitterness or aftertaste. I prefer fine sea salt for cooking because it dissolves more easily, and I save the premium coarser salts for the table. For a more in-depth discussion of how to use salt, see pages 26–27.

Pepper Italian cooking does not as much depend on pepper as do some other cuisines. Black pepper is pretty much the only type I use; it has a rich, full flavor. It is very important, however, to always grind it fresh from a peppermill. With preground pepper you get the heat from the pepper but none of its fragrance.

Dried herbs Have some dried herbs on hand for when the supermarket seems to have every fresh herb imaginable except the one you need. Rosemary, sage, thyme, oregano, and marjoram are all herbs that can be used dry in a pinch. Make sure you buy cut or whole dried leaves and not crushed or crumbled herbs, which are harsher and less fragrant. When using dried herbs, always chop them a little to release the flavor. Bay leaves are the exception because their edges are sharp and small pieces could scratch the throat and esophagus.

Spices Spices are used sparingly in Italian cooking. The principal ones are salt, black pepper, hot red pepper (I prefer whole dried chili peppers but crushed red pepper flakes are fine), whole nutmeg, and juniper berries. If you make desserts on a regular basis, keep pure vanilla extract and baking powder in the pantry.

Bread crumbs The bread crumbs used in these recipes are plain, fine, and dry. If you have the inclination to make them yourself, follow the recipe on page 42; it is easy and requires little time. Otherwise, make sure you buy plain bread crumbs, not seasoned.

Flour The only flour you'll need here is all-purpose flour. I prefer using unbleached.

Sugar For most things you'll be using granulated sugar. Some desserts call for confectioner's sugar. Use 10X (ultrafine or superfine), not 6X (very fine) or 4X (fine).

Beans I am a firm believer in good-quality canned beans. I do not find dried beans worth the time and effort. Fresh beans, when available, are certainly superior, but otherwise I highly recommend the convenience of canned beans. The principal varieties used in Italian cooking are cannellini, chickpeas, and cranberry beans (*borlotti* in Italian).

Canned tuna Whereas in the States making a meal out of a can of tuna would be considered the antithesis of a gourmet meal, in Italy canned tuna is a delicacy. The very best tuna is *ventresca,* made only from the belly of the tuna and packed in extra virgin olive oil. It is available here in specialty markets and online sources. Be prepared to pay at least thirty dollars for a 12-ounce jar.

Canned tomatoes I use canned tomatoes when I want rich tomato flavor, in a tomato sauce for pasta for example, and flavorful fresh locally grown tomatoes are not available. The best imported Italian tomatoes come from a town near Naples called San Marzano, famous for its sweet, flavorful pear-shaped tomatoes. In any case, always buy whole peeled tomatoes because their flavor is closer to a perfect fresh tomato than chopped or crushed canned tomatoes.

Dried porcini Not really a substitute for fresh porcini, the luscious Italian wild mushroom, dried porcini deliver a concentrated burst of wild porcini mushroom flavor. They can be used to add porcini flavor to fresh cultivated mushrooms or on their own as in the Risotto with Porcini on page 209. Dried mushrooms will keep several months.

Wine My rule of thumb when cooking with wine is that it should be good enough that you would not mind drinking the rest of the bottle with the meal. Use dry whites and medium-bodied reds that are not too tannic.

In the Pantry, Perishables

Garlic An Italian pantry without garlic is inconceivable; however, less garlic than most people believe is actually used in Italian cooking. Garlic's rich and slightly pungent flavor should complement a dish, not dominate it. When you buy garlic, make sure it is firm with no green shoots sprouting. Store garlic in a dry ventilated spot, not in the refrigerator, for no more than a couple of weeks.

Onions I use sweet yellow onions predominantly, but unless sweet onions are specifically called for, regular yellow onions are fine for any recipe. Onions should be stored just like garlic. If you have a cut piece of onion left over, wrap in plastic wrap and refrigerate it.

Fresh tomatoes In season, look for locally grown tomatoes whenever possible because they usually have the best flavor. Out of season, when you are limited to supermarket tomatoes, use plum tomatoes (sometimes referred to as Romas). The most important thing is not to put them in the refrigerator, as it will rob them of what little flavor they do have.

In the Refrigerator

Parmigiano-Reggiano Considered by cheese lovers the "king" of cheeses, Parmigiano-Reggiano is a cow's milk cheese of incomparable flavor, texture, and richness. It is prized both as a table cheese and a grating cheese. Made the same way for eight centuries, its production is still dependent on the skill of the cheesemaker, passed on from generation to generation. As part of a cheese plate served at the end of a meal, it is excellent paired with dried fruit or *mostarda,* a spicy fruit preserve. For an hors d'oeuvre, serve bite-sized pieces with a drop of good balsamic vinegar; or grate it, mix it with softened butter, and partially coat walnut halves with the mixture.

Parmigiano-Reggiano should be aged at least two years and occasionally you may find wheels that are three, even four, years old. These are referred to as *stravecchio,* meaning "very old." The older the cheese, the richer and more complex its flavor. Only buy cheese that has the words "Parmigiano-Reggiano" imprinted on the rind. If you can, buy a piece that is cut from a wheel for you rather than a precut piece. It will not have lost any of its fragrance and richness and will keep longer. A choice piece will easily keep for several months. When you get home, divide it into two or three pieces so that you only unwrap and wrap one smaller piece. The other pieces will keep better without being opened all the time. Keep the pieces in resealable plastic bags, making sure to squeeze all the air out. If mold forms on the surface, scrape it off with a knife.

Always grate Parmigiano-Reggiano as close to using it as possible. Never buy pregrated cheese. Even if you are certain it is the real thing, it will have dried and lost much of its fragrance by the time you use it.

Mozzarella Originally all mozzarella was made from water buffalo milk. It is a specialty of the Campania region, of which Naples is the capital. Now mozzarella is made predominantly from cow's milk in most regions of Italy. Whereas cow's milk mozzarella is fairly bland, buffalo milk mozzarella is sweet, slightly tangy, and richer in flavor. It is more expensive and perishable than cow's milk but certainly worth the extra cost. Recently it has been much easier to find in the States. Even our local supermarket carries it now.

Pancetta Pancetta is basically Italian bacon. The main difference is that pancetta is not smoked but is air cured just like prosciutto and can be eaten as is. In fact, a good pancetta in Italy is often part of a cold cut platter. If it is well wrapped, pancetta will keep up to a week in the refrigerator.

Prosciutto One of Italy's most glorious cured meats, prosciutto is a ham that is salted and air cured for ten to twelve months, depending on its size. Several regions in Italy are famous for their prosciutto, the most well known being Prosciutto San Daniele, from the northern Friuli region, and Prosciutto di Parma, made in a government-designated geographic area within Parmigiano-Reggiano's production zone. Prosciutto di Parma benefits from its proximity to Parmigiano factories because the pigs are fed whey obtained from the cheesemaking process. Prosciutto is used in cooking, of course, but it is also superb served on its own or in the classic pairing with cantaloupe melon. Either way, do not discard the ribbon of fat surrounding the meat. Its sweetness balances the savory lean part.

Pecorino romano Often simply called "romano," pecorino romano is an aged sheep's milk cheese that is intensely flavored and a bit sharper than Parmigiano-Reggiano. It is best suited to savory olive oil–based sauces and more boldly flavored dishes.

Butter I use unsalted butter exclusively. First of all, I prefer the flavor. Second, salt is used primarily as a preservative so the butter will keep longer; consequently, unsalted butter is likely to be fresher. That said, even unsalted butter keeps well for several weeks, so I always have a "backup pound" on hand. Premium European butter undoubtedly has a richer, sweeter flavor, but it is a distinction most notice only when using it uncooked. For cooking, a good domestic brand is fine.

Heavy cream Ultrapasteurized heavy cream often has expiration dates of thirty days or more, so I always keep a half pint on hand.

Eggs If you plan on making desserts or egg pasta on a fairly regular basis, then always have eggs on hand. Otherwise buy them only when you need them.

Carrots and celery Carrots and celery are often used in flavor bases. Since I usually do not use a whole head of celery before it gets old, I use the more tender ribs from the center first and work my way out. That way, if I don't use all of it, at least it's the outer, tougher ribs that get thrown away. Always peel the backs of the celery ribs to remove the tough strings (page 33).

Fresh herbs If you have the inclination, growing your own herbs is the easiest way to always have some on hand. Basil, mint, rosemary, sage, thyme, marjoram, and oregano are all fairly easy to grow, even indoors on a windowsill, and make up the majority of the herbs you are likely to use in Italian food. Bay leaves are also useful but better suited to growing outdoors. If it is not practical to grow your own herbs, then buy them as you need them. Most supermarkets now have a pretty good selection year round. Either keep herbs in the refrigerator with their stems immersed in a small cup of water or in a resealable plastic bag. Wrapping them in damp paper towels keeps the leaves too wet and causes them to rot faster.

Parsley Parsley is one herb I have found impractical to grow, mostly because I use it faster than it grows. Parsley is the most common fresh herb in Italian cuisine. In Italy there is a saying that if you run into someone all the time they are "like parsley." The only parsley I use is flat-leaf Italian parsley. Curly parsley is rather harsh and not as fragrant. After rinsing parsley, make sure to pat the leaves dry with paper towels before chopping or it will all clump together. Parsley keeps in the refrigerator for several days, even a week if it is very fresh.

Capers Capers are available preserved both in salt and in vinegar. The advantage of those preserved in vinegar is that they last a long time, even after the jar is opened. Unfortunately, capers in vinegar inevitably take on a vinegar flavor that will not go away even if you rinse them. Capers preserved in salt do not last as long, but because the salt imparts no flavor, they taste only of capers. You can tell when they spoil because the salt turns yellow. When using salted capers, first soak them in several changes of water to rinse away the salt.

Anchovies When anchovies are used in Italian cooking, it is not for the anchovy taste, but for the added richness of flavor. Look for anchovies packed in glass jars, which are usually of better quality than those packed in tins and much easier to store in the refrigerator once opened. The best anchovies are whole anchovies packed in salt. Rinse away the salt, fillet them, and scrape off the skin. If placed in a container with enough olive oil to cover, they will keep in the refrigerator for several weeks. Anchovies packed in salt are worth the trouble if you are going to eat them as is; they are excellent on good bread with sweet butter. For cooking, oil-packed anchovies are perfectly adequate.

Olives I find pitted olives in brine tend to lose their flavor because the hole in the center, where the flesh is not protected by skin, soaks up the watery brine. Since I always slice olives anyway, it does not take any more time or work to slice the flesh from the pit. Buy olives only as needed because they do not keep long outside their brine, even in the refrigerator.

Bottarga A Sardinian specialty, *bottarga* is mullet roe that is first dried for twelve hours, pressed flat, soaked in salt water, then hung to dry for thirty days. It is a delicacy whose luscious, rich flavor makes for a heavenly pasta sauce (page 122), a wonderful topping for canapés (page 48), or adds a delightful element to a salad (page 386). Buy it in gourmet specialty stores or online.

In the Freezer

For the most part, my freezer is populated with ice cream, ice cubes, teethers, and a booboo bear for my tottering seventeen-month-old. When I make pesto (page 107), I usually make a large batch and freeze it. Sometimes I'll also freeze meat sauces for pasta and the simple tomato sauce with butter and onion on page 106. Other than that I am not fond of freezing. I find that freezing damages food. The following are a couple of exceptions.

Bread To most Italians, good bread is an essential accompaniment to any dish except pasta and risotto. Bread is served with the meal as opposed to before it. Bread is never served with butter (or olive oil for that matter). Ideally, you would buy it daily from the corner bakery, but that's not possible for most of us. Unless you are going to bake your own (something few Italians would consider doing), freezing bread is an excellent alternative. Freeze it as soon as you get it home, and it will keep fresh for up to two weeks. When you are ready to serve it, thaw (I find the microwave useful for this), then heat it in a 400° oven for 5 to 6 minutes. It's the next best thing to buying it every day.

Homemade broth There is no question that homemade Italian meat broth is the best whenever broth is called for in a recipe, and for certain soups there is no substitute. For instructions on how to make and store homemade broth, see page 46. For those times that you are out of homemade broth and pressed for time, have some good-quality bouillon cubes on hand. I much prefer them to canned broth, and they more closely approximate an Italian broth than the stocks or demi-glaces that you can buy. They should be diluted with more water than the directions on the package indicate: Use at least 5 to 6 cups water per cube. Since Italian broth is made with a combination of meats, use one-half beef and one-half chicken bouillon cube.

How to Shop for Meats, Seafood, and Vegetables

Meats In general, when buying steaks or shoulder cuts for roasts and stews, look for meat that is well marbled without large chunks of fat. Do not buy excessively lean meats. Ground meats for pasta sauces, meat-balls, and meatloaf if too lean will end up dry. When buying veal for scaloppine, look for a nicely trimmed piece of top round, then slice it yourself across the grain to ensure the scaloppine will be the most ten-der. If you must buy slices, make sure that there is as little gristle or mem-branes as possible and that the meat has been sliced across the grain. Poultry is best if it is free range (sometimes labeled cage free) because it tends to have less fat and more flavor.

Seafood The best way to be sure what you are buying is fresh is to become friendly with whomever you buy seafood from, whether it's a fish market or just the fish counter of your local supermarket. A good rule of thumb is that the fresher the fish, the less "fishy" it smells. Whether whole or filleted, the fish should look bright and fresh, not dull and opaque. Read the signs in the case carefully. Just because it's not frozen in the case doesn't mean that it hasn't been previously frozen. If in doubt, ask. Some seafood you should expect to be previously frozen, such as shrimp, which is almost never fresh, and squid. Buy shrimp in the shell because the shell protects the flesh, keeping it firmer and better tasting.

Don't buy clams or mussels if quite a few are open. You should only use them if they are closed or shut when tapped. Fresh scallops are available "wet" or "dry." Wet scallops are more common and may look more appealing because they are white and shiny and coated in a milky liquid. The liquid, however, is water mixed with sodium tripolyphosphate, which increases shelf life and reduces moisture loss. Dry scallops have nothing added and are more of a cream color. When fresh, dry scallops are much better than wet scallops and also easier to sear because they do not release as much moisture. Since they do have a shorter shelf life, make sure you smell them before buying to ensure freshness.

Vegetables Just because produce looks good does not necessarily mean it is good, but at least it's probably reasonably fresh. The need for perfect appearance at all costs in grocery stores has made for some sad results, such as the perfectly round and flavorless supermarket tomato. However, unless you have easy access to a wonderful farmers' market, the supermarket is where you'll buy produce. If you can, shop at a store with lots of traffic because it is likely to have more frequent deliveries. For the most part, when choosing vegetables, smaller is better, as they are younger, sweeter, and more tender. Artichokes, mushrooms, and lettuces are exceptions to this rule. When buying eggplant, choose the lightest ones. They will have the smallest and least amount of seeds and taste sweeter.

BASIC TECHNIQUES

Italian cuisine is mostly done on top of the stove. It probably evolved that way because ovens were not always commonplace in Italian kitchens. Because the stovetop is the primary heat source, the food can be seen, heard, and smelled at all times. What you get is a style of cooking that involves the cook much more because small adjustments to the heat or amount of liquid in the pan are easily made. It is a direct and intuitive style of cooking that is not complex but requires attention and nurturing. This chapter covers the principal cooking techniques you'll use in this book and some tips on how to chop, slice, peel, and trim commonly used ingredients.

Sautéing

Sautéing is probably used most often in Italian cooking. Most Italian recipes begin by making a flavor base, whether it's with onions, garlic, carrots, or celery, or a combination thereof, which is sautéed. Sautéing is cooking something in a minimal amount of butter or oil over medium-high heat, causing the food to almost hop on the surface of the pan (*sauté* is French for "jumped" or "skipped"). The purpose of sautéing is to intensify flavor through caramelization and to reduce the food's water content through evaporation. It is important to differentiate sautéing from frying, which requires more cooking fat to envelop the food and for that fat to be very hot when the food comes in contact with it. This makes the food crispy on the outside while sealing its moisture in. Sautéing is a more gradual process. When sautéing, it is better not to wait for the oil or butter to get hot. Remember, the point of sautéing onions, garlic, carrots, and celery is to create a flavor base through evaporation, not to seal the flavor in by creating a browned crust. Be patient and allow vegetables to sauté gradually to extract the most flavor.

Frying

Unfortunately, frying has gotten quite a bad reputation, due perhaps to the prevalence of overly greasy, poorly fried fast foods. When food is fried properly, it is light, crispy, and flavorful. Unlike sautéing, frying is dependent on the food making initial contact with the oil when it is very hot, searing the food's surface to make it crispy, while sealing in moisture and flavor. You can fry in either a saucepan or a skillet. The wider the pan you use, the more food you can fry at one time, but you will need more oil and you will have to work faster to prevent the food from burning. Ideally, fried food should absorb little or no oil as long as you follow some simple guidelines.

1. Use plenty of oil, enough to allow the food to float. I prefer using a neutral-tasting vegetable oil.

2. Do not crowd the pan by frying too many pieces at once. There should be enough room for the oil to circulate freely around each piece. Adding too much food at once lowers the temperature of the oil too much. To keep the temperature fairly constant, replace each piece you remove rather than emptying the pan and then refilling it.

3. Gauge the correct oil temperature by what's happening in the pan rather than with a thermometer. If the food is burning before it is cooked through, lower the heat. If it's not browning enough, raise the heat a little.

4. Turn pieces only once if possible. Each time you turn them, they absorb a little more oil.

5. If it's necessary to add oil, wait until the current batch is out of the pan, then allow the new oil to heat before resuming.

6. When lifting cooked pieces out of the pan, allow all the excess oil to drip back into the pan, then place the pieces on a platter lined with paper towels. Serve as soon as possible.

Searing and Browning

Usually the first step in pan roasting is browning the meat. This provides a tasty layer of caramelization on both the meat and the surface of the pan. Those browned bits on the bottom of the pan will be essential in creating the sauce later. Fish fillets and scallops are also often pan seared. Unlike frying, searing and browning is done with a minimal amount of cooking fat, similar to sautéing, but the food is placed in oil or butter that is already hot. Be aware that when cold meat comes in contact with a hot pan it will inevitably stick to the bottom (do not use a nonstick pan because it will not allow caramelization). Resist the temptation to move it immediately as you will only succeed in tearing the meat. Once the meat has browned, it should loosen from the pan surface quite easily. In fact, when it releases easily from the pan is a good indication that the meat or fish is browned and ready to turn.

Pan Roasting and Braising

These are actually very similar techniques and the principal way that meats are prepared in Italian cooking. Braising involves cooking with more liquid than pan roasting does, but both use the moist-heat cooking method. When cooking with dry heat, the meat is seared, such as cooking a steak on a grill or a roast beef in the oven, and usually it is not cooked all the way through, leaving the center at least pink. With moist-heat cooking, meat is cooked using gentle heat in a moist environment. When the meat passes the point of being cooked through, it becomes more and more tender as the fibers break down and it absorbs the flavors of the juices in which it is cooking.

The basic method for pan roasting and braising is simple. The meat is usually first browned in a hot pan, then removed from the pan and seasoned with salt and pepper. Herbs and spices are added to the pan as well as the liquid the meat will cook in. For pan roasts the liquid is most often wine. For braising it might be broth or tomatoes or even red wine vinegar. Add liquid to the pan when it is quite hot so that the browning residue will loosen from the bottom of the pan and flavor the sauce. In the case of wine, the high heat allows the alcohol to evaporate, preventing an unpleasant, strong winy flavor in the dish. The meat is then returned to the pan, the heat is lowered to a gentle but steady simmer, and the pan is covered with the lid slightly askew. Turn the meat approximately every 20 minutes and check to see if the liquid has evaporated. The meat is done once it feels tender when prodded with a fork. If the pan has dried out before the meat is tender, add some water and continue cooking. Do not add more of whatever liquid you began with because there is already enough of that flavor in the pan. All you need is water.

Grilling

Grilling is actually a perfect manifestation of the Italian approach to cooking. Italian cooking is all about bringing out the flavor of the ingredients, and grilling accomplishes that perfectly. Sometimes Italians simply season vegetables or meat with salt and pepper before grilling, then drizzle with some olive oil afterwards. Meats sometimes are marinated before grilling, and seafood may be coated with a seasoned breading. Rarely are heavy sauces added to grilled food. If there is a sauce, it is usually olive oil mixed with fresh herbs.

How to Use Salt

Using salt judiciously is crucial in cooking, but you must develop a feel for it. The exact amount to use is difficult to determine, which is why I have purposely avoided giving measurements in these recipes. How much depends on the type you use, how much food you are seasoning, and finally your own sensitivity to salt. For a discussion of the different types of salt to use, see page 13. When used properly, salt coaxes out flavor without adding the taste of salt itself. If you are unsure as to whether something needs salt, add a tiny pinch to a small amount of the dish and taste it. If it just tastes salty, then don't add more. If the flavor is richer and fuller, then the dish needs more salt.

When to salt is also important. The sooner in the cooking process you add salt, the better it can be absorbed and enhance flavors. However, salt draws out moisture from food, so sometimes it is best not to add it in the beginning. When browning zucchini or peppers, for instance, adding salt right away releases too much moisture to brown the vegetables. In that case, wait until the vegetables begin to brown and then add salt. The same thing applies to browning meat in a pan. If you are grilling a steak, however, salt it just before it goes on the grill. The salt will penetrate the meat better, and any moisture released will simply drip through the grill. In a pan, however, the additional moisture would prevent the meat from browning. For a dish with ingredients added at different times, season each one as it goes in the pan. This is called layering with salt, and it ensures that each ingredient contributes its flavor fully to the dish.

Increasing and Decreasing
Number of Servings

When a recipe serves four people but you want to cook for two or maybe eight or twelve, don't simply divide or multiply the quantities of ingredients. In general, the ingredients that make up the bulk of the dish, such as meats, vegetables, or tomatoes, as well as herbs and spices, can all be multiplied, but ingredients such as oil, butter, and wine should not be doubled or halved. The amount of these ingredients is determined not just by the quantity of the main ingredients but also by the size and shape of the pan. A good rule of thumb is that for each time you increase the recipe you should increase oil, butter, or wine by only 50%; if you are halving the recipe, decrease them by only 25%.

Sharpening Your Knives

Keep your knives sharp. It is one of the most important things you can do to make life in the kitchen easier. A knife quickly loses its edge because in chopping, microscopic dents are created on the blade. It does not mean the knife needs grinding, however. A honing steel is all that's needed to make the edge smooth and straight again, and the knife will regain its original sharpness. Some honing steels have a ridged steel rod and some have a fine diamond coating. I have found the latter to be the most effective. Everyday use of a steel will not shorten the life of the knife. In fact, it lengthens it because you won't need to have your knives sharpened and ground as often.

1. Place the knife on top of the steel at a slight angle with the blade facing you and the knife handle near the steel handle. Slide the knife away from you diagonally until the knife tip is near the steel tip.

2. Repeat with the knife under the steel. Alternate sides until you have done each side five or six times.

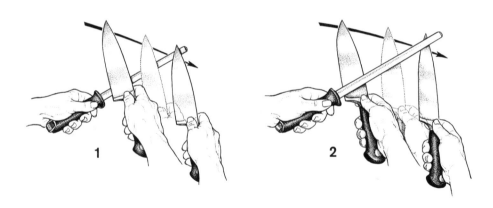

When the steel no longer restores a knife's edge, it's time to use a knife sharpener or grinder. A sharpening stone requires considerable skill because the blade must be kept at the correct angle, which changes as you grind. I use an electric grinder with two or three stages. Magnets grab the blade and ensure it is ground at the proper angle in each stage. Place the knife in the slot and pull it through with an even, smooth motion. Unless you have found a really good professional knife sharpener, I do not recommend sending your knives out to be sharpened. They tend to come back rather smaller than they were and often the original rounded shape of the blade is lost.

Basic Technique for Using a Chef's Knife

1. Hold the knife close to the blade with your index finger on the blade itself for better control.

2. Hold the food with your fingers curled in so that your knuckles, not your fingertips, are touching the blade.

3. Always move the knife in a sawing motion rather than just pressing down with the blade. You will use considerably less pressure, making cutting safer, easier, and more precise.

4. Whenever possible, keep the tip of the knife on the cutting board, using the knife in a rocking motion. Anchoring your knife keeps it steadier and gives you more control.

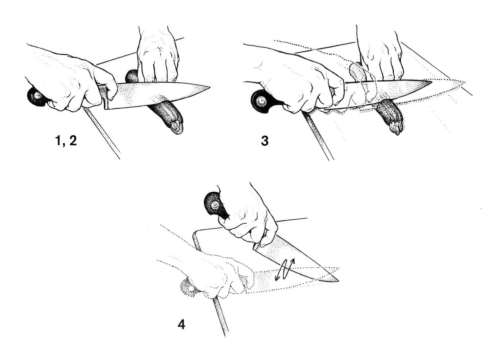

Easy Way to Finely Chop an Onion

1. Cut off the top of the onion, but not the root end, with a chef's knife. Cut the onion lengthwise in half and remove the skin.

2. Place the onion half cut side down and use the tip of your knife to make lengthwise cuts close together, from the outside of the onion to the center, making lots of narrow wedges.

3. Thinly slice the onion crosswise. You now have finely chopped onion.

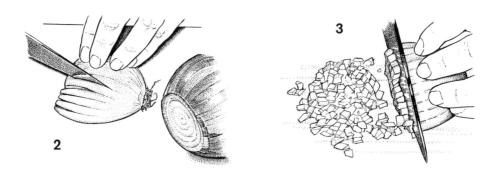

Peeling and Dicing Tomatoes

Many advocate peeling tomatoes by first scoring the top with an X and dipping the tomatoes in boiling water long enough for the skin to separate from the flesh. But then you must take them out and burn your fingers to remove the skin while it's hot, and wash the pot. Using a peeler as illustrated below is actually much easier.

1. Use the peeler in a sawing motion to cut through the skin of the tomato easily.

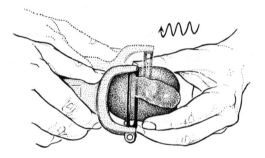

2. If instructed to remove the seeds, cut the tomato in half crosswise (lengthwise if using a plum tomato) and remove the seeds by scooping them out with your fingers.

Peeling Peppers

There are two reasons why Italians peel peppers. The first is that the skin remains tough no matter how long the pepper is cooked. The second, and more important, is that the skin has a bitter flavor that can permeate a dish.

1. Cut the pepper open by cutting along the grooves from the bottom to the top.

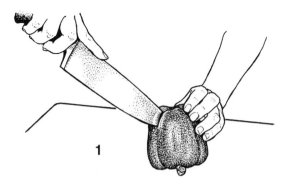

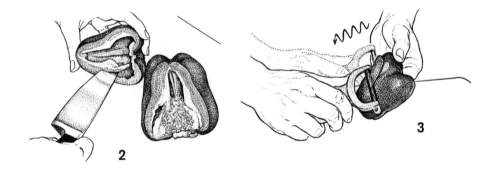

2. Trim the white pith and remove the stem, core, and seeds.

3. Peel the pepper using a sawing motion with the peeler.

Dicing Carrots

1. Cut off the ends and peel the carrot. Cut the carrot into lengths no more than 2 inches long.

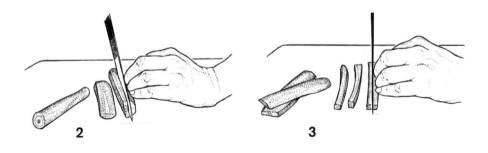

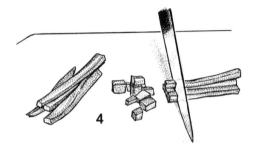

2. Cut each length into 3 or more lengthwise slices, depending on the thickness.

3. Cut each slice into ¼-inch-thick sticks.

4. Line the sticks up and cut crosswise into dice.

Dicing Celery

1. Trim the ends of the rib and peel the back of the rib to remove the tough strings.

2. Cut the rib into ¼-inch-thick sticks.

3. Line the sticks up and cut crosswise into dice.

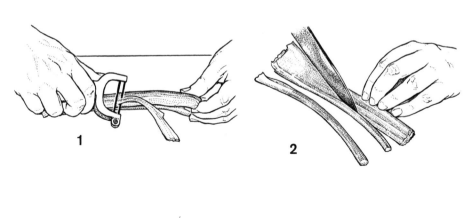

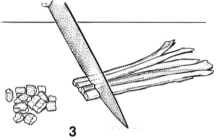

Trimming Artichokes

1. Fold each leaf back, snapping it where the tender part at the bottom of the leaf ends. Pull down to remove. Continue until the lighter, tender part comes about halfway up the leaf.

2. Cut across the remaining leaves with a chef's knife or a serrated bread knife and discard the top half. Cut off the stem. Always rub any cut parts immediately with a lemon half, so the exposed flesh does not oxidize and turn brown.

3. Trim the outer part of the stem so only the inner core remains. Put the stem into a bowl of cold water and add the juice of half a lemon.

4. Use a paring knife to trim the outside of the artichoke, removing all the dark green parts.

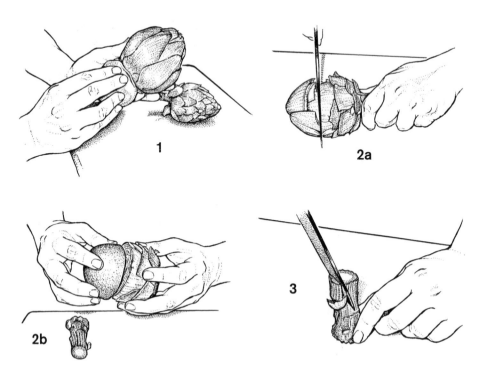

1

2a

2b

3

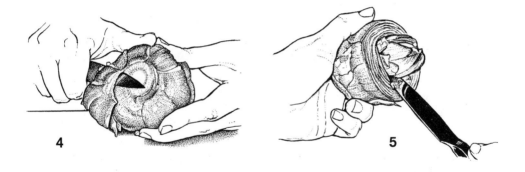

4   **5**

5. Use a knife with a rounded tip, such as a dinner knife, to pry out the choke and scrape away all the white fuzz in the center. Slice the artichoke as directed in the recipe and place the pieces in the bowl of lemon water.

Trimming Leeks

1. Slice off the root of the leek.

2. The dark green part of the leaves is the tough part that must be discarded. The closer you are to the center of the leek, the more light tender part of the leaf there is. If you simply remove the top of the leek where the leaves turn dark green, you'll also lose some of the tender leaves inside. That's why I remove the dark part one layer at a time. Use a sharp chef's knife to cut one layer of leaves at a time where the whiter tender part ends and the tough dark green part begins.

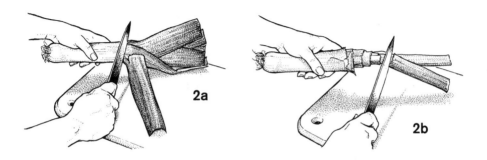

2a   **2b**

Peeling and Deveining Shrimp

1. Pry open the shell from the belly of the shrimp, working your way to the tail.

2. Snap the center part of the tail back, then gently pull the shell off by grabbing the very tip of the tail. The flesh from the tail should still be attached to the shrimp.

3. Use a paring knife to make an incision along the back of the shrimp and pull out the black vein if there is one.

When deveining cooked shrimp, the vein may not come out as easily as when they are raw. Wiping it away with a paper towel may help. Do not worry if some traces remain.

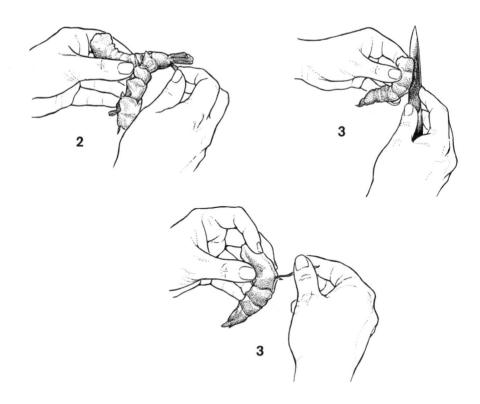

Cutting a Chicken into 12 Pieces

1. Pull the legs away from the body and cut at the upper joint with a heavy knife or cleaver to remove the leg and thigh from the body.

2. Run your finger on the inside of the leg to find the joint that attaches the drumstick to the thigh, then cut them apart.

3. Cut the wings from the breast.

4. Cut the back away from the breast, then cut the back in half.

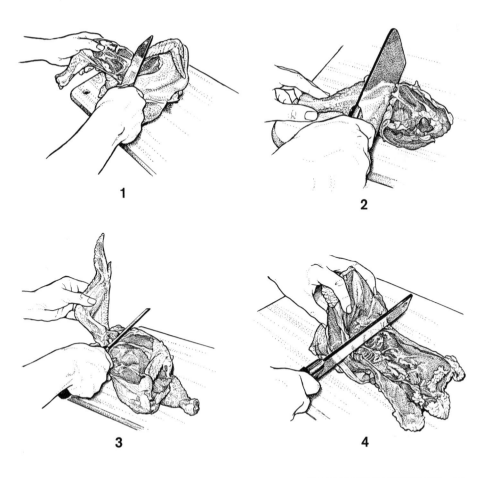

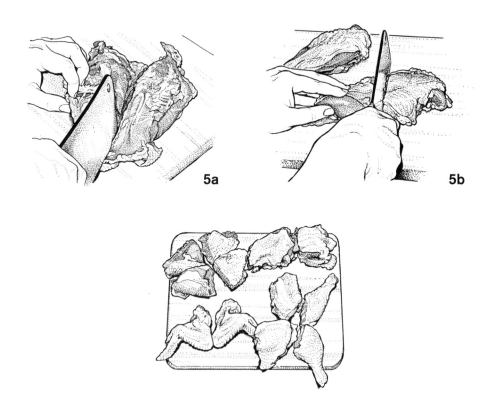

5a

5b

5. Cut the breast in half along the breastbone, then cut each half in half again.

Pounding Meat

Use a meat pounder that has the handle perpendicular to the disk. Aim the edge of the pounder at the center of the meat and direct the pounder down

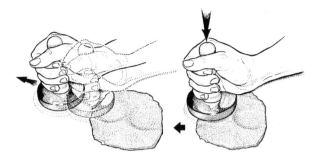

and away from the center of the meat in smooth even strokes, as if you were tracing the spokes of a wheel.

Making Coffee with a Moka

1. Fill the bottom reservoir with water up to the valve.

2. Put the filter in and fill it with very finely ground coffee for espresso. Do not press the coffee down.

3. Screw on the top tightly and place over medium heat. When you hear a gurgling sound, the coffee should be ready. Open the lid to make sure, then remove from the heat.

BASE RECIPES

- **Homemade Bread Crumbs**
- **Béchamel Sauce**
- **Mayonnaise**
- **Homemade Sausage**
- **Homemade Meat Broth**

These are recipes for sauces or items that may be used as basic components in this book.

HOMEMADE BREAD CRUMBS

Total time: 15 minutes

1 loaf day-old Italian or Cuban white bread

1. Preheat the oven to 250°.

2. Cut away the crust and cut the loaf lengthwise in half. Place it in the oven and bake for about 5 minutes on each side. Take it out of the oven and let it cool.

3. Cut the bread into chunks small enough to easily fit in a food processor. Run the processor until you have fairly even crumbs that are not too fine. Use the same day if fresh bread crumbs are called for. For recipes that call for fine dry crumbs, process them finer, then sift them through a medium-mesh strainer. Store the dry crumbs in a jar in the pantry where they'll keep for several weeks.

BÉCHAMEL SAUCE

Balsamella

Balsamella, a creamy, rich white sauce, is used in many baked pasta dishes, particularly lasagne, and sometimes in gratinéed vegetable dishes. It is simple to make but requires a little patience. Do not be discouraged if it does not thicken right away and don't be tempted to add more flour. The proportions listed below ensure a fine, delicate, and smooth béchamel sauce.

Total time: 20 minutes

Makes about 2½ cups

> 2 cups whole milk
> 4 tablespoons butter
> 4 tablespoons all-purpose flour
> Salt

1. Pour the milk in a small saucepan and place over medium heat. Heat until steam is released when the milk is stirred, just before it boils.

2. While the milk is heating, melt the butter in a 2-quart saucepan over medium-low heat. Add the flour and whisk until the mixture is smooth. Cook, whisking constantly, for about 1 minute. Do not brown. Remove from the heat.

3. When the milk is hot, transfer it to a measuring cup or pitcher with a spout. Place the pan with the flour mixture over medium heat. Begin adding the hot milk, very slowly at first, mixing with the whisk. Do not be concerned if the mixture becomes quite thick at first. Continue adding the milk slowly while mixing with the whisk. As the consistency becomes thinner, add the remaining milk more rapidly.

4. Season with salt. Cook, whisking constantly, over medium heat until the sauce begins to thicken, about 15 minutes. The sauce is done when it thickly coats the whisk. Béchamel is best when used the same day but will keep overnight in the refrigerator if necessary. It's not necessary to reheat before using.

MAYONNAISE

Maionese

Homemade mayonnaise is delicious with seafood and is an essential ingredient for *Vitello Tonnato* (page 278). It takes less than 15 minutes to make and is, in my opinion, far superior to anything you buy in a jar. Some people use olive oil, but I prefer the lighter mayonnaise you get with vegetable oil. If you want the flavor of extra virgin olive oil, just drizzle some in the dish along with the mayonnaise.

Total time: 15 minutes

Makes about 1¼ cups

> 2 large eggs
> Salt
> 1½ cups vegetable oil
> 2 tablespoons fresh lemon juice

1. Take the eggs out of the refrigerator and allow them to warm to room temperature.

2. Separate the eggs, putting the yolks in the bowl of an electric mixer and discarding the whites.

3. Sprinkle a little salt over the yolks and begin beating with the whisk attachment on medium-high speed. Beat until the yolks become paler and creamy in consistency, 2 to 3 minutes.

4. Begin adding the oil, very slowly at first, pausing periodically to allow it to be incorporated into the eggs. After about ¼ cup of the oil has been added, add only about ½ tablespoon lemon juice. Don't be concerned if the mixture becomes softer. Beat in more oil (the mayonnaise will firm up again), then add another ½ tablespoon lemon juice. Continue until all the oil and lemon juice have been incorporated. Taste and add more salt if desired. The mayonnaise will keep refrigerated for 2 to 3 days.

HOMEMADE SAUSAGE

Sausage that resembles that of Italy is one of the hardest products to find in the States. The Italian sausage in the States is mostly based on recipes the early immigrants brought from southern Italy. This kind of sausage tends to be much more heavily spiced, particularly with fennel, than the pork sausage of central and northern Italy, which almost never has fennel. The recipe below approximates the flavor of sausage that you might get in Italy. It is not real sausage, of course, because it has no casing, but for those times when crumbled sausage is called for, it works remarkably well.

Preparation time: 5 minutes
Total time from start to finish: 12 hours

Makes 1 pound

> 1 pound ground pork
> 1 teaspoon salt
> 1 teaspoon freshly ground black pepper
> 1 teaspoon chopped fresh rosemary
> ½ teaspoon finely chopped garlic
> 2 tablespoons dry white wine

1. Put all the ingredients in a bowl and mix thoroughly with your hands.

2. Wrap in plastic wrap and refrigerate overnight to allow the flavors to blend. Use within 2 days or freeze for up to 2 months.

HOMEMADE MEAT BROTH

Preparation time: 15 minutes
Total time from start to finish: 3¼ hours

Makes about 2 quarts

2 carrots
1 ripe fresh tomato *or* 1 peeled canned tomato
1 medium yellow onion
8 beef marrow bones
1½ to 2 pounds veal neck or rib bones
1 pound veal breast or shoulder
1 pound beef chuck
1 small frying chicken
1 tablespoon salt
2 to 3 ribs celery
1 sprig flat-leaf Italian parsley
1 tablespoon whole black peppercorns

1. Peel the carrots and the fresh tomato if using. Peel the onion and cut it in half. Put all the ingredients in a large stockpot and add enough cold water to cover by 2 inches. Cover the pot and place over high heat. When the water begins to boil, reduce the heat to very low. Use a skimmer to remove the scum that has risen to the surface. Cover the pot and cook at a very gentle simmer for at least 3 hours.

2. Pour the broth through a strainer and, once the steam has subsided, put it in the refrigerator. The broth will keep in the refrigerator for only 2 days, so it is best to freeze it. As soon as the broth is chilled and the fat is solidified on the surface, take it out of the refrigerator and lift the fat off with a slotted spatula or spoon. Pour the broth into ice cube trays. Once the cubes are frozen, you can pop them out and store them in resealable freezer bags in the freezer for up to 2 months.

APPETIZERS AND BUFFET ITEMS

Antipasti

- **Bottarga and Mozzarella Canapés**
- **Whipped Striped Bass Canapés**
- **Roasted Eggplant Salad**
- **Seafood Salad with Cannellini Beans**
- **Shrimp with Pistachio Sauce**
- **Shrimp with Oil and Lemon**
- **Shrimp and Beans**
- **Baked Stuffed Onions**
- **Piedmontese "Steak Tartare"**
- **Frittata with Onions and Prosciutto**
- **Frittata with Potatoes and Pancetta**
- **Frittata with Leeks and Red Peppers**
- **Pizza**

Antipasto, which translates as "that which comes before the meal," is usually served at more formal meals or for guests. The portions should be small because they are followed by several courses and are meant to stimulate, not satiate, the appetite. These dishes are also well suited to a buffet because almost all can be served at room temperature.

BOTTARGA AND MOZZARELLA CANAPÉS

Crostini di Bottarga

These are delicious hors d'oeuvres to pass before sitting down to dinner. *Bottarga,* a Sardinian specialty, is mullet roe that is first dried for 12 hours, pressed flat, soaked in salt water, then hung to dry for 30 days. If it is not available, these canapés are also very good with anchovies instead. Using buffalo milk mozzarella instead of cow's milk will make a significant difference.

Preparation time: 10 minutes
Total time from start to finish: 20 minutes

Makes 12 canapés

> **6 slices white bread**
> **6 ounces buffalo milk mozzarella**
> **1 ounce *bottarga or* 6 anchovy fillets**
> **1 tablespoon butter**

1. Preheat the oven to 375°.

2. Trim the crusts from the bread and cut the slices diagonally in half. Place on a baking sheet.

3. Cut the mozzarella into 12 slices, about ¼ inch thick, and place a slice on each piece of bread, taking care not to let it overhang.

4. Grate the *bottarga* (the easiest way is with a drum-type grater) and sprinkle it over the mozzarella. If using anchovies, cut the fillets in half and place one half on each piece of bread. Dot each canapé with butter.

5. Bake until the bread begins to brown and the mozzarella begins to melt, about 10 minutes. Serve warm.

WHIPPED STRIPED BASS CANAPÉS

Branzino Mantecato

Total time: 30 minutes

Makes 12 canapés

½ medium carrot
¼ medium yellow onion
½ rib celery
1 teaspoon salt
1 teaspoon red wine vinegar
8 ounces striped bass or snapper fillet
¼ cup homemade mayonnaise (page 44)
1 tablespoon extra virgin olive oil
1 tablespoon fresh lemon juice
2 tablespoons capers
6 thin slices white bread

1. Peel the carrot and onion and put them with the celery in a pan that is wide enough to accommodate the fish. Fill two-thirds full with water, place over high heat, and bring to a boil. Add the salt and vinegar, then slide the fish fillet into the water. Bring the water back to a boil, lower the heat, and gently simmer for about 10 minutes for a 1-inch-thick fillet. Remove the fish with a slotted spoon and set it aside on a plate to cool.

2. While the fish is cooking, make the mayonnaise.

3. Remove any skin and bones from the fish. Put the fish and mayonnaise in a food processor and run the processor until you get a smooth consistency. Transfer to a mixing bowl and stir in the olive oil, lemon juice, and capers. You can make this ahead of time and refrigerate it; let warm to room temperature before continuing.

4. Lightly toast the bread. Cut the slices diagonally in half and spread each piece with some of the fish mixture. Serve at room temperature.

ROASTED EGGPLANT SALAD

Melanzane Arrosto

This fragrant and refreshing salad is perfect for a picnic or summer buffet. If the eggplant is finely diced, it also makes a delicious topping for toast to serve as a canapé.

Total time: 30 minutes

Serves 6

> 1½ pounds eggplant
> 1 red bell pepper *or* ½ red and ½ yellow bell pepper
> ⅓ English cucumber
> ¼ small red onion
> ½ small clove garlic
> 3 tablespoons extra virgin olive oil
> 2 tablespoons fresh lemon juice
> Salt
> Freshly ground black pepper

1. To roast the eggplants, preheat a charcoal or gas grill or a broiler. Alternatively, you can simply use the open flame of a gas burner.

2. Roast the eggplants, turning as needed, until the skin is charred on all sides. The time will vary depending on the cooking method you choose. The eggplant is cooked when it is soft and looks somewhat deflated. Place it on a plate to cool.

3. Trim and seed the pepper, then cut into ¼-inch dice. Cut the cucumber lengthwise in half, scoop out the seeds with a spoon, and cut into ¼-inch dice. Peel and finely chop the onion. Peel and finely chop the garlic.

4. When the eggplant is cool enough to handle, remove as much of the skin as possible along with any large, dark seeds. Cut the eggplant into 1-inch squares (or smaller if using it as a spread) and place it in a colander in the

sink or over a bowl for 5 to 10 minutes, or until you are ready to serve, to allow the excess liquid to drain.

5. Transfer the eggplant to a bowl and add the pepper, cucumber, onion, and garlic. Stir in the olive oil and lemon juice and season with salt and pepper. Serve at once or the salt will draw out too much moisture from the vegetables.

SEAFOOD SALAD
WITH CANNELLINI BEANS

Insalata di Mare con i Fagioli

Total time: 25 minutes

Serves 4

Salt
3 teaspoons red wine vinegar
8 ounces large (16 to 20 count) shrimp in the shell
8 ounces squid tubes and tentacles
8 ounces sea scallops
1 small tomato
½ cup drained canned cannellini beans
1 or 2 sprigs fresh marjoram
3 tablespoons extra virgin olive oil

1. Fill a medium saucepan (large enough to hold each of the types of seafood) two-thirds full with water and bring to a boil. Add 1 teaspoon salt and 1 teaspoon of the vinegar, then add the shrimp. Cover the pot to bring the water back to a boil as quickly as possible. As soon as the shrimp turn pink through and through, less than 1 minute after the water comes back to a boil, scoop them out with a slotted spoon and transfer them to a bowl. Add the squid to the pot and scoop them out 1 minute after the water returns to

a boil. Transfer them to another bowl. Put the scallops in the pot and after the water comes back to a boil, cook 2 to 3 minutes, depending on the size. Transfer them to a shallow bowl.

2. Peel the shrimp, cut them lengthwise in half, and devein. Cut the squid tubes into ¼-inch rings. Cut the scallops horizontally in half. Place all the seafood in a shallow bowl.

3. Cut the tomato into small wedges and add it along with the cannellini beans to the bowl. Chop enough of the marjoram leaves to measure 1 teaspoon and sprinkle it over the top. Season with salt. Add the olive oil and remaining 2 teaspoons vinegar and toss well. Taste and adjust the seasoning if necessary and serve.

> **Note:** You can cook the seafood a couple of hours ahead of time but do not refrigerate it. Assemble and season the salad just before serving.

SHRIMP WITH PISTACHIO SAUCE

Gamberi con Salsa di Pistacchi

Usually one hears of a restaurant giving a loyal customer the recipe for one of their favorite dishes. When my wife and I had this delicious and unusual appetizer at a restaurant on the Italian Riviera, we discovered it was a loyal customer who had given the restaurant the recipe!

Total time: 15 minutes

Serves 4

> Salt
> 1 teaspoon red wine vinegar
> 1 pound large (16 to 20 count) shrimp in the shell

2 ounces shelled pistachios
4 anchovy fillets
1 tablespoon capers
3 tablespoons extra virgin olive oil
1 tablespoon fresh lemon juice, or more to taste

1. Bring 3 quarts water to a boil in a medium pot. Add 1 teaspoon salt and the vinegar, then add the shrimp. Cover the pot to bring the water back to a boil as quickly as possible. As soon as the shrimp are pink through and through, less than 1 minute after the water comes back to a boil, they are done. Drain them but do not rinse with cold water.

2. Shell the shrimp and devein.

3. Put the pistachios, anchovies, capers, 2 tablespoons of the olive oil, and the lemon juice in a food processor. Run the processor until you get a creamy consistency. Add 2 tablespoons water and run the processor again until it is well incorporated.

4. Put the shrimp and the sauce together in a bowl, add the remaining 1 tablespoon olive oil, and toss well. Taste and add additional salt or lemon juice if necessary. Serve at room temperature.

SHRIMP WITH OIL AND LEMON

Gamberi all'Olio e Limone

The most prized, and often most expensive, produce and seafood in markets in Italy have signs next to them that say *nostrano.* It literally means "ours," or local, and that is what Italians value most when buying food. One of the perks of living in Florida is being able to buy fresh pink Key West shrimp off the back of a truck on the side of the road. When shrimp are that fresh, this is my favorite way of preparing them. Adding vinegar to the water the shrimp cook in is a little trick that gives boiled seafood a fresh, vibrant flavor. When simply seasoned with extra virgin olive oil and lemon, the shrimp's sweet flavor comes through. Of course, this recipe is also very good with high-quality frozen shrimp.

Total time: 20 minutes

Serves 4 as a light lunch or 8 as an appetizer

> 4 quarts water
> Salt
> 1 tablespoon red wine vinegar
> 2 pounds large (16 to 20 count) shrimp in the shell
> ¼ cup extra virgin olive oil
> 2 tablespoons fresh lemon juice

1. Bring the water to a boil in a large pot. Add 1 tablespoon salt and the vinegar, then add the shrimp. Cover the pot to bring the water back to a boil as quickly as possible. As soon as the shrimp are pink through and through, less than 1 minute after the water comes back to a boil, they are done. Drain them but do not rinse with cold water.

2. Shell the shrimp and devein. Place the shrimp in a serving bowl and season with salt. Add the olive oil and lemon juice and toss well. Serve warm or at room temperature with some good crusty bread.

SHRIMP AND BEANS

Gamberi e Fagioli

Total time: 25 minutes

Serves 4 as a light lunch or 8 as an appetizer

> 4 quarts water
> Salt
> 1 teaspoon red wine vinegar
> 1 pound medium (21 to 25 count) shrimp in the shell
> 3 or 4 sprigs flat-leaf Italian parsley
> 1 cup drained canned Great Northern or cannellini beans
> 3 tablespoons extra virgin olive oil
> 1 tablespoon fresh lemon juice

1. Bring the water to a boil in a large pot. Add 1 tablespoon salt and the vinegar, then add the shrimp. Cover the pot to bring the water back to a boil as quickly as possible. As soon as the shrimp are pink through and through, less than 1 minute after the water comes back to a boil, they are done. Drain them but do not rinse with cold water.

2. Finely chop enough parsley leaves to measure 1 tablespoon. Shell the shrimp and devein. Put the shrimp and beans in a serving bowl. Season with salt. Add the parsley, olive oil, and lemon juice and toss well. Serve slightly warm or at room temperature.

BAKED STUFFED ONIONS

Cipolle al Forno Ripiene

This versatile dish can be served as a side dish, appetizer, or as part of a buffet. The onions are equally good served warm or at room temperature.

Preparation time: 20 minutes
Total time from start to finish: 1 hour 20 minutes

Serves 6

> 3 large sweet onions, such as Vidalia or Walla Walla
> Salt
> 2 slices white bread
> 2 tablespoons whole milk
> 1 tablespoon capers
> 3 anchovy fillets
> 1 large egg
> 2 teaspoons butter

1. Preheat the oven to 325° on convection heat or 350° on regular bake.

2. Trim the tops and bottoms of the onions, cut them horizontally in half, and peel. Put them cut side up on a baking sheet and sprinkle lightly with salt. Place in the oven and bake until tender, about 45 minutes. Remove from the oven and set aside to cool. Raise the oven temperature by 25°.

3. While the onions are baking, remove the crusts from the bread. Place the bread in a small shallow bowl with the milk.

4. When the onions are cool enough to handle, scoop out the centers leaving only the outer 3 layers. Put the centers in a food processor, add the capers and anchovies, and finely chop.

5. Beat the egg in a medium bowl. Mash the bread and milk with your fingers to form a pulp and mix it with the egg. Add the contents of the food proces-

sor to the bowl and mix everything together. Spoon the mixture into the hollowed-out onion halves and dot with butter.

6. Bake until the tops are golden brown, 15 to 20 minutes. Serve warm or at room temperature.

PIEDMONTESE "STEAK TARTARE"

Carne Cruda alla Piemontese

Because the meat is eaten raw, it goes without saying that the freshest, highest-quality veal should be used here. Top round is the best cut. It is the same cut used for scaloppine, so buy scaloppine if your butcher does not have a piece of top round. Do not have the meat put through a grinder, because the texture is much better when chopped by hand. Ideally, this would be served with thin shavings of fresh white truffle, but it is also very good on its own or with thinly sliced white mushrooms. Serve with a good crusty bread.

Total time: 15 minutes

Serves 4

> 12 ounces veal top round
> Salt
> Freshly ground black pepper
> Optional: 2 ounces white mushrooms *or* a generous sprinkling
> of white truffle shavings
> ¼ cup extra virgin olive oil
> 3 tablespoons fresh lemon juice
> 1 teaspoon Dijon mustard

Use a knife to cut the meat into very fine dice, no larger than ⅛ inch. Put the meat in a bowl and season with salt and pepper. If using the mushrooms, slice them very thin and add them to the bowl. Add the olive oil, lemon juice, and mustard and mix thoroughly. Serve at once or the lemon juice will begin cooking the meat and it will become tough. If you are using truffles instead of mushrooms, shave them directly over each serving.

FRITTATE

A frittata is basically an open-faced omelet. The number of variations is limited only by your imagination. A frittata can be served either hot, warm, or cold and is delicious in a sandwich. It is easier to make than an omelet because it does not require folding. The "filling" is mixed with the eggs before cooking, and the mixture is poured into an ovenproof nonstick skillet in which some butter has been heated. Once the bottom of the frittata browns well and only the top is runny, the skillet is placed under the broiler for 2 to 3 minutes until the top is golden brown and the frittata is done. For the recipes that follow, a 10-inch skillet is the perfect size, making a ½-inch-thick frittata which serves 4 as an appetizer or more as part of a buffet.

FRITTATA WITH ONIONS AND PROSCIUTTO

Frittata di Cipolle e Prosciutto

Total time: 35 minutes

Serves 4

> 2 large sweet yellow onions
> 2 tablespoons butter
> Salt
> Freshly ground black pepper

2 ounces thinly sliced prosciutto

1 or 2 sprigs fresh marjoram

1 10-ounce ripe tomato

5 large eggs

6 to 8 fresh basil leaves

¼ cup freshly grated pecorino romano

1. Peel and thinly slice the onions crosswise. Put the onions with 1½ table-spoons of the butter in a 10-inch ovenproof nonstick skillet. Season with salt and pepper and place over medium-high heat. Sauté, stirring occasionally, until the onion begins to brown, 10 to 15 minutes.

2. While the onion is sautéing, cut the prosciutto into thin strips. When the onions begin to brown, add the prosciutto and sauté for about 1 minute. Coarsely chop enough of the marjoram leaves to measure 1 teaspoon and add it to the pan. Lower the heat to medium and continue cooking until the onions are completely wilted and quite tender, 5 to 10 more minutes.

3. Peel the tomato (pages 30–31), remove the seeds, and cut into ½-inch dice. When the onions are done, add the tomato and cook until all the liquid it releases evaporates, 10 to 15 minutes.

4. Beat the eggs in a bowl. Coarsely chop the basil and add it to the eggs along with the pecorino. Mix well, then season lightly with salt and pepper. Pour the contents of the pan into the eggs and mix thoroughly.

5. Preheat the broiler.

6. Put the remaining ½ tablespoon butter in the skillet and place over medium heat. When the butter is hot, pour in the egg mixture. Cook for 6 to 8 minutes until the bottom is well browned and only the top is runny. Put the skillet under the broiler for 2 to 3 minutes until the top of the frittata is firm and golden brown. Remove from the oven and slide the frittata onto a serving platter. Serve warm or at room temperature.

FRITTATA WITH POTATOES AND PANCETTA

Frittata con le Patate e Pancetta

Total time: 50 minutes

Serves 4

> 12 ounces Yukon Gold or large red potatoes
> 2 medium sweet yellow onions
> 2 tablespoons butter
> Salt
> Freshly ground black pepper
> Pinch crushed red pepper flakes
> 6 ounces pancetta, sliced ¼ inch thick
> 5 large eggs

1. Scrub the potatoes, put them in a pot, and cover with water. Cover the pot and place over high heat. When the water comes to a boil, lower the heat so that it simmers steadily, and cook until the potatoes are tender when pierced, 20 to 35 minutes depending on the type and size.

2. While the potatoes are cooking, peel the onions and thinly slice them crosswise. You should have about 2 cups. Put the onions with 1½ tablespoons of the butter in a 10-inch ovenproof nonstick skillet. Season with salt and pepper, and the crushed red pepper and place over medium-high heat. Sauté, stirring occasionally, until the onions begin to brown, 10 to 15 minutes.

3. While the onions are cooking, unravel the pancetta and cut into thin strips 1 inch long. When the onions begin to brown, add the pancetta and sauté until it begins to brown, about 2 minutes. Lower the heat to medium and continue cooking until the onions are completely wilted and quite tender, 10 to 15 minutes.

4. When the potatoes are done, transfer them to a plate. As soon as they are cool enough to handle, remove the skins. Cut the potatoes into ½-inch dice. Add the potatoes to the onions and mix gently.

5. Beat the eggs in a bowl and season lightly with salt and pepper. Add the contents of the skillet and mix thoroughly.

6. Preheat the broiler.

7. Put the remaining ½ tablespoon butter in the skillet and place over medium heat. When the butter is hot, pour in the egg mixture. Cook for 6 to 8 minutes until the bottom is well browned and only the top is runny. Put the skillet under the broiler for 2 to 3 minutes until the top of the frittata is firm and golden brown. Remove from the oven and slide the frittata onto a serving platter. Serve warm or at room temperature.

FRITTATA WITH LEEKS AND RED PEPPERS

Frittata ai Porri e Peperoni

Total time: 40 minutes

Serves 4

> 1 red bell pepper
> 2 tablespoons butter
> 2 medium leeks
> Salt
> Freshly ground black pepper
> ¼ cup water
> 5 large eggs
> ½ cup freshly grated Parmigiano-Reggiano

1. Trim, seed, and peel the pepper (pages 31–32), then cut it into narrow ¼-inch strips.

2. Put 1½ tablespoons of the butter in a 10-inch ovenproof nonstick skillet and place over medium-high heat. When the butter foam has subsided add the pepper. Sauté, stirring occasionally, until the pepper begins to brown, 10 to 15 minutes.

3. While the pepper is sautéing, trim the root ends and tough dark green tops from the leeks (page 35). Cut the leeks lengthwise in half (or in quarters if they are more than 1 inch thick), then slice them crosswise into ½-inch chunks. Place the leeks in a large bowl of cold water and swish them around to loosen any dirt that is clinging to them.

4. When the peppers are done, lift the leeks out of the water and add them to the pan. Season with salt and pepper, stir for about 1 minute, then add ¼ cup water. Cover the pan and cook until the leeks are wilted and tender, about 15 minutes.

5. Beat the eggs in a bowl. Add the grated cheese and season lightly with salt and pepper. Add the contents of the pan and mix thoroughly.

6. Preheat the broiler.

7. Put the remaining ½ tablespoon butter in the skillet and place over medium heat. When the butter is hot, pour in the egg mixture. Cook for 6 to 8 minutes until the bottom is well browned and only the top is runny. Put the skillet under the broiler for 2 to 3 minutes until the top of the frittata is firm and golden brown. Remove from the oven and slide the frittata onto a serving platter. Serve warm or at room temperature.

PIZZA

This recipe is not meant to replicate the pizza at a pizzeria in Italy. For that you would need a wood-burning pizza oven capable of very high temperatures. This pizza is a "baker's pizza," which you might find at a bakery or in someone's home. It is meant to be baked in a home oven on a baking sheet, and the dough is more similar to focaccia or bread than the chewy pizzeria dough. The topping here, with tomato and mozzarella, makes the classic Pizza Margherita, but you can substitute any topping you wish (see box). A stand mixer fitted with a dough hook works best to make this dough; alternatively, you can use a food processor.

Preparation time: 55 minutes
Total time: at least 9 hours

Serves 4 as a main dish or 8 as an appetizer

PIZZA TOPPINGS

This is a list of the most common toppings, but the possibilities are limited only by your imagination.

Marinara–tomato, sliced garlic, and olive oil
Napoletana–tomato, mozzarella, and anchovies (only called this outside of Naples)
Quattro Stagioni–this "four seasons" pizza has a different topping in each of its four quarters
Al Prosciutto–tomato, mozzarella, and prosciutto
Alla Salsiccia–tomato, mozzarella, and sausage
Ai Funghi–tomato, mozzarella, and sautéed mushrooms, ideally fresh porcini
Vegetariana–a combination of grilled or roasted vegetables, usually eggplant, peppers, and zucchini

---

FOR THE DOUGH
¼ cup lukewarm water
1 package (¼ ounce) active dry yeast
1 teaspoon sugar
4¼ cups all-purpose flour
1 cup plus 2 tablespoons cool (not ice) water
1 tablespoon plus 2 teaspoons salt
1 tablespoon plus 2 teaspoons extra virgin olive oil

1. Combine the lukewarm water, yeast, and sugar in a small bowl to make the starter; set aside for 10 minutes.

2. Put the flour, cool water, salt, and olive oil in a stand mixer fitted with a dough hook or in a food processor. Add the starter and mix at moderate speed or run the processor just until a homogeneous dough is formed, about 1 minute in the mixer or less than 1 minute in the processor. Coat the inside of a mixing bowl with a little olive oil and place the dough in the bowl. Cover with plastic wrap and let the dough rise for at least 8 hours or up to 12 hours. Alternatively, after the dough has risen for 8 hours, you can refrigerate it for up to 24 hours. Take it out of the refrigerator at least 30 minutes before using it.

FOR THE TOPPING
2 cups canned whole peeled tomatoes with their juice
2 tablespoons extra virgin olive oil
Salt
1 pound buffalo milk mozzarella (if unavailable, use cow's milk
   mozzarella)
1 teaspoon dried oregano leaves

1. Coarsely chop the tomatoes. Heat 1 tablespoon of the olive oil in a 10-inch skillet over medium-high heat. When the oil is hot, add the tomatoes with their juice and season with salt. Cook until the tomatoes are no longer watery, 10 to 15 minutes.

2. Preheat the oven to the highest temperature possible, preferably on the convection bake setting if available.

3. While the tomatoes are cooking, cut the mozzarella into ¼-inch dice.

4. Gather dough into a ball and roll the dough about ¼ inch thick, sprinkling flour on the work surface and the rolling pin as needed to prevent the dough from sticking. If using a rectangular baking sheet to cook the pizza, roll it into an oval shape; if your baking sheet is square, roll the dough into a circle. Lightly coat the baking sheet with olive oil. Transfer the dough to the baking sheet and stretch it with your fingers to fit. You should be able to easily cover a 16 x 12-inch pan or the equivalent.

5. Spread the tomatoes over the dough and sprinkle the diced mozzarella on top. Season lightly with salt and sprinkle with the dried oregano. Finish by drizzling the remaining 1 tablespoon olive oil on top. Bake until the dough around the edges begins to brown, 10 to 15 minutes. Cut into pieces and serve hot.

SOUPS

Zuppe

- **Chilled Tomato Soup with Cucumber and Goat Cheese**
- **Tuscan Tomato Bread Soup**
- **Italian Onion Soup**
- **Artichoke Soup**
- **Egg-Drop Zucchini Soup**
- **Leek and Fennel Soup with Black-Eyed Peas**
- **Cannellini and Swiss Chard Soup**
- **Red Cabbage and Cannellini Soup**
- **Rita's Sardinian Lentil Soup**
- **Leek and Chickpea Soup**
- **Pasta e Fagioli**
- **Neapolitan Pasta and Potato Soup**
- **Porcini, Potato, and Pasta Soup**
- **Spring Vegetable Soup with Barley**
- **Farro Soup with Carrots, Celery, and Rosemary**
- **Shrimp and Butternut Squash Soup**
- **Shrimp and Zucchini Soup**
- **Veal Meatballs in Broth**

Italian soups are rarely puréed and are generally fairly substantial. They are served as a first course in an Italian meal, taking the place of a pasta or risotto, but most can easily be a meal by themselves.

CHILLED TOMATO SOUP
WITH CUCUMBER AND GOAT CHEESE

Zuppa di Pomodoro Fredda

I first tasted this delightful cold tomato soup at the Trattoria di Giovanni Rana in Verona. I loved the contrasting flavors and textures of the full-flavored tomato, the fresh, crunchy cucumber, and tangy, creamy goat cheese. The version below is my recreation of this delicious summer dish.

Preparation time: 10 minutes
Total time from start to finish: 3 hours

Serves 4

> 3 tablespoons extra virgin olive oil, plus extra for serving
> ½ small yellow onion
> 1¾ pounds ripe tomatoes
> Salt
> 1 cup water
> 1 seedless cucumber
> 4 ounces fresh goat cheese

1. Peel and finely chop the onion and put it with 2 tablespoons of the olive oil in a deep sauté pan. Place over medium-high heat and sauté, stirring occasionally, until the onion turns a rich golden color, about 5 minutes.

2. While the onion is sautéing, peel the tomatoes (pages 30–31) and coarsely chop them. When the onion is ready, add the tomatoes to the pan and season with salt. Sauté for about 5 minutes, then lower the heat to medium-low. Add the water, cover the pan, and continue cooking for 25 minutes.

3. Purée the soup using an immersion blender or a regular blender. Set aside to cool, then refrigerate.

4. While the soup is chilling, peel and dice enough of the cucumber to measure 5 tablespoons.

5. When ready to serve, stir the cucumber into the soup. Ladle the soup into bowls and place a dollop, about 2 teaspoons, of the goat cheese in the center of each serving. Drizzle a little olive oil on top and serve.

Note: Since the soup is refrigerated, you can easily make this up to 2 days ahead of time. Add the cucumber just before serving.

TUSCAN TOMATO BREAD SOUP

Pappa al Pomodoro

In this classic poor man's soup, day-old bread is cooked together with enough tomato and meat broth to flavor it. This simple combination of basic ingredients is so good that today it can be found at some of the finest restaurants (priced at many times the actual cost of its ingredients, by the way). *Pappa* also refers to baby food, and this soup makes an excellent meal for the one-year-old crowd (ours certainly approved).

Preparation time: 15 minutes
Total time from start to finish: 45 minutes

Serves 4

> 1 pound ripe tomatoes
> 4 cloves garlic
> 3 tablespoons extra virgin olive oil
> Salt
> Freshly ground black pepper
> 18 to 20 fresh basil leaves
> 3½ cups homemade meat broth (page 46) *or* ½ each beef and
>   chicken bouillon cube dissolved in 3½ cups water
> 4 ounces day-old bread

1. Peel the tomatoes (pages 30–31) and coarsely chop them.

2. Lightly crush the garlic cloves and peel them. Put the garlic and olive oil in a small soup pot over medium-high heat and lightly brown the garlic on all sides, 1 to 2 minutes. Remove and discard the garlic.

3. Add the tomatoes to the oil and season with salt and pepper. Shred the basil with a knife and add it to the pot. Pour in the broth.

4. Cut the bread into approximately ¾-inch chunks and add it to the soup. Cover the pot and bring the soup to a boil. Lower the heat to medium-low and simmer for 10 minutes. Remove from the heat and allow to rest, covered, for another 20 minutes. Serve warm.

ITALIAN ONION SOUP

Zuppa di Cipolle

This Italian version of the classic onion soup is made with olive oil, a light Italian-style broth rather than French stock, and pecorino cheese. Also, it is not gratinéed; instead the cheese is thinly shaved and allowed to melt on top of the soup.

Preparation time: 20 minutes
Total time from start to finish: 1½ hours

Serves 4

> 1½ pounds sweet yellow onions
> 2 tablespoons extra virgin olive oil
> 1 tablespoon butter
> Salt

Freshly ground black pepper

⅓ cup dry white wine

3 cups homemade meat broth (page 46) *or* 1 beef bouillon cube
    dissolved in 3 cups water

4 slices crusty Italian bread

2 ounces pecorino cheese (use a medium-aged cheese, such as
    Crosta Rossa di Pienza, not the aged pecorino romano)

1. Peel and thinly slice the onions crosswise. Put them in a soup pot with the olive oil and butter and season with salt and pepper. Place over medium-high heat and cook, stirring often, until the onions begin to brown, about 5 minutes. Lower the heat to medium-low and continue cooking until the onions are wilted completely and have started caramelizing, about 30 minutes.

2. Raise the heat to medium-high and add the wine. Let it bubble away until you no longer smell the alcohol. Add the broth and bring to a boil. Reduce the heat to low, cover the pot, and cook for 45 minutes.

3. When you are ready to serve, toast the bread slices and put one in each of 4 soup bowls. Ladle the hot soup over the bread. Using a vegetable peeler, shave thin slices of the cheese over each serving. Serve at once.

Note: This soup can be made through step 2 the day before. Store, covered, in the refrigerator and reheat before proceeding.

ARTICHOKE SOUP

Zuppa di Carciofi

During a week-long stay in Sardinia, we had the privilege of being chaperoned by the noted Italian food journalist Gilberto Arru. He took us to some of his favorite restaurants, trattorias where the food is as good as home cooking.

One was Trattoria Da Riccardo in Magomadas where we shared an extraordinary artichoke soup. The secret, we were told, was not some unusual ingredient but simply using artichokes at their peak.

Preparation time: 30 minutes
Total time from start to finish: 50 minutes

Serves 4

    1 lemon
    4 medium artichokes
    ½ medium yellow onion
    3 tablespoons extra virgin olive oil
    1 small clove garlic
    8 ounces ripe tomatoes
    Salt
    Freshly ground black pepper
    2 cups water

1. Squeeze the lemon juice into a medium bowl and fill the bowl halfway with cold water. Trim the artichokes as described on pages 34–35. Cut them into wedges about ¼ inch thick and put them in the bowl of lemon water to prevent them from discoloring.

2. Peel and finely chop the onion. Put it with the olive oil in a soup pot over medium-high heat. Sauté, stirring occasionally, until the onion turns a dark golden color, about 5 minutes.

3. While the onion is sautéing, finely chop the garlic. Peel (pages 30–31) and chop the tomatoes.

4. When the onion is done, add the garlic and sauté for about 1 minute. Add the tomatoes and cook for 2 to 3 minutes.

5. Drain the artichokes, add them to the pot, and season with salt and pepper. Add the water, cover the pot, and bring to a boil. Lower the heat so the soup simmers and cook until the artichokes are quite tender, 20 to 25 minutes.

6. Using a slotted spoon, take out about one-third of the artichokes and purée them with a food mill or in a food processor. Stir the puréed artichokes back into the soup. Serve hot with crusty bread.

Note: You can make the soup up to 2 hours ahead of time without refrigerating it. The artichokes will not taste the same if kept longer.

EGG-DROP ZUCCHINI SOUP

Stracciatella alle Zucchine

Preparation time: 25 minutes
Total time from start to finish: 45 minutes

Serves 4

½ medium yellow onion
2 tablespoons extra virgin olive oil
1 tablespoon butter
1½ pounds zucchini
Salt
Freshly ground black pepper
3 cups homemade meat broth (page 46) *or* ½ each beef and
    chicken bouillon cube dissolved in 3 cups water
3 or 4 sprigs flat-leaf Italian parsley
6 fresh basil leaves
2 large eggs
¼ cup freshly grated young pecorino cheese (preferably aged 45
    days or less)

1. Peel and finely chop the onion. Put it with the olive oil and butter in a soup pot over medium-high heat. Sauté, stirring occasionally, until the onion turns a rich golden color, about 5 minutes.

2. While the onion is sautéing, cut the zucchini into ½-inch chunks. When the onion is done, put in the zucchini and sauté until it begins to brown, 10 to 15 minutes. Season with salt and pepper and add the broth. Bring to a boil, then adjust the heat so that the soup simmers. Cook, covered, for 30 minutes.

3. Finely chop enough parsley leaves to measure 1 tablespoon. Cut the basil into narrow strips. Beat the eggs in a bowl and mix in the parsley, basil, and grated cheese.

4. When you are ready to serve the soup, slowly pour in the egg mixture while stirring. Remove from the heat and serve at once.

Note: You can make the soup through step 3 up to 2 hours ahead of time. Do not refrigerate. The zucchini will not taste the same if kept longer.

LEEK AND FENNEL SOUP WITH BLACK-EYED PEAS

Zuppa di Porri coi Fagioli all'Occhio

Although we think of black-eyed peas as a distinctively southern U.S. phenomenon, they are part of the Italian tradition as well, though not as common as cranberry and cannellini beans.

Preparation time: 30 minutes
Total time from start to finish: 1 hour

Serves 4

> 3 medium leeks
> ½ small yellow onion
> 3 tablespoons extra virgin olive oil

1 small clove garlic
2 ounces pancetta, sliced ¼ inch thick
¼ cup celery leaves
¼ cup green feathery fennel tops
½ head escarole
Salt
Freshly ground black pepper
2 cups drained canned black-eyed peas
3 cups homemade meat broth (page 46) *or* ½ each beef and
    chicken bouillon cube dissolved in 3 cups water

1. Trim the root ends and dark green tops from the leeks (page 35). Cut the leeks into 2-inch lengths. Cut each piece lengthwise in half, then into strips about ¼-inch wide. Place the cut leeks in a large bowl of cold water and swish them around to loosen any dirt that is clinging to them.

2. Peel and finely chop the onion. Put it in a heavy-bottomed soup pot and add 2 tablespoons of the olive oil. Place over medium-high heat and sauté, stirring occasionally, until the onion turns a rich golden color, about 5 minutes.

3. While the onion is sautéing, peel and finely chop the garlic. Unravel the pancetta and cut it into thin strips about ½ inch long. Coarsely chop the celery leaves and fennel tops. When the onion is done, add the pancetta and garlic to the pan and sauté until the pancetta begins to color, 2 to 3 minutes. Add the celery leaves and fennel tops; cook for about 1 minute. Lift the leeks out of the water and add them to the pot. Cook for about 5 minutes until they are wilted.

4. While the leeks are cooking, rinse the escarole and coarsely shred it with a knife. You should get about 2 cups. After the leeks have wilted, add the escarole. Season with salt and pepper and continue cooking for 2 to 3 minutes.

5. Add the black-eyed peas and broth. Raise the heat to high and bring to a boil. Lower the heat and simmer gently for 30 minutes. Add the remaining 1 tablespoon olive oil (or drizzle some over the individual servings) and serve hot.

Note: You can keep this soup up to 2 days in the refrigerator.

CANNELLINI
AND SWISS CHARD SOUP

Zuppa di Fagioli e Biete

Preparation time: 20 minutes
Total time from start to finish: 1 hour

Serves 4

½ medium yellow onion
1 medium carrot
1 rib celery
3 tablespoons extra virgin olive oil
1 pound Swiss chard
1 sprig fresh rosemary
1 ounce thinly sliced pancetta
1½ cups drained canned cannellini beans
Salt
Freshly ground black pepper
3 cups homemade meat broth (page 46) *or* ½ each beef and
  chicken bouillon cube dissolved in 3 cups water

1. Peel and finely chop the onion. Peel the carrot and celery and cut into ¼-inch dice.

2. Put 2 tablespoons of the olive oil, the onion, carrot, and celery in a heavy-bottomed soup pot and place over medium-high heat. Sauté, stirring occasionally, until the vegetables are lightly browned, about 10 minutes.

3. Rinse the Swiss chard, then tear the green leaves from the stalks. Coarsely chop the leaves and cut the stalks into 1 x ¼-inch strips.

4. Finely chop enough of the rosemary to measure 1 teaspoon. Finely chop the pancetta. When the vegetables are browned, add the rosemary and pancetta to the pot and continue cooking for about 2 minutes.

5. Add the Swiss chard leaves and stalks and the cannellini beans to the pot and season with salt and pepper. Add the broth and bring to a boil. Lower the heat so that the soup simmers, cover the pot, and cook for 40 minutes. Add the remaining 1 tablespoon olive oil (or drizzle some over the individual servings) and serve hot.

Note: You can make the soup up to 2 hours ahead of time without refrigerating it. The Swiss chard will not taste the same if kept longer.

RED CABBAGE
AND CANNELLINI SOUP

Zuppa di Cavoli e Fagioli

Preparation time: 30 minutes
Total time from start to finish: 1¼ hours

Serves 4

½ small yellow onion
1 medium carrot
1 rib celery
2 tablespoons extra virgin olive oil
1 small clove garlic
2 ounces pancetta, sliced about ⅛ inch thick
8 ounces ripe tomatoes
8 ounces red cabbage
8 ounces Savoy cabbage
Salt
Freshly ground black pepper
1½ cups drained canned cannellini beans
3 cups homemade meat broth (page 46) *or* ½ each beef and
    chicken bouillon cube dissolved in 3 cups water

1. Peel and finely chop the onion. Peel the carrot and celery and cut into ¼-inch dice.

2. Put the olive oil, onion, carrot, and celery in a heavy-bottomed soup pot over medium-high heat and sauté, stirring occasionally, until the vegetables are lightly browned, about 10 minutes.

3. While the vegetables are browning, peel and finely chop the garlic. Finely dice the pancetta. Peel the tomatoes (pages 30–31) and coarsely chop.

4. Add the garlic and pancetta to the pot and cook until the pancetta begins to brown, 1 to 2 minutes. Add the tomatoes and cook for 5 minutes.

5. Finely shred the red and Savoy cabbages. Add the cabbages to the pot and season with salt and pepper. Cook, stirring occasionally, until the cabbage is wilted, about 10 minutes.

6. Add the cannellini beans and broth. Cover the pot and bring to boil. Adjust the heat so that the soup simmers and cook for 45 minutes. Serve hot.

   Note: This soup will keep up to 3 days refrigerated.

RITA'S SARDINIAN
LENTIL SOUP

La Zuppa di Lenticchie di Rita

Rita d'Enza, owner of the restaurant and inn Gallura in Olbia, gave me this delicious Sardinian lentil soup recipe. The Sardinian greens she used are not available here, so I use mustard greens instead.

Preparation time: 20 minutes
Total time from start to finish: 1 hour

Serves 4

> 2 small sweet onions, such as Vidalia or Walla Walla
> 3 tablespoons extra virgin olive oil
> Salt
> 1 medium clove garlic
> 8 ounces mustard greens
> Pinch crushed red pepper flakes
> Freshly ground black pepper
> 8 ounces lentils (1¼ cups)
> 6 cups homemade meat broth (page 46) *or* ½ each beef and
>   chicken bouillon cube dissolved in 6 cups water

1. Peel, halve, and thinly slice the onions lengthwise. Put the onions and olive oil in a heavy-bottomed soup pot and place over medium-high heat. Season with salt and sauté, stirring occasionally, until the onion is lightly browned, about 5 minutes. Lower the heat to medium and continue cooking until the onion is wilted, about 5 minutes.

2. While the onion is sautéing, peel and finely chop the garlic. Coarsely chop the mustard greens.

3. When the onion is done, add the garlic and crushed red pepper. Sauté for about 1 minute, then add the mustard greens. Season with salt and fairly gen-

erously with black pepper. Cook until the greens are wilted, about 5 minutes, then add the lentils and broth. Cover the pot and bring to a boil. Lower the heat so that the soup simmers and cook until the lentils are tender, 30 to 40 minutes. Serve hot.

Note: You can make the soup up to 2 hours ahead of time without refrigerating it. The mustard greens will not taste the same if kept longer.

LEEK AND CHICKPEA SOUP

Zuppa di Porri e Ceci

Preparation time: 20 minutes
Total time from start to finish: 1 hour

Serves 4

> 3 or 4 medium leeks
> 2 ounces pancetta, sliced ¼ inch thick
> 2 tablespoons extra virgin olive oil
> 1 small clove garlic
> 1 to 2 fresh sage leaves
> 1 sprig fresh rosemary
> Salt
> Freshly ground black pepper
> 1½ cups drained canned chickpeas
> 5 cups homemade meat broth (page 46) *or* ½ each beef and
>   chicken bouillon cube dissolved in 5 cups water
> 6 ounces tubetti or another small pasta suitable for soup
> ¼ cup freshly grated pecorino romano

1. Trim the root ends and dark green tops from the leeks (page 35). Cut the leeks lengthwise in half (or in quarters if they are more than 1 inch thick), then

slice them crosswise in ½-inch chunks. Place the cut leeks in a large bowl of cold water and swish them around to loosen any dirt that is clinging to them.

2. Unravel the pancetta and cut into thin strips. Put the pancetta and olive oil in a soup pot over medium-high heat and sauté, stirring occasionally, until the pancetta just begins to brown.

3. While the pancetta is sautéing, peel and finely chop the garlic and coarsely chop enough of the sage and rosemary leaves to get 1 teaspoon of each.

4. When the pancetta begins browning, add the garlic and herbs. Stir for about 30 seconds. Lift the leeks from the bowl of water and add them to the pot. Season with salt and pepper and cook, stirring occasionally, for 2 to 3 minutes.

5. Add the chickpeas and broth to the pot and bring to a boil. Lower the heat so that the soup simmers, cover the pot, and cook for 30 minutes.

6. Add the pasta to the pot and cook until the pasta is done. Serve at once, sprinkling some grated pecorino on top of each serving.

Note: You can make this soup through step 5 up to 2 days in advance. Store, covered, in the refrigerator. Reheat the soup before proceeding.

PASTA E FAGIOLI

This is probably one of the best-known soups in Italian cooking. It is found all over Italy in an incredible number of variations. Perhaps the only thing all of them have in common is beans and some kind of pasta. But even the pasta varies. More northern regions use homemade egg pasta, while central and southern Italy favor flour-and-water pasta, as in this recipe. Some people purée the beans completely, some not at all. This is simply one of the many variations, but one I like for its flavor and ease of preparation.

Preparation time: 20 minutes
Total time from start to finish: 1 hour

Serves 4

> ½ medium yellow onion
> 1 small carrot
> 1 small celery
> 4 cloves garlic, peeled
> 3 tablespoons extra virgin olive oil
> ¾ cup canned whole peeled tomatoes with their juice
> 3 cups drained canned cranberry or cannellini beans
> Salt
> Freshly ground black pepper
> 5 cups homemade meat broth (page 46) *or* ½ each beef and
>   chicken bouillon cube dissolved in 5 cups water
> 6 ounces tubetti or another small pasta suitable for soup
> ¼ cup freshly grated Parmigiano-Reggiano

1. Peel and finely chop the onion. Peel the carrot and celery and cut into ¼-inch dice (you should get about a ¼ cup of each). Put the onion, carrot, celery, garlic, and olive oil in a heavy-bottomed soup pot and place over medium heat. Sauté, stirring occasionally, until the vegetables turn a rich golden color, about 10 minutes. Discard the garlic cloves.

2. Coarsely chop the tomatoes. Add the tomatoes with their juices and the beans to the pot and season with salt and pepper. Add the broth and bring to

a boil. Lower the heat so that the soup simmers, cover the pot, and cook for 45 minutes.

3. Scoop up about one-quarter of the beans and purée them using a food mill or a food processor. Return the puréed beans to the pot. Check to make sure there is enough liquid to cook the pasta. If necessary, add a little more broth or water.

4. Raise the heat to medium-high and bring the soup to a boil. Add the pasta and cook until done. Remove the soup from the heat and stir in the Parmigiano. Serve at once.

Note: You can make this soup through step 3 up to 2 days ahead of time. Store, covered, in the refrigerator. Reheat the soup before proceeding.

NEAPOLITAN PASTA AND POTATO SOUP

Zuppa di Patate e Pasta alla Napoletana

Preparation time: 30 minutes
Total time from start to finish: 1 hour and 20 minutes

Serves 4

> ½ medium yellow onion
> 1 medium carrot
> 1 rib celery
> 1 pound large red potatoes
> ¾ pound ripe tomatoes
> 3 tablespoons extra virgin olive oil
> 3 ounces thinly sliced prosciutto
> ¼ cup dry white wine
> Salt
> Freshly ground black pepper
> 5 cups homemade meat broth (page 46) *or* ½ each
>   beef and chicken bouillon cube dissolved in 5 cups
>   water
> 12 fresh basil leaves
> 6 ounces tubetti or another small pasta suitable
>   for soup
> 4 ounces smoked mozzarella

1. Peel and finely chop the onion. Peel the carrot and celery and cut into ¼-inch dice (you should get about ⅓ cup of each). Peel the potatoes, cut them into ½-inch cubes, and put them in a bowl of cold water to prevent them from discoloring. Peel the tomatoes (pages 30–31), then coarsely chop.

2. Put the onion, carrot, celery, and olive oil in a soup pot and place over medium-high heat. Sauté, stirring occasionally, until the vegetables begin to brown, about 10 minutes.

3. While the vegetables are sautéing, chop the prosciutto. When the vegetables begin to brown, add the prosciutto and cook until it loses its raw pink color.

4. Add the wine, bring to a boil, and cook for about 30 seconds to let the alcohol evaporate. Add the tomatoes and drained potatoes and season lightly with salt and pepper. Add the broth, cover the pot, and bring to a boil. Adjust the heat so that the broth simmers and cook for 45 minutes.

5. Coarsely chop the basil and add it to the soup. Add the pasta and cook until it is done.

6. While the pasta is cooking, grate the smoked mozzarella. Serve the soup hot with some grated cheese sprinkled on top of each serving.

Note: You can make this soup through step 4 up to 2 days ahead. Store, covered, in the refrigerator. Reheat the soup before proceeding.

PORCINI, POTATO, AND PASTA SOUP

Minestra di Pasta, Porcini, e Patate

Preparation time: 20 minutes
Total time from start to finish: 50 minutes

Serves 4

> 1 ounce dried porcini mushrooms
> 2 cups water
> ½ medium yellow onion
> 1 rib celery
> 1 pound white or Yukon Gold potatoes
> 2 tablespoons extra virgin olive oil
> 1 to 2 fresh sage leaves
> Salt
> Freshly ground black pepper
> 4 cups homemade meat broth (page 46) *or* ½ each beef and
>   chicken bouillon cube dissolved in 4 cups water
> 6 ounces tubetti or another small pasta suitable for soup

1. Put the dried porcini in a bowl with the water and soak for at least 15 minutes.

2. Peel and finely chop the onion. Peel and cut the celery into ¼-inch dice. Peel the potatoes and cut into ½ -inch dice. Put the potatoes in a bowl and cover with cold water to prevent them from discoloring.

3. Put the onion, celery, and olive oil in a soup pot and place over medium-high heat. Sauté, stirring occasionally, until the onion and celery are lightly browned, about 10 minutes.

4. While the vegetables are sautéing, chop enough of the sage to measure about 1 teaspoon.

5. Lift the porcini from the water and squeeze out the excess back into the bowl. Do not discard the water. Rinse the mushrooms under running water and coarsely chop them. When the onion and celery are done, add the sage, porcini, and drained potatoes. Season with salt and pepper and stir for 30 seconds, then add the broth. Add the porcini water carefully as there may be some sand at the bottom. If you want, you can pour it through a paper towel. Bring to a boil, then lower the heat so that the broth simmers. Cover the pot and cook until the potatoes are tender, about 20 minutes.

6. Add the pasta and continue cooking until it is done. Serve at once.

Note: You can make the soup about 1 hour ahead of time without refrigerating it. The potatoes will start to break down if kept much longer.

SPRING VEGETABLE SOUP WITH BARLEY

Zuppa d'Orzo alle Verdure

A delicate-tasting, quick, and delicious spring vegetable soup.

Preparation time: 30 minutes
Total time from start to finish: 1½ hours

Serves 4

> ½ medium yellow onion
> 2 tablespoons extra virgin olive oil
> 8 ounces small zucchini
> 4 ounces carrots
> 6 ounces green beans
> 12 ounces large red potatoes
> Salt
> Freshly ground black pepper
> 5 cups homemade meat broth (page 46) *or* ½ each
>   beef and chicken bouillon cube dissolved in 5 cups
>   water
> ½ cup pearl barley
> 12 fresh basil leaves

1. Peel and finely chop the onion. Put it with the olive oil in a soup pot over medium-high heat. Sauté, stirring occasionally, until the onion turns a rich golden color, about 5 minutes.

2. While the onion is sautéing, cut the zucchini into ½-inch dice. Peel the carrots and cut into ½-inch dice. Snap or cut off the ends of the green beans and cut into ½-inch lengths. Peel the potatoes and cut into ½-inch dice.

3. When the onion is done, add the vegetables to the pot. Season with salt and pepper and sauté for about 5 minutes.

4. Add the broth and bring to a boil. Lower the heat so that the broth simmers, then cover the pot and cook for 15 minutes. Use a slotted spoon to lift out about half of the vegetables and purée in a food mill or food processor. Return the puréed vegetables to the pot. Bring the soup back to a simmer and add the barley. Cook, covered, for 20 minutes.

5. Coarsely shred the basil with a knife and add it to the soup. Cook until the barley is tender, about 10 minutes. Serve at once.

FARRO SOUP WITH CARROTS, CELERY, AND ROSEMARY

Zuppa di Farro alle Carote, Sedano, e Rosmarino

Farro is actually a form of spelt, an ancient Etruscan grain. It has recently gained more popularity in the States and is becoming more available. You can also get pasta made with farro (a wonderful alternative for the wheat intolerant). If you can't find farro in your local market, pearl barley is a good substitute.

Preparation time: 20 minutes
Total time from start to finish: 1 hour

Serves 4

> 3 medium carrots
> 3 ribs celery
> 3 cloves garlic
> 2 tablespoons extra virgin olive oil
> 1 sprig fresh rosemary
> Salt
> Freshly ground black pepper
> 5 cups homemade meat broth (page 46) *or* ½ each beef and
>   chicken bouillon cube dissolved in 5 cups water
> ½ cup farro

1. Peel the carrots and celery and cut them into ½-inch chunks.

2. Lightly crush and peel the garlic cloves. Put them with the olive oil in a soup pot over medium-high heat. Cook the garlic cloves until they are lightly browned on all sides, then remove and discard them.

3. While the garlic is browning, chop enough of the rosemary leaves to measure 1 teaspoon. After removing the garlic, add the carrots, celery, and rosemary to the oil. Season with salt and pepper and sauté, stirring occasionally, until the vegetables begin to brown, 10 to 15 minutes.

4. Add the broth, raise the heat to high, cover the pot, and bring to a boil. Add the farro and lower the heat so that the soup simmers. Cook, covered, until the farro is tender, about 30 minutes. Serve at once.

Note: You can make the soup up to 2 hours ahead of time without refrigerating it. Wait to cook the farro until 30 minutes before serving, or it will soak up all the broth and become too soft.

SHRIMP AND
BUTTERNUT SQUASH SOUP

Minestra di Zucca e Gamberi

Sweet butternut squash and shrimp make a wonderful combination. I like egg pasta with the delicate flavor of this soup. If you make your own egg pasta, you can cut some into maltagliati, which are shaped like triangles approximately 1 inch on each side; once dry they will keep for months.

Total time: 35 minutes

Serves 4

> ½ medium yellow onion
> 2 tablespoons extra virgin olive oil
> 1 butternut squash, about 1¾ pounds
> Salt
> Freshly ground black pepper
> 4 cups water
> 1 pound medium (21 to 25 count) shrimp in the shell
> 4 ounces dried egg pasta, homemade (pages 170–176), or
>   store-bought fettuccine or pappardelle, broken into
>   1-inch pieces (about ¾ cup)

1. Peel and finely chop the onion and put it in a soup pot with the olive oil. Place over medium-high heat and sauté, stirring occasionally, until it turns a rich golden color, about 5 minutes.

2. While the onion is sautéing, peel the butternut squash, halve lengthwise, and remove the seeds. Cut the flesh into ½-inch cubes. When the onion is done, add the squash and season with salt and pepper. Stir, then add the water and bring to a boil. Lower the heat so that the soup simmers, cover, and cook until the squash is tender, 15 to 20 minutes.

3. While the squash is cooking, peel and devein the shrimp, then cut them into ½-inch pieces.

4. When the squash is done, add the pasta and shrimp and season with a little more salt. Cook until the pasta and shrimp are done, about 3 minutes. Serve at once.

Note: You can make the soup through step 2 up to 2 hours ahead of time without refrigerating it. Wait to cook the pasta and shrimp until ready to serve.

SHRIMP AND ZUCCHINI SOUP

Zuppa di Gamberi e Zucchine

I am particularly fond of dishes that pair seafood with vegetables. Zucchini and shrimp are wonderfully suited to each other and make this a delicious, light, fragrant soup you can prepare in less than 45 minutes.

Total time: 40 minutes

Serves 4

> ½ medium yellow onion
> 1 medium carrot
> 1 rib celery
> 12 ounces small zucchini
> 3 tablespoons extra virgin olive oil
> 1 small clove garlic
> 1 tablespoon green feathery fennel tops
> Salt
> Freshly ground black pepper
> 3 cups water
> 1 pound medium (21 to 25 count) shrimp in the shell

1. Peel and finely chop the onion. Peel the carrot and celery and cut into ¼-inch dice. Cut the zucchini into ½-inch dice.

2. Put the onion, carrot, celery, and olive oil in a soup pot and place over medium-high heat. Sauté, stirring occasionally, until the vegetables begin to brown, about 10 minutes.

3. While the vegetables are sautéing, peel and finely chop the garlic. Finely chop enough of the fennel tops to measure 1 tablespoon. When the vegetables are ready, add the garlic and fennel. Sauté for about 1 minute, then add the zucchini. Season with salt and pepper, stir well, and add the water. Cover the pot and bring to a boil. Lower the heat so that the soup simmers and cook for 20 minutes.

4. While the soup is cooking, peel and devein the shrimp. Cut each shrimp into 4 pieces. After the soup has cooked for 20 minutes, add the shrimp, season with salt, and cook until the shrimp are pink through and through, 2 to 3 minutes. Serve at once.

VEAL MEATBALLS IN BROTH

Polpettine in Brodo

Since the broth is a principal ingredient here, a good homemade meat broth will make all the difference in this simple, comforting soup.

Total time: 25 minutes

Serves 4

> 4 cups homemade meat broth (page 46)
> 1 slice white bread
> 1 tablespoon milk
> 6 ounces ground veal
> 1 large egg
> 2 tablespoons freshly grated Parmigiano-Reggiano, plus more for
>   serving
> Pinch freshly grated nutmeg
> Salt

1. Put the broth in a soup pot, cover, and bring to a boil over high heat. Lower the heat so that the broth simmers steadily.

2. Remove and discard the crust from the bread. Put the bread and milk in a small bowl.

3. Put the veal, egg, cheese, and nutmeg in a medium bowl. Mash the bread and milk together with your hands until it is a smooth pulp, then add it to the meat. Season with salt. Mix everything together thoroughly with your hands. Shape the mixture into little meatballs, about ½ inch in diameter.

4. Put the meatballs into the simmering broth and cook for 10 minutes. Serve with a sprinkling of freshly grated Parmigiano on top.

PASTA AND PASTA SAUCES

- **Simple Butter and Tomato Sauce**
- **Genoese Basil Pesto**
- **Classic Bolognese Meat Sauce**
- **Bolognese with Porcini Mushrooms**
- **Tuscan Ragù**
- **Classic Meat Sauce of the Marches**
- **Spaghettini with Olive Oil and Garlic**
- **Spaghettini with Tomato, Olive Oil, Garlic, and Basil**
- **Spaghettini with Olives and Capers, Vesuvius Style**
- **Spaghettini with Fake Clam Sauce**
- **Spaghetti with Clams**
- **Spaghetti with Clams and Porcini**
- **Spaghetti with Bottarga**
- **Spaghetti with Fresh Tomato, Eggplant, and Mozzarella**
- **Spaghetti with Eggplant and Shrimp**
- **Spaghetti Carbonara**
- **Spaghettoni with Fresh Tomato, Pancetta, and Marjoram**
- **Bucatini with Spicy Tomato Sauce**
- **Square Spaghetti with Zucchini, Tomato, and Fresh Mint**

- Square Spaghetti with Kale, Pecorino, and Mint
- Square Spaghetti with Fava Beans
- Square Spaghetti with Clams, Zucchini, and Carrots
- Linguine with Pesto and Tomatoes
- Penne with Asparagus and Salmon
- Penne with Porcini, Fresh Tomatoes, and Cream
- Fusilli with Zucchini Pesto
- Fusilli with Roasted Peppers
- Fusilli with Eggplant and Peppers
- Fusilli with Eggplant and Ricotta
- Fusilli with Savoy Cabbage and Pancetta
- Fusilli with Lamb and Pepper Sauce
- Small Maccheroni with Swordfish
- Small Maccheroni with Peas and Pancetta
- "Macaroni and Cheese"
- Maccheroni with Asiago Cheese
- Maccheroni with Olives, Anchovies, and Bread Crumbs
- Maccheroni with Neapolitan Pork Ragù
- Baked Maccheroni
- Farfalle with Peas, Sausage, and Tomato
- Farfalle with Sautéed Vegetables
- Orecchiette with Broccoli Rabe
- Egg Pasta of Emilia Romagna
- Fettuccine with Gorgonzola
- Fettuccine with Walnut Pesto
- Fettuccine with Artichokes
- Classic Tortelloni of Emilia Romagna with a Simple Tomato Sauce
- Spinach and Ricotta Tortelloni in a Porcini Cream Sauce

- **Tortelloni Filled with Radicchio**
- **Ricotta-and-Parsley–Filled Tortelloni with a Pink Tomato Sauce**
- **"Pumpkin"-Filled Tortelli with Butter and Sage**
- **Tortellini/Cappelletti**
- **Tortellini in Broth**
- **Tortellini with Cream**
- **Lasagne with Bolognese Meat Sauce**
- **Leek and Porcini Lasagne**
- **Potato Gnocchi**

To deprive an Italian of pasta would be cruel punishment indeed. I experience withdrawal if I go for more than four or five days without it. And variations of shapes and sauces are almost endless. As my mother once wrote, if Scheherazade had been an Italian girl, she might have saved her life by making a different pasta dish each night.

The many pasta shapes available are not simply for variety's sake but also because certain shapes are better suited to certain sauces. Although a long smooth pasta is good with tomato sauces, it is not well suited to meat and other chunky sauces, which are better with tubular and twisted shapes with cavities to catch the sauce. Taste sensations are also affected by texture. A smooth sauce tastes better with a smooth pasta shape, another reason for the variety in pasta.

As you travel throughout Italy, you will find pasta made with buckwheat, chickpea flour, and farro, a type of spelt. It is flour-and-water pasta and flour-and-egg pasta, however, which are by far the most widely used. The latter is best when made by hand and is commonly referred to as "homemade pasta." Flour-and-water pasta, instead, is best suited to factory production and is referred to as "factory-made" or "store-bought" pasta. One is not necessarily better than the other; they are simply different and used for different types of sauces.

Flour-and-water pastas include spaghetti, penne, and rigatoni, and are made with durum wheat (hard-wheat) flour. The dough is quite stiff and requires machine kneading. Shapes are produced by extruding the dough through dies, making a compact pasta with a sturdy body and texture best suited to olive-oil–based sauces and more robustly flavored sauces, such as those with capers, anchovies, olives, or hot red pepper. Certain flour-and-water pastas, such as orecchiette from Apulia, pici from Tuscany, and trofie from Liguria, to name a few, are still often made by hand, although they usually are not made entirely with hard-wheat flour.

Not all factory-made pastas are created equal. Better brands employ bronze dies that give the pasta a particular texture not possible with the Teflon dies mass-produced brands use. Mass-produced pasta is also dried at higher temperatures to save time but that almost toasts the pasta in the process. Producers of premium pastas use much lower temperatures and dry their pasta over a period of one to two days instead of just hours. Finally, the quality of the wheat is crucial. The makers of Latini pasta, for example, have grown wheat for generations and constantly fine-tune the blend of wheat varieties they use. They even make single varietal pastas using heirloom wheat types. Although the premium brands can cost three or four times as much as the mass-produced kind, they are still less than $2 a portion and their flavor is far superior.

Egg pasta is best homemade. The slower and gradual process of hand kneading, as well as the warmth from your hands, greatly enhances the elasticity and texture of the dough. Unlike factory-made flour-and-water pastas, such as spaghetti, egg pasta is not extruded to create noodles but rather rolled out thin and then cut into different shapes. Since the dough is stretched instead of compressed, the result is a pasta that is much more delicate and absorbent and so is better suited to butter-based sauces, sauces with cream, and sweeter, milder-flavored sauces in general.

HOW TO COOK PASTA

For perfectly cooked pasta follow these simple rules:

1. Use plenty of water, at least 6 quarts for 1 pound pasta. Without enough water, the pasta will not cook evenly and can stick together.

2. Add about 2 tablespoons salt for 6 quarts water after it boils and before putting the pasta in. Salting it before it boils will make it take longer to boil. If you don't salt the water, the pasta will have no flavor.

3. Put the pasta in and cook, uncovered, until done. Italians like their pasta al dente, meaning firm to the bite. How firm depends on where you are in Italy. The farther south you travel, the firmer the pasta becomes. It should never be crunchy in the middle, however. Cooking time varies by shape and manufacturer. Some brands offer fairly reliable cooking times on the packaging; some do not. Tasting is the only surefire method of determining if it's done.

4. Stir the pasta occasionally while it's cooking, especially in the first few minutes when its starch is at its stickiest. As long as you have plenty of water, you keep it at a rolling boil, and you stir periodically, there is no need to add any oil.

5. When the pasta is done, drain it and toss it with the sauce right away. Never rinse the pasta because it washes away the coating of starch that allows a sauce to cling to it. Adding pasta water to the sauce is rarely done in Italy.

THE PRINCIPAL PASTA SHAPES
USED IN ITALIAN COOKING

It is almost impossible to create a definitive list of pasta shapes and their names. For one thing, names for the same shapes change from one region to another. Furthermore, in the case of factory-made pasta, the names of some shapes are the fanciful invention of the pasta maker. The following is a list of the most common shapes used in Italian cooking with suggestions for what kinds of sauces are best suited to them. I have listed long shapes from thin to thick, then tubular and special shapes from small to large.

Flour-and-Water Pasta Shapes

Spaghettini Literally little or thin spaghetti. It's especially important not to overcook spaghettini. It goes well with simple but savory sauces, such as olive oil and garlic or spicy tomato sauces, but not with heavy sauces.

Spaghetti Probably the best known of all pasta shapes, spaghetti are a masterful invention. Their sturdy texture make them a perfect vehicle for a wide variety of sauces but not meat sauces or ones with large chunks.

Spaghetti alla Chitarra This wonderful pasta, whose shape resembles square spaghetti, originated in Abruzzi. *Chitarra* in Italian means "guitar." These square spaghetti, when done by hand, are made with a tool that somewhat resembles a guitar or harp. A thick sheet of pasta is pressed on top of parallel taut wires with a rolling pin, causing the wires to cut the pasta into long square strands. It is made with either egg or flour-and-water pasta. You can buy it in specialty markets.

Linguine *Linguine* means "little tongues" and is far more popular outside of Italy than it is there, where it is found mostly in the southern part of the country. Although linguine are often mistaken for fettuccine, linguine are not flat, but slightly convex, just like a tongue.

Bucatini Also called perciatelli by some manufacturers, these hollow spaghetti are wonderful with the robust sauces found in south-central Italy, such as the spicy Amatriciana sauce on page 130.

Fusilli Lunghi This amusing shape resembles a coiled telephone cord and is great with sauces with chunky bits that cling well to the pasta, such as the eggplant and pepper sauce on page 148.

Penne Penne are probably the most commonly used of the tubular pastas. They are named "pens" in Italian for their pointed quill-shaped ends. Penne are available either smooth or ridged and in a variety of sizes. Penne are best with tomato sauces, and the ridged penne with sauces that have small chunks, such as the porcini mushroom sauce on page 143.

Maccheroni Historically the name was synonymous with *pasta* when it first made its appearance in the aristocratic courts of southern Italy. Now maccheroni refers to a straight-edged tubular pasta which, like penne, can be either smooth or ridged. I prefer the ridged maccheroni for its texture.

Rigatoni These large, wonderfully chewy and satisfying tubes are a popular shape in Italy. They are traditionally served with meat sauces but are also good with chunky vegetable sauces. I serve them with the butter and Parmigiano-Reggiano sauce on page 158 because I like how the rich sauce coats them inside and out.

Orecchiette A specialty of Apulia, the name means "little ears." They are traditionally made by hand from a flour-and-water dough pressed between the thumb and palm.

Ruote Also called *ruote di carro*, which means "cartwheels," this pasta shape is traditionally served with a spicy sausage and tomato sauce. They are also good with chunky vegetable sauces and other meat sauces.

Farfalle *Farfalle* in Italian means "bow ties." Their convoluted shape makes them excellent for meat sauces and chunky vegetable sauces.

Cavatappi Their name means "corkscrews," and they are like an enlarged section of the long fusilli. Their twisted shape wraps itself around chunky vegetable sauces wonderfully.

Fusilli As an example of how confusing names of pasta shapes can be, there is a short pasta that is also called fusilli. Some are very similar to cavatappi, and some look a little more like a thick drill bit than a corkscrew. They are all spiral shaped, however, which enables sauces to cling to them remarkably well.

Strozzapreti The name, which literally translates as "priest stranglers," supposedly came about after a priest's gluttony led to a fatal encounter with this pasta. They are in fact quite harmless and are traditionally made by hand from flour-and-water dough in the south or from egg pasta in Romagna. They are about 1½ inches long and resemble a piece of stretched telephone cord.

Lumache *Lumache* is Italian for "snails," and they resemble the curled shape of a snail's shell. Meat sauces go especially well with this pasta.

Conchiglie The name means "shells," and conchiglie are available in a variety of different sizes. The smallest ones are usually used in soups, the larger ones for sauces. The very large stuffed shells are more of an Italian-American phenomenon. For the Italian palate, the quantity of stuffing that is necessary overwhelms the pasta.

Egg Pasta Shapes

Capelli d'Angelo The name means "angel hair" because capelli d'angelo are extremely thin. They are traditionally served in a soup of homemade meat broth. In Italy this pasta is never served with sauce because it is too light and delicate.

Tagliolini Except for capelli d'angelo this is the narrowest of the ribbon pastas. They are occasionally paired with a sauce but more commonly served in homemade broth.

Fettuccine Probably the best known ribbon pasta, fettuccine are a bit narrower than tagliatelle and are suited to delicate cream-based sauces.

Tagliatelle Bologna is the home of tagliatelle, flat noodles slightly wider than fettuccine. In fact in 1972 the Accademia della Cucina Italiana, an organization devoted to preserving authentic Italian cuisine, created a replica of the "ideal" tagliatella in gold. Its width was determined to be exactly 1/12,270th the height of the Torre Asinelli, Bologna's famous medieval tower, or about 6½ millimeters. Its most classic match is with Bolognese meat sauce.

Pappardelle These are wide ribbons and in Bologna are also known as *larghissime,* which means "very wide." They can be cut with either a straight- or fluted-edged cutting wheel.

Lasagne Except for the Veneto (where *lasagne* refers to what the rest of Italy calls *tagliatelle*), these are large sheets of pasta used to make the layered pasta dish by the same name (except again in the Veneto where it is called *pasticcio*).

SIMPLE BUTTER
AND TOMATO SAUCE

Sugo al Burro e Pomodoro

This sauce has been a favorite since my mother made it when I was a little boy. Now it is a favorite of my five-year-old daughter, Gabriella. Nothing could be simpler, or more delicious. When flavorful ripe fresh tomatoes are in season, by all means use them. If it is winter and only mediocre tomatoes are available, a good-quality canned tomato (page 15) is best. When tossing pasta with it, mix in some freshly grated Parmigiano-Reggiano cheese. I like this sauce with spaghetti, bucatini, and penne, but my favorite is with tortelloni filled with Swiss chard (page 181).

Preparation time: 5 minutes
Total time from start to finish: 45 minutes

Makes enough for 1 pound dried pasta

> 2 pounds ripe tomatoes *or* 3 cups canned whole peeled
>   tomatoes with their juice
> 6 tablespoons butter
> Salt
> 1 medium yellow onion

1. If using fresh tomatoes, peel them (pages 30–31). Coarsely chop the tomatoes and put them in a sauce pot. Place over medium heat, add the butter, and season with salt.

2. Peel the onion, trim away the root end, cut it in half, and add it to the pot. When the tomatoes begin to bubble, lower the heat and simmer until the tomatoes are no longer watery and the sauce is reduced, 30 to 45 minutes depending on the size and shape of the pot. The sauce will cook faster in a wider pot. When the sauce is done, you should not see any more liquid in the pan.

Note: Once cool, the sauce will keep in the refrigerator for 2 to 3 days, or you can freeze it for up to 2 months.

GENOESE BASIL PESTO

Pesto di Basilico alla Genovese

Pesto comes from the Italian word *pestare,* which means "to mash," because traditionally pesto was made with a mortar and pestle. With the invention of the food processor, the painstakingly slow process has become incredibly quick and easy. To experience truly authentic Genoese pesto, you have to go to Liguria, the region of Italy called the Italian Riviera, where you can find the tiny fragrant sweet basil for which the region is famous. Elsewhere, we must make do with locally available basil which, although it will not produce quite the same flavor, still makes a delicious pasta sauce. The traditional pairing is with trenette, a narrow fettuccine, a few boiled green beans, and sliced potatoes. Pesto is also delicious with spaghetti, spaghettini, linguine, maccheroni alla chitarra (square spaghetti), and potato gnocchi.

Total time: 15 minutes

Makes enough for 1 pound dried pasta or 1 recipe homemade pasta (pages 170–176)

> 1⅓ cups fresh basil leaves
> 1 small garlic clove
> ⅓ cup pine nuts
> 1¼ teaspoons salt
> ⅓ cup extra virgin olive oil
> ¼ cup freshly grated Parmigiano-Reggiano
> 3 tablespoons freshly grated pecorino romano
> 1 tablespoon plus 1 teaspoon butter

1. Rinse the basil leaves and spin dry. Peel the garlic and place it with the basil, pine nuts, salt, and olive oil in a food processor. Run the processor until the mixture is smooth and creamy. Transfer the contents to a mixing bowl and mix in the grated cheeses with a spoon or rubber spatula.

2. While the pasta you will serve with the pesto is cooking, add 2 tablespoons of the pasta water and the butter to the pesto and mix well. When the pasta is done, toss it with the pesto and serve at once.

Note: Pesto can be made ahead of time and frozen for up to 2 months. After adding the cheeses, place the pesto in a freezer container and coat the surface with olive oil before sealing and placing in the freezer. Defrost before adding the pasta water and butter.

CLASSIC BOLOGNESE MEAT SAUCE

Ragù alla Bolognese

Ragù is a generic term for a slow-cooked meat sauce usually with tomatoes. This is the famous meat sauce of Emilia Romagna (of which Bologna is the capital). Practically everyone from this region makes their own version with subtle changes from one generation to another. My family is from Emilia Romagna and we are no exception. I learned to make the sauce from my mother, Marcella, who learned it from my grandmother Mary. This recipe is how I make it now.

Its classic pairing is with homemade tagliatelle or pappardelle, and I would be hard pressed to think of a more satisfying dish. It is also very good with rigatoni, shells, or any substantial pasta shape, preferably one with ridges, that has nooks and cavities to trap the sauce. When tossing with pasta, add a generous sprinkling of freshly grated Parmigiano-Reggiano and a tablespoon of butter.

Preparation time: 25 minutes
Total time from start to finish: 3½ hours

Makes enough for 1 pound dried pasta or 1 recipe homemade pasta
(pages 170–176)

> ½ small yellow onion
> 1 small carrot
> 1 rib celery
> 3 tablespoons butter
> 2 tablespoons extra virgin olive oil
> 12 ounces ground beef chuck
> Salt
> 1 cup dry white wine
> ½ cup whole milk
> ⅛ teaspoon freshly grated nutmeg
> 2 cups canned whole peeled tomatoes with their juice

1. Peel and finely chop the onion. Peel the carrot and celery and cut into ¼-inch dice to get ¼ cup each. Put the onion, carrot, celery, butter, and olive oil in a heavy-bottomed sauce pot and place over medium-high heat. Sauté, stirring occasionally, until the vegetables are lightly browned, about 10 minutes.

2. Add the ground beef and break it up with a wooden spoon. Season with salt and continue stirring until the meat has lost its raw red color.

3. Add the wine and cook, stirring occasionally, until it is almost completely evaporated. Add the milk and nutmeg and cook, stirring occasionally, until the milk is mostly evaporated.

4. Coarsely chop the tomatoes and add them to the pot. Season with salt. Once the tomatoes have started bubbling, turn the heat down very low so that the sauce is barely simmering. Cook, uncovered, for 3 hours, stirring occasionally. If all the liquid evaporates before the cooking time is up, add ½ cup water as needed. After 3 hours, make sure all the liquid is evaporated before you remove the sauce from the heat.

> **Note:** You can prepare the sauce ahead of time and refrigerate it for 2 to 3 days or freeze it for up to 2 months.

BOLOGNESE WITH PORCINI MUSHROOMS

Ragù alla Bolognese con i Porcini

Dried porcini add a unique dimension to this classic sauce. Put 1 ounce dried porcini in a bowl, cover with water, and soak for at least 15 minutes. Lift the porcini out of the water and squeeze the excess back into the bowl; do not discard the soaking water. Rinse the reconstituted mushrooms under running water, then coarsely chop. When you add the tomatoes, add the mushrooms along with the water in which they soaked. Be aware that there may be some sand at the bottom of the bowl, so pour carefully or strain through a paper towel.

TUSCAN RAGÙ

Ragù Toscano

This is a Tuscan-style meat sauce that I learned from a local resident of Montepulciano, a small town about an hour south of Florence. It differs from Bolognese meat sauce in that it's made with red wine instead of white; no milk; olive oil and no butter; and both beef and pork. Its classic pairing is with pici, the thick handmade spaghetti typical of Tuscany, but it is also excellent with rigatoni, shells, or any short stubby pasta with a cavity for catching the sauce.

Preparation time: 25 minutes
Total time from start to finish: 2½ hours

Makes enough for 1 pound dried pasta or 1 recipe homemade pasta
(pages 170–176)

> ½ small yellow onion
> 1 medium carrot

3 tablespoons extra virgin olive oil
1 small bunch flat-leaf Italian parsley
8 ounces ground beef chuck
8 ounces ground pork
1½ cups canned whole peeled tomatoes with their juice
Salt
Freshly ground black pepper
½ cup red wine

1. Peel and finely chop the onion. Peel the carrot and cut into ¼-inch dice to get ¼ cup. Put the onion and carrot in a heavy-bottomed sauce pot with the olive oil and place over medium-high heat. Sauté, stirring occasionally, until the onion and carrot begin to brown, about 10 minutes.

2. While the vegetables are browning, finely chop the parsley leaves. When the onion and carrots are done, add the chopped parsley and sauté for another minute.

3. Add both ground meats and break them up with a wooden spoon. Cook until the meat begins to brown a little.

4. While the meat is cooking, coarsely chop the tomatoes.

5. When the meat is lightly browned, season it with salt and pepper. Raise the heat to high and add the red wine. Let the wine boil until it is reduced by about half to evaporate the alcohol. Add the tomatoes, season them lightly with salt, and lower the heat so that the sauce simmers gently. Cook, uncovered, for 2 hours, stirring occasionally. If all the liquid evaporates before the cooking time is up, add a little water.

Note: The sauce will keep in the refrigerator for up to 3 days or in the freezer for up to 2 months.

CLASSIC MEAT SAUCE
OF THE MARCHES

Ragù Marchigiano

While visiting The Marches, the region of Italy situated on the central Adriatic coast (Ancona is its capital), we ate at a simple trattoria called La Pianella, which we miraculously found off a narrow winding mountain road in the minuscule town of Serra S. Quirico. The food was simple but wonderful, its flavor genuinely satisfying. When our pasta arrived, it was tossed with a delicious local meat sauce, whose ingredients can change according to the cook's whim. Its flavor, however, is always dependent on a generous base of sautéed carrots and celery, and the slow, patient cooking that is essential to intensify the flavor of meats and vegetables. Serve this sauce with maccheroni or rigatoni.

Preparation time: 25 minutes
Total time from start to finish: 2 hours

Makes enough for 1 pound dried pasta

> ½ medium yellow onion
> 1 carrot
> 1 rib celery
> 3 tablespoons extra virgin olive oil
> 1½ cups canned whole peeled tomatoes with their juice
> 2 or 3 fresh sage sprigs
> Pinch crushed red pepper flakes
> 1½ pounds country-style pork ribs
> 1¼ pounds chicken wings
> Salt
> ⅓ cup dry white wine

1. Peel and finely chop the onion. Peel the carrot and celery. Cut into ¼-inch dice to get ½ cup carrot and ⅓ cup celery. Put the onion, carrot, celery, and olive oil in a large heavy-bottomed sauce pot and place over medium heat.

Sauté, stirring occasionally, until the vegetables begin to brown, about 10 minutes.

2. While the vegetables are sautéing, coarsely chop the tomatoes. Chop enough of the sage leaves to measure about 1 tablespoon.

3. When the vegetables are done, add the sage, crushed red pepper, pork ribs, and chicken wings. Season with salt and raise the heat to high. Stir well, then add the white wine. Allow the wine to boil for about a minute to evaporate the alcohol, then add the tomatoes. Once they begin to bubble, lower the heat to medium-low. Cook, uncovered, stirring occasionally, until the meat is about to fall off the bone and the sauce is no longer watery, about 1½ hours. If the sauce dries out before the meats are done, add a little water.

4. Remove the pork ribs and chicken wings from the pot. Pull the meat from the bones and cut into small pieces. Return the meat to the pot and simmer with the sauce for about 2 minutes.

   Note: This sauce will keep well in the refrigerator for up to 3 days or in the freezer for up to 2 months.

SPAGHETTINI WITH OLIVE OIL
AND GARLIC

Spaghettini Aglio e Olio

This is the classic midnight snack of the Roman *dolce vita*. In its purest form it is made simply with fresh young garlic, full-flavored extra virgin olive oil, and a hint of hot red pepper. I like to add parsley but you can omit it. This is Italian cooking at its best, with a few impeccable ingredients quickly and artfully combined. Its successful rendition is predicated on careful and loving preparation, making sure the garlic is sautéed long enough to release its rich flavor but not so long that it browns and becomes burnt.

Total time: 25 minutes

Serves 4 as a main course or 6 as part of a multicourse Italian meal

> 1 medium clove garlic
> 6 to 8 sprigs flat-leaf Italian parsley
> Salt
> 1 pound spaghettini
> 6 tablespoons extra virgin olive oil
> 1 whole dried hot red pepper *or* ⅛ teaspoon crushed red
>   pepper flakes

[handwritten: Add 1 zucchini shedded, cooked w/ garlic]

[handwritten: 2·3F]

1. Fill a pot for the pasta with at least 6 quarts water, place over high heat, and bring to a boil.

2. Peel and finely chop the garlic. Finely chop enough of the parsley leaves to measure 2 tablespoons.

3. Add 2 tablespoons salt to the boiling water, put in the spaghettini, and stir until all the strands are submerged. Cook until al dente.

4. While the pasta is cooking, put the olive oil, garlic, parsley, and hot red pepper in a medium skillet and season lightly with salt. Place over medium-high heat and cook until the garlic begins to sizzle and the smallest pieces just

Penne with Asparagus and Salmon, page 141

Chilled Tomato Soup with Cucumber and Goat Cheese, page 68

Square Spaghetti with Clams,
Zucchini, and Carrots, page 138

Shrimp with Red and Yellow Peppers, page 254

Arugula, Fennel, and Avocado Salad, page 377

Grilled Salmon with Thyme and Parsley Sauce, page 236

Linguine with Pesto and Tomatoes, page 140

Spring Vegetable Soup with Barley, page 88

Whole Artichokes Braised Roman Style, page 344

Braised Chicken with Peppers
and Eggplant, page 263

Sliced Steak with Arugula and Pecorino, page 322

Classic Tortelloni of Emilia Romagna, page 181

Veal Slices Topped with Prosciutto and Sage, page 274

Risotto with Zucchini, page 216

Beef Short Ribs Braised with Tomatoes and Potatoes, page 332

Pan-Roasted Lamb with Artichokes, page 310

begin to turn color, 1 to 2 minutes. Discard the hot pepper if using whole. Remove from the heat and set aside.

5. When the pasta is done, drain it well, toss it with the sauce, and serve at once.

SPAGHETTINI WITH TOMATO, OLIVE OIL, GARLIC, AND BASIL

Spaghettini al Pomodoro e Basilico

Most Italian recipes begin with either olive oil or butter, depending on whether the dish is delicate and sweet or more robustly flavored. Whether butter or olive oil is used also affects how the recipe evolves. This tomato sauce and the Simple Butter and Tomato Sauce on page 106 are perfect examples of the difference between the two approaches. In the butter sauce, the sweeter flavor of onion is used and the sauce is cooked longer for a deep, rich flavor. This olive oil sauce, however, is made with garlic and cooked quickly with just the flesh of fresh tomatoes to give it a vibrant, bright flavor.

Preparation time: 30 minutes
Total time from start to finish: 40 minutes

Serves 4 as a main course or 6 as part of a multicourse Italian meal

> 2 pounds ripe tomatoes
> 2 medium cloves garlic
> 4 tablespoons extra virgin olive oil
> Pinch crushed red pepper flakes (enough to make the sauce
>   lively, not spicy)
> Salt
> 12 medium basil leaves
> 1 pound spaghettini

1. Fill a pot for the pasta with at least 6 quarts water, place over high heat, and bring to a boil.

2. Peel the tomatoes (pages 30–31), scoop out and discard the seeds, and cut the flesh into 1½ x ½-inch strips.

3. Peel and thinly slice the garlic. Put the garlic with 3 tablespoons of the olive oil and the crushed red pepper in a 12-inch skillet over medium-high heat. Sauté until the garlic begins to sizzle, 1 to 2 minutes. Add the tomatoes and season with salt. Cook until all the liquid is evaporated and the tomatoes separate from the oil, 10 to 20 minutes.

4. Tear the basil leaves into pieces and add them to the sauce. Cook for 1 to 2 minutes, then remove from the heat.

5. Add 2 tablespoons salt to the boiling water, put in the spaghettini, and stir until all the strands are submerged. Cook until al dente, then drain it well. Toss with the sauce and the remaining 1 tablespoon olive oil. Serve at once.

SPAGHETTINI WITH OLIVES AND CAPERS, VESUVIUS STYLE

Spaghettini alla Vesuviana

This savory pasta dish is from the area around Naples, hence the name "Vesuvius Style." The rich flavor of tomato is necessary here, so good-quality canned tomatoes (page 15) are best.

Total time: 35 minutes

Serves 4 as a main course or 6 as part of a multicourse Italian meal

2 cups canned whole peeled tomatoes with their juice
1 medium clove garlic
Pinch crushed red pepper flakes
3 tablespoons extra virgin olive oil
Salt
8 Sicilian-style green olives
12 Kalamata olives
1 to 2 sprigs fresh oregano
2 tablespoons capers
1 pound spaghettini

1. Coarsely chop the canned tomatoes.

2. Peel and thinly slice the garlic. Put the garlic, crushed red pepper, and olive oil in a 12-inch skillet and place over medium-high heat. When the garlic begins to sizzle, 1 to 2 minutes, add the tomatoes and lower the heat to medium. Season lightly with salt and cook until the tomatoes are reduced and no longer watery, 15 to 20 minutes.

3. Fill a pot for the pasta with at least 6 quarts water, place over high heat, and bring to a boil.

4. While the tomatoes are cooking, slice the flesh of the olives from the pits. Coarsely chop enough of the oregano leaves to measure 1½ teaspoons. When the tomatoes are done, add the olives, capers, and oregano. Stir and cook for another 5 minutes, then remove from the heat.

5. Add 2 tablespoons salt to the boiling water, put in the spaghettini, and stir until all the strands are submerged. Cook until al dente, then drain it well. Toss the pasta with the sauce and serve at once.

Note: The sauce can be made through step 2 of the recipe up to 2 days ahead and refrigerated. Reheat the sauce before proceeding.

SPAGHETTINI
WITH FAKE CLAM SAUCE

Spaghettini alle Finte Vongole

This was a favorite in our house when I was growing up, and the following recipe is not very different from one my mother included in her first cookbook, *The Classic Italian Cookbook.* We used to call it "fake" clam sauce because it's actually made with anchovies, although it tastes remarkably like clam sauce.

Total time: 45 minutes

Serves 4 as a main course or 6 as part of a multicourse Italian meal

> 2 pounds fresh ripe tomatoes *or* 3 cups canned whole peeled
>   tomatoes with their juice
> 1 small clove garlic
> 3 to 4 sprigs flat-leaf Italian parsley
> 5 anchovy fillets
> 4 tablespoons extra virgin olive oil
> Salt
> 1 pound spaghettini

1. If using fresh tomatoes, peel them (pages 30–31). Coarsely chop the tomatoes. Peel and finely chop the garlic. Finely chop enough of the parsley leaves to measure 1 tablespoon.

2. Fill a pot for the pasta with at least 6 quarts water, place over high heat, and bring to a boil.

3. Chop the anchovy fillets and put them in a medium skillet with 3 tablespoons of the olive oil. Place over medium-high heat. Stir with a wooden spoon until the anchovies are dissolved, 1 to 2 minutes. Add the garlic and parsley and sauté for about 1 minute. Add the tomatoes and season with salt. Cook until the tomatoes are reduced and no longer watery, 15 to 20 minutes.

4. Add 2 tablespoons salt to the boiling water, put in the spaghettini, and stir until all the strands are submerged. Cook until al dente, then drain it well. Toss the pasta with the sauce and remaining 1 tablespoon olive oil. Serve at once.

SPAGHETTI WITH CLAMS

Spaghetti alle Vongole

One of the things I yearn for when I return to Italy after I have been away for a while is a dish of spaghetti with clams. The spicy flavor of the tiny, tender Italian clams is unlike that of any clam in North America. Of course, you can make a very respectable clam sauce in the States, but somewhat more forceful seasoning is necessary, such as hot red pepper which is not used in Italy. Also I cut the larger American clams into smaller pieces so that they are less chewy. Finish cooking the pasta in the sauce to allow the spaghetti to fully absorb the clam flavor.

Total time: 40 minutes

Serves 4 as a main course or 6 as part of a multicourse Italian meal

> 3 dozen small littleneck, Manila, or mahogany clams
> 8 ounces ripe tomatoes
> 1 small clove garlic
> 3 to 4 sprigs flat-leaf Italian parsley
> ¼ cup extra virgin olive oil
> Pinch crushed red pepper flakes
> ¼ cup dry white wine
> Salt
> 1 pound spaghetti

1. Rinse the clams in several changes of cold water until you do not see any sand at the bottom of the bowl. Peel the tomatoes (pages 30–31), scoop out

and remove the seeds, and cut into ¼-inch dice. Peel and finely chop the garlic. Finely chop enough of the parsley leaves to measure 1 tablespoon.

2. Fill a pot for the pasta with at least 6 quarts water, place over high heat, and bring to a boil.

3. Put the olive oil, garlic, parsley, and crushed red pepper in a 12-inch skillet or a 10-inch sauteuse. Place over medium-high heat and sauté until the garlic sizzles and the smallest pieces just begin to turn color, 1 to 2 minutes. Add the wine and let it bubble for about 30 seconds to let the alcohol evaporate. Add the tomatoes and cook for 5 minutes. Season with salt, add the clams, and cover the pan. Cook until all the clams are open, 3 to 5 minutes. Don't be concerned if some clams take longer to open; they are the freshest ones. Remove the clams from the pan and set aside. The sauce should have a thick, soupy consistency at this point. If it is liquidy, cook, uncovered, until it reduces, then remove the pan from the heat.

4. Add about 2 tablespoons salt to the boiling water, put in the spaghetti, and stir until all the strands are submerged.

5. Take the clams out of the shell and cut them into pieces about the size of a large pea.

6. When the pasta is just shy of al dente, drain it well. Return the pan with the sauce to medium-high heat, add the clams and pasta, and toss well. Cover the pan. (If the sauce looks too thin once the pasta is in, leave the pan uncovered.) Cook for a minute or so until the pasta is done and has absorbed some of the sauce. Serve at once.

   Note: You can make the sauce up to 2 hours ahead of time but wait to add the clams until you are ready to cook the pasta. Do not refrigerate.

SPAGHETTI WITH CLAMS
AND PORCINI

Spaghetti alle Vongole e Porcini

Total time: 45 minutes

Serves 4 as a main course or 6 as part of a multicourse Italian meal

1 ounce dried porcini mushrooms
12 littleneck, Manila, or mahogany clams
8 ounces ripe tomatoes
1 small clove garlic
3 to 4 sprigs flat-leaf Italian parsley
3 tablespoons extra virgin olive oil
Pinch crushed red pepper flakes
2 tablespoons dry white wine
Salt
1 pound spaghetti

1. Put the dried porcini in a bowl, cover with water, and soak for at least 15 minutes.

2. While the porcini are soaking, rinse the clams in several changes of cold water until you do not see any sand at the bottom of the bowl. Peel the tomatoes (pages 30–31) and cut into ½-inch dice. Peel and finely chop the garlic. Finely chop enough of the parsley leaves to measure 1 tablespoon.

3. Fill a pot for the pasta with at least 6 quarts water, place over high heat, and bring to a boil.

4. Lift the porcini out of the water and squeeze the excess back into the bowl; do not discard the water. Rinse the mushrooms under running water, then coarsely chop them.

5. Put the olive oil, garlic, parsley, and crushed red pepper in a 12-inch skillet or a 10-inch sauteuse and place over medium-high heat. Once the garlic

begins to sizzle, add the porcini. Stir well, then add the wine and cook for 1 to 2 minutes to evaporate the alcohol. Add the porcini water. Be aware that there may be some sand at the bottom of the bowl, so pour carefully or strain through a paper towel. Cook until all the liquid is evaporated, then add the tomatoes. Season with salt and cook until any liquid the tomatoes release is evaporated, about 10 minutes.

6. Add the clams and cover the pan. Cook until all the clams open, 3 to 5 minutes. Don't be concerned if some clams take longer to open; they are the freshest ones. Remove the clams from the pan and set aside. Continue cooking the sauce until most of the liquid the clams released is evaporated. When the clams are cool enough to handle, take the clams out of the shell and cut them into 3 or 4 pieces, about the size of a pea. Return the clams to the pan, stir for about 1 minute, and remove from the heat.

7. Add about 2 tablespoons salt to the boiling water, put in the spaghetti, and stir until all the strands are submerged. Cook until al dente, then drain well. Toss the pasta with the sauce and serve at once.

> **Note:** You can make the sauce up to 2 hours ahead of time but wait to add the clams until you are ready to cook the pasta. Do not refrigerate.

SPAGHETTI WITH BOTTARGA

Spaghetti alla Bottarga

It was late, and my wife, Lael, and I had just taken a six-hour ferry ride to Sardinia when we arrived at Gallura, Rita D'Enza's restaurant and inn. We would have been perfectly happy to just go to our room and fall asleep, but Rita, a good friend of my parents, would have nothing of it. "You can't go to bed on an empty stomach!" She ushered us into the dining room for "just a light supper," then set before us two plates of spaghetti with *bottarga* whose steamy fragrance magically wiped away fatigue as it enveloped us. Thus began a week of gastronomic bliss.

Bottarga (dried mullet roe described on page 20) is a delicacy that, when grated, makes a sublime pasta sauce. Some people sauté garlic and parsley in olive oil before tossing it and then add the *bottarga,* but I like this uncooked version best. This way, the rich flavor of *bottarga* comes through. When I tested this recipe at home, I held back some of the pasta without the sauce for our then three-year-old daughter, Gabriella, but she ignored us and went for the bowl with the *bottarga,* complaining, "You took too much! I want more." She proceeded to polish off two servings.

Preparation time: 5 minutes
Total time from start to finish: 25 minutes

Serves 4 as a main course or 6 as part of a multicourse Italian meal

> **Salt**
> **1 pound spaghetti**
> **4 ounces *bottarga***
> **¼ cup extra virgin olive oil**

1. Fill a pot for the pasta with at least 6 quarts water, place over high heat, and bring to a boil. Add about 2 tablespoons salt to the boiling water, put in the spaghetti, and stir until all the strands are submerged. Cook until al dente.

2. While the pasta is cooking, grate the *bottarga.* When the pasta is done, drain it well and transfer to a serving bowl. Pour in the olive oil and toss. Add the *bottarga* and continue tossing until the pasta is well coated with the sauce. Season with salt if necessary (the *bottarga* may be salty enough already) and serve at once.

SPAGHETTI WITH FRESH TOMATO, EGGPLANT, AND MOZZARELLA

Spaghetti alla Norma

This is a classic Sicilian pasta dish. Almost every restaurant on the island has it on the menu, each with subtle differences. Basically, it is a quintessentially Italian combination of eggplant and tomato. Often the eggplant is fried before it is added to the sauce, but I prefer adding it raw and cooking it gently, covered, until tender. It has a sweeter flavor and absorbs less oil.

Total time: 45 minutes

Serves 4 as a main course or 6 as part of a multicourse Italian meal

> 1½ pounds ripe tomatoes
> 1 small clove garlic
> 2 tablespoons extra virgin olive oil
> Salt
> 1 pound eggplant
> 1 pound spaghetti
> 6 ounces whole milk mozzarella
> 10 to 12 fresh basil leaves

1. Peel the tomatoes (pages 30–31) and cut them into ½-inch dice. Peel and finely chop the garlic.

2. Put the olive oil and garlic in a 12-inch skillet over medium-high heat. As soon as the garlic begins to sizzle, after 1 to 2 minutes, add the tomatoes and season with salt. Cook until the liquid the tomatoes release is evaporated, about 10 minutes.

3. While the tomatoes are cooking, peel the eggplant and cut into ¾-inch dice.

4. Fill a pot for the pasta with at least 6 quarts water, place over high heat, and bring to a boil.

5. When the liquid from the tomatoes is evaporated, add the diced eggplant to the pan. Cover and cook until the eggplant is tender, about 15 minutes. Uncover the pan and, if the sauce seems watery, raise the heat and cook until it is reduced. Remove from the heat and set aside.

6. Add about 2 tablespoons salt to the boiling water, put in the spaghetti, and stir until all the strands are submerged. Cook until al dente.

7. While the pasta is cooking, cut the mozzarella into ¼-inch dice. Put the pan with the sauce over medium heat. Coarsely shred the basil (by hand or with a knife) and add it to the pan. When the pasta is done, drain it well. Toss it with the sauce and the diced mozzarella and serve at once.

Note: You can make the sauce through step 5 up to 1 day ahead of time. Store, covered, in the refrigerator and reheat before proceeding.

SPAGHETTI WITH EGGPLANT AND SHRIMP

Spaghetti alle Melanzane e Gamberi

Total time: 50 minutes

Serves 4 as a main course or 6 as part of a multicourse Italian meal

> 1 pound ripe tomatoes
> 8 ounces eggplant
> ½ small yellow onion
> 4 tablespoons extra virgin olive oil
> 1 small clove garlic
> 6 to 8 sprigs flat-leaf Italian parsley
> Salt
> Freshly ground black pepper
> 8 ounces large (16 to 20 count) shrimp
> 1 pound spaghetti

1. Peel the tomatoes (pages 30–31) and coarsely chop. Peel the eggplant and cut into ½-inch dice. Peel and finely chop the onion.

2. Put the onion and 3 tablespoons of the olive oil in a 10-inch skillet and place over medium-high heat. Sauté, stirring occasionally, until the onion turns a rich golden color, about 5 minutes.

3. While the onion is sautéing, peel and finely chop the garlic. Finely chop enough of the parsley leaves to measure 2 tablespoons. When the onion is done, add the garlic and parsley, stir for about 1 minute, then add the tomatoes and eggplant. Season with salt and pepper and cook until the tomatoes are no longer watery and the eggplant is tender, 15 to 20 minutes.

4. While the eggplant and tomatoes are cooking, peel the shrimp, devein, and cut into ½-inch pieces.

5. Fill a pot for the pasta with at least 6 quarts water, place over high heat, and bring to a boil. When the eggplant and tomatoes are done, add about 2 tablespoons salt to the boiling water, put in the spaghetti, and stir until all the strands are submerged. Cook until al dente.

6. While the pasta is cooking, add the shrimp to the sauce, season with salt and pepper, and cook until they are pink, 2 to 3 minutes. Remove from the heat.

7. Drain the pasta, toss it with the sauce and the remaining 1 tablespoon olive oil, and serve at once.

Note: You can make the sauce through step 3 up to 1 day ahead of time. Store, covered, in the refrigerator. Reheat the sauce before proceeding.

SPAGHETTI CARBONARA

Spaghetti alla Carbonara

This is the famous Roman pasta dish whose creaminess is achieved by tossing hot pasta with raw eggs. The hot pasta partially cooks the egg, but if eating raw eggs concerns you, this dish may not be for you. Some people use only yolks, which gives more richness to the dish, and others use whole eggs. In my first book, *The Classic Pasta Cookbook,* I used only yolks, but here I use a combination of whole eggs and yolks which I find makes the dish both richer and creamier. Actual cream should never be used, nor should the pasta be finished in a skillet.

Total time: 25 minutes

Serves 4 as a main course or 6 as part of a multicourse Italian meal

4 ounces pancetta, sliced ¼ inch thick
2 tablespoons extra virgin olive oil
2 tablespoons butter
¼ cup dry white wine
Salt
1 pound spaghetti
3 to 4 sprigs flat-leaf Italian parsley
¼ cup freshly grated Parmigiano-Reggiano
2 tablespoons freshly grated pecorino romano
2 large eggs
2 large egg yolks
Freshly ground black pepper

1. Fill a pot for the pasta with at least 6 quarts water, place over high heat, and bring to a boil.

2. Unravel the pancetta and cut into thin ½-inch strips. Put the olive oil, butter, and pancetta in a 10-inch skillet and place over medium-high heat. Cook until the pancetta begins to brown but not long enough to make it crisp, 3 to 5 minutes. Add the wine and cook until it is reduced by half. Remove from the heat and set aside.

3. Add about 2 tablespoons salt to the boiling water, put in the spaghetti, and stir until all the strands are submerged. Cook until al dente.

4. While the pasta is cooking, finely chop enough of the parsley leaves to measure 1 tablespoon. Put the parsley and the grated cheeses in a serving bowl. Add the eggs and yolks and season lightly with salt and generously with pepper. Mix thoroughly.

5. Put the skillet with the pancetta back over high heat to get it hot quickly. Drain the pasta, put it in the bowl with the egg mixture, and toss vigorously. Pour the contents of the skillet into the bowl and toss again. Serve at once.

SPAGHETTONI WITH FRESH TOMATO, PANCETTA, AND MARJORAM

Spaghettoni Rustici alla Pancetta

Spaghettoni are simply extra-thick spaghetti. Regular spaghetti and bucatini are also good here.

Total time: 30 minutes

Serves 4 as a main course or 6 as part of a multicourse Italian meal

> 2 pounds ripe tomatoes
> ½ medium yellow onion
> 3 tablespoons butter
> 3 ounces pancetta, thinly sliced
> 3 to 4 sprigs fresh marjoram leaves
> Salt
> 1 pound spaghettoni

1. Fill a pot for the pasta with at least 6 quarts water, place over high heat, and bring to a boil.

2. Peel the tomatoes (pages 30–31) and coarsely chop them.

3. Peel and finely chop the onion. Put it with the butter in a 12-inch skillet over medium heat and sauté, stirring occasionally, until it turns a rich golden color, about 5 minutes.

4. Chop the pancetta. Coarsely chop enough of the marjoram leaves to measure 1 tablespoon. When the onion is ready, add the pancetta and marjoram to the pan. Cook until the pancetta begins to brown, 2 to 3 minutes. Add the tomatoes and season with salt. Raise the heat to medium-high and cook until the tomatoes are no longer watery, about 15 minutes. Remove from the heat and set aside.

5. Add about 2 tablespoons salt to the boiling water, put in the spaghettoni, and stir until all the strands are submerged. Cook until al dente, then drain well. Toss the pasta with the sauce and serve at once.

Note: You can make the sauce up to 1 day ahead and refrigerate it.

BUCATINI WITH SPICY TOMATO SAUCE

Bucatini all'Amatriciana

This is a classic Roman pasta dish and one of the few Italian dishes that is spicy. How spicy depends entirely on the person making it.

Preparation time: 15 minutes
Total time from start to finish: 45 minutes

Serves 4 as a main course or 6 as part of a multicourse Italian meal

> ½ medium yellow onion
> 4 tablespoons butter
> 3 ounces pancetta, sliced ¼ inch thick
> ¼ teaspoon crushed red pepper flakes, or more to taste
> 2 cups canned whole peeled tomatoes with their juice
> Salt
> 1 pound bucatini
> ¼ cup freshly grated Parmigiano-Reggiano
> 2 tablespoons freshly grated pecorino romano

1. Peel and finely chop the onion. Put it with 3 tablespoons of the butter in a medium saucepan over medium-high heat. Sauté, stirring occasionally, until the onion has turned a rich golden color, about 5 minutes.

2. While the onion is sautéing, unravel the pancetta and cut it into thin strips. When the onion is done, add the pancetta and red pepper flakes. Cook until the pancetta is lightly browned but not crisp, 2 to 3 minutes.

3. Coarsely chop the tomatoes and add them to the pan. Season with salt. Once the tomatoes start bubbling, lower the heat to medium. Cook until the tomatoes are no longer watery, 20 to 30 minutes.

4. Fill a pot for the pasta with at least 6 quarts water, place over high heat, and bring to a boil. When the sauce is done, add about 2 tablespoons salt to the boiling water, put in the bucatini, and stir until all the strands are submerged. Cook until al dente. Drain well and toss the pasta with the sauce in a serving bowl. Add the remaining 1 tablespoon butter and both cheeses and stir vigorously until creamy. Serve at once.

Note: This sauce can be prepared ahead of time and refrigerated for 2 to 3 days or frozen for up to 2 months.

SQUARE SPAGHETTI WITH ZUCCHINI, TOMATO, AND FRESH MINT

Spaghetti alla Chitarra con Zucchine, Pomodoro, e Menta

This is a light and fragrant summer pasta sauce. Use only fresh tomatoes here. If flavorful vine-ripe tomatoes are not available, use fresh plum tomatoes.

Preparation time: 15 minutes
Total time from start to finish: 45 minutes

Serves 4 as a main course or 6 as part of a multicourse Italian meal

> 1 pound zucchini
> 1 medium clove garlic
> 3 tablespoons extra virgin olive oil
> 8 ounces ripe tomatoes
> 2 to 3 sprigs fresh mint
> Salt
> 1 pound spaghetti alla chitarra (page 102), spaghetti, or
>   spaghettini

1. Cut the zucchini crosswise into 1½-inch-long pieces. Slice each piece lengthwise ¼ inch thick, then lengthwise again to make sticks.

2. Fill a pot for the pasta with at least 6 quarts water, place over high heat, and bring to a boil.

3. Peel and thinly slice the garlic. Put it with the olive oil in a 12-inch skillet and place over medium-high heat. When the garlic is sizzling, after about 1 minute, add the zucchini and cook, stirring occasionally, until the zucchini begins to brown, 5 to 10 minutes.

4. While the zucchini are cooking, peel the tomatoes (pages 30–31) and cut into ¾-inch dice. When the zucchini are browned, add the tomatoes and cook until they are no longer watery, 10 to 15 minutes.

5. Coarsely chop enough of the mint leaves to measure 1 tablespoon and add it to the pan. Season with salt and cook, stirring, for 1 to 2 minutes. Remove from the heat and set aside.

6. Add about 2 tablespoons salt to the boiling water, put in the spaghetti, and stir until all the strands are submerged. Cook until al dente. Drain well, toss the pasta with the sauce, and serve at once.

Note: You can make the sauce up to 2 hours ahead of time. Keep it in the pan until you are ready to cook the pasta.

SQUARE SPAGHETTI WITH KALE, PECORINO, AND MINT

Spaghetti alla Chitarra alle Ortiche

Ortiche are nettles and, although they don't sound like something you want to get near, let alone eat, the leafy tops are actually delicious and not uncommon in Italian cooking. I had the pleasure of tasting this sauce for pasta at a wonderful simple restaurant in Ancona called Osteria del Teatro Strabacco. Since the produce section of your local supermarket is unlikely to carry nettles, I experimented with possible substitutes and found that kale is a remarkably good stand-in.

Total time: 40 minutes

Serves 4 as a main course or 6 as part of a multicourse Italian meal

> 12 ounces kale
> Salt
> ½ medium yellow onion
> 5 tablespoons butter
> 1 pound spaghetti alla chitarra (page 102) or spaghetti
> 12 to 14 fresh mint leaves
> 2 ounces young pecorino cheese (not romano),
>   freshly grated

1. Rinse the kale leaves and remove the tough center ribs. Place the leaves in a pot over medium-high heat and add about 1 cup water and a generous sprinkling of salt. Cover the pot and cook, stirring occasionally, until the kale is tender, 8 to 10 minutes.

2. While the kale is cooking, peel and finely chop the onion and put it in a 12-inch skillet with 2 tablespoons of the butter. Sauté, stirring occasionally, over medium-high heat until the onion turns a rich golden color, about 5 minutes.

3. Fill a pot for the pasta with at least 6 quarts water, place over high heat, and bring to a boil.

4. When the kale is tender, drain it in a colander, pressing down with a spoon to squeeze out as much water as possible. Transfer the kale to a cutting board and coarsely chop. When the onion is ready, lower the heat to medium, add the kale, and sauté for about 10 minutes. It is important to sauté long enough so that the flavors will be rich enough to season the pasta.

5. Add about 2 tablespoons salt to the boiling water, put in the spaghetti, and stir until all the strands are submerged. Cook until al dente.

6. While the pasta is cooking, coarsely chop the mint. Drain the pasta well and toss with the kale in a serving bowl. Cut the remaining 3 tablespoons butter into small chunks and add to the pasta along with the cheese and mint. Toss again and serve at once.

SQUARE SPAGHETTI
WITH FAVA BEANS

Spaghetti alla Chitarra alle Fave

This recipe comes from The Marches region, where I ate it in a restaurant called Giardino in the town of S. Lorenzo in Campo. Fresh fava beans, which are in season in May and June, are delicious raw, dipped in sea salt, or cooked. Normally I do not remove the skin of the fava beans, but here it important because this is a sauce. Since only the green tops of the fennel are used, you can serve the bulb thinly sliced in a salad.

Preparation time: 25 minutes
Total time from start to finish: 45 minutes

Serves 4 as a main course or 6 as part of a multicourse Italian meal

> 1¼ pounds fresh fava beans in the pod
> ½ medium yellow onion
> 3 tablespoons extra virgin olive oil
> 2 ounces pancetta sliced ¼ inch thick
> 1 pound ripe tomatoes
> 4 to 6 sprigs green feathery fennel tops
> Salt
> 1 pound spaghetti alla chitarra (page 102) or spaghetti
> ¼ cup freshly grated pecorino romano

1. Remove the fava beans from the pods and peel the skins from the beans.

2. Peel and finely chop the onion. Put the olive oil and onion in a 12-inch skillet over medium-high heat. Sauté, stirring occasionally, until the onion turns a rich golden color, about 5 minutes.

3. While the onion is sautéing, unravel the pancetta and cut into thin strips. Peel the tomatoes (pages 30–31) and coarsely chop. Chop enough of the fennel tops to measure 2 tablespoons.

4. When the onion is ready, add the pancetta and cook until it begins to brown, 2 to 3 minutes. Add the tomatoes, fava beans, and fennel tops. Season with salt, lower the heat to medium-low, and cook until the fava beans are tender, 20 to 25 minutes. If all the liquid in the pan evaporates before the fava beans are cooked, add some water.

5. Fill a pot for the pasta with at least 6 quarts water, place over high heat, and bring to a boil.

6. Add about 2 tablespoons salt to the boiling water, put in the spaghetti, and stir until all the strands are submerged. Cook until al dente, then drain well. Toss the pasta with the sauce and pecorino cheese. Serve at once.

Note: You can make the sauce up to 1 day ahead and refrigerate it.

SQUARE SPAGHETTI WITH CLAMS, ZUCCHINI, AND CARROTS

Spaghetti alla Chitarra con Vongole, Zucchine, e Carote

Italians often pair vegetables with seafood. This combination of clams with zucchini and carrots is a particular favorite at our house.

Total time: 1 hour

Serves 4 as a main course or 6 as part of a multicourse Italian meal

> 1 pound small zucchini
> 2 medium carrots
> ½ medium yellow onion
> 3 tablespoons extra virgin olive oil
> 1 small clove garlic
> 6 to 8 sprigs flat-leaf Italian parsley
> Salt
> Freshly ground black pepper
> 2 dozen littleneck or Manila clams
> 1 pound spaghetti alla chitarra (page 102) or spaghetti

1. Cut the zucchini into ½-inch dice. Peel the carrots and cut into ¼-inch dice.

2. Peel and finely chop the onion. Put it in a 12-inch skillet with the olive oil. Place over medium-high heat and sauté, stirring occasionally, until the onion turns a rich golden color, about 5 minutes.

3. While the onion is sautéing, peel and finely chop the garlic. Finely chop enough of the parsley leaves to measure 2 tablespoons. When the onion is done, add the garlic and parsley and cook for another minute. Add the carrots and zucchini and season with salt and pepper. Lower the heat to medium and cook until the vegetables are very tender and some have begun to brown around the edges, about 30 minutes.

4. Fill a pot for the pasta with at least 6 quarts water, place over high heat, and bring to a boil.

5. While the vegetables are cooking, rinse the clams in several changes of cold water until you do not see any sand at the bottom of the bowl. Put them in a saucepan with about ½ inch water and place over medium-high heat. Cook, covered, until all the clams are open, 3 to 5 minutes. Don't be concerned if some clams take longer to open, they are the freshest ones. Remove the clams from the pan and set aside, saving the liquid in the pan. As soon as they are cool enough to handle, take the clams out of the shell and cut them into pieces about the size of a large pea. Put the clams in a small bowl with the liquid from the saucepan.

6. Once the vegetables are done, add about 2 tablespoons salt to the boiling water, put in the spaghetti, and stir until all the strands are submerged. Cook until just shy of al dente.

7. Lift the clams from the liquid and add them to the vegetables. Carefully pour in the clam liquid, taking care not to add any sand that may have settled at the bottom. Raise the heat to high and cook until most of the liquid is evaporated. The pasta will finish cooking in the sauce, so reserve a little of the liquid in the pan.

8. When the pasta is ready, drain it well and transfer to the skillet with the sauce. Cook for about 1 minute until the pasta is completely done and it has absorbed the remaining liquid in the sauce. Serve at once.

Note: You can make the sauce up to 2 hours ahead of time but wait to add the clams until you are ready to cook the pasta. Do not refrigerate.

LINGUINE WITH PESTO AND TOMATOES

Linguine al Pesto e Pomodori

Basil pesto mixed with fresh raw tomatoes makes a truly delicious summer pasta sauce.

Preparation time: 10 minutes
Total time from start to finish: 25 minutes

Serves 4 as a main course or 6 as part of a multicourse Italian meal

> ½ cup Genoese Basil Pesto (page 107)
> Salt
> 1 pound linguine
> 8 ounces ripe tomatoes

1. Make the Genoese Basil Pesto.

2. Fill a pot for the pasta with at least 6 quarts water, place over high heat, and bring to a boil. Add about 2 tablespoons salt to the boiling water, put in the linguine, and stir until all the strands are submerged. Cook until al dente.

3. While the pasta is cooking, peel the tomatoes (pages 30–31), remove the seeds, and cut into ¼-inch dice. Place the tomatoes and pesto in the serving bowl. Add about 2 tablespoons of the pasta cooking water and stir well.

4. When the pasta is done, drain it well. Toss the pasta with the sauce and serve at once.

PENNE WITH ASPARAGUS
AND SALMON

Penne agli Asparagi e Salmone

Seafood and vegetables are a typical Italian combination, and asparagus and salmon complement each other perfectly.

Total time: 45 minutes

Serves 4 as a main course or 6 as part of a multicourse Italian meal

> 8 ounces asparagus
> Salt
> ½ medium yellow onion
> 2 tablespoons extra virgin olive oil
> 12 ounces ripe tomatoes
> Freshly ground black pepper
> 1 pound penne
> ⅓ cup heavy cream
> 8 ounces skinless salmon fillet

1. Fill a sauté pan wide enough to accommodate the asparagus with water, place over high heat, and bring to a boil.

2. Cut off the woody bottom part of the asparagus spears, then peel the remaining bottom third. Add 1 teaspoon salt to the boiling water, then gently slide in the asparagus. Cook until the asparagus are tender, 5 to 6 minutes, then lift them out and set aside.

3. While the asparagus are cooking, peel and finely chop the onion. Put it in a 12-inch skillet with the olive oil over medium-high heat. Sauté, stirring occasionally, until it turns a rich golden color, about 5 minutes.

4. While the onion is sautéing, cut the asparagus into ¾-inch lengths. When the onion is ready, add the asparagus and sauté for about 5 minutes.

5. Fill a pot for the pasta with at least 6 quarts water, place over high heat, and bring to a boil.

6. While the asparagus are sautéing, peel the tomatoes (pages 30–31) and coarsely chop. Add the tomatoes to the asparagus and season with salt and pepper. Cook until the liquid the tomatoes release is evaporated completely.

7. Add about 2 tablespoons salt to the boiling water, put in the penne, and stir well. Cook until al dente.

8. Add the cream to the sauce and cook for 1 to 2 minutes until it thickens a bit. Cut the salmon into strips 2 to 3 inches long and about ¼ inch thick. Add them to the pan, season with salt and pepper, and cook for 2 to 3 minutes until the fish is cooked and flakes easily.

9. When the pasta is done, drain it well, toss with the sauce, and serve at once.

   Note: You can make the sauce through step 6 up to 1 day ahead of time. Store, covered, in the refrigerator. Reheat before proceeding.

PENNE WITH PORCINI, FRESH TOMATOES, AND CREAM

Penne ai Porcini, Pomodori, e Panna

Total time: 40 minutes

Serves 4 as a main course or 6 as part of a multicourse Italian meal

> 1 ounce dried porcini mushrooms
> ½ medium yellow onion
> 2 tablespoons butter
> 8 ounces cremini or white mushrooms
> Salt
> Freshly ground black pepper
> 1 pound ripe tomatoes
> 1 pound penne
> ½ cup heavy cream

1. Put the dried porcini in a bowl, cover with water, and soak for at least 15 minutes.

2. Fill a pot for the pasta with at least 6 quarts water, place over high heat, and bring to a boil.

3. Peel and finely chop the onion. Put it in a 12-inch skillet with the butter over medium-high heat. Sauté, stirring occasionally, until the onion turns a rich golden color, about 5 minutes.

4. While the onion is sautéing, brush any dirt off the fresh mushrooms and thinly slice them.

5. When the porcini have finished soaking, lift them out of the water and squeeze the excess water back into the bowl; do not discard the water. Rinse the porcini under running water, then coarsely chop them. Add the porcini to the onions along with the soaking water. Be aware that there may be some

sand at the bottom of the bowl, so pour carefully or strain through a paper towel. Cook until the liquid is evaporated, then add the fresh mushrooms. Season with salt and pepper and cook until all the liquid the mushrooms release is evaporated, 10 to 15 minutes.

6. While the mushrooms are cooking, peel the tomatoes (pages 30–31) and coarsely chop. When the mushrooms are done, add the tomatoes, season with salt, and cook until they are no longer watery, about 10 minutes.

7. Add about 2 tablespoons salt to the boiling water, put in the penne, and stir well. Cook until al dente.

8. Add the cream to the sauce and cook until it is thick enough to coat a spoon. When the pasta is done, drain it well, toss with the sauce, and serve at once.

> *Note:* You can make the sauce through step 6 up to 2 days ahead. Store, covered, in the refrigerator. Reheat before proceeding.

FUSILLI WITH ZUCCHINI PESTO

Fusilli al Pesto di Zucchine

In Italian *pesto* means anything that is finely ground or chopped. Here is a wonderfully fragrant pesto of zucchini, mint, garlic, and olive oil.

Total time: 35 minutes

Serves 4 as a main course or 6 as part of a multicourse Italian meal

> Salt
> 1 pound zucchini
> 3 tablespoons pine nuts

1 small clove garlic
1 pound short or long fusilli
12 fresh mint leaves
3 tablespoons extra virgin olive oil
¾ cup freshly grated Parmigiano-Reggiano

1. Preheat the oven to 350°, or 325° if convection heat is available.

2. Fill a pot that will comfortably hold the zucchini with water and place it over high heat. Fill a pot for the pasta with at least 6 quarts water, place over high heat, and bring to a boil.

3. Add 1 teaspoon salt to the boiling water for the zucchini, then put in the zucchini. Cook until tender, about 10 minutes, then lift the zucchini out and set aside.

4. Put the pine nuts on a baking sheet and toast them in the oven until lightly browned, about 5 minutes.

5. While the zucchini are cooking, finely chop the garlic.

6. After the zucchini are cooked, add about 2 tablespoons salt to the boiling pasta water, put in the fusilli, and stir well. Cook until al dente.

7. While the pasta is cooking, cut the zucchini into chunks and peel the garlic. Put the zucchini, garlic, mint leaves, olive oil, and pine nuts in a food processor or blender, season with salt, and chop very fine. Transfer the mixture to a serving bowl and mix in ½ cup of the Parmigiano.

8. When the pasta is done, drain it well and toss it with the sauce in the bowl. Mix in the remaining ¼ cup cheese and serve at once.

FUSILLI WITH
ROASTED PEPPERS

Fusilli ai Peperoni Arrosto

When I first made this pasta sauce, I knew it would become a favorite. Simple to prepare, its flavors are perfectly balanced. It is an ideal aromatic summer dish.

Total time: 40 minutes

Serves 4 as a main course or 6 as part of a multicourse Italian meal

> 2 red bell peppers
> 2 green bell peppers
> ½ small bunch flat-leaf Italian parsley
> 8 to 10 sprigs fresh thyme
> 3 to 4 sprigs fresh marjoram
> Salt
> 1 pound short or long fusilli
> 6 tablespoons extra virgin olive oil
> ¼ cup freshly grated pecorino romano

1. To roast the peppers, preheat a charcoal or gas grill or a broiler. Alternatively, you can simply use the open flame of a gas burner. Roast the peppers, turning as needed, until the skin is charred on all sides. The time will vary depending on the cooking method you choose. Put the hot peppers in a plastic bag and tie it shut. Let them sit for 5 minutes to allow the steam from the peppers to loosen the skin.

2. Fill a pot for the pasta with at least 6 quarts water, place over high heat, and bring to a boil.

3. Finely chop enough of the parsley leaves to measure ¼ cup, and enough of the thyme and marjoram leaves to measure 2 teaspoons each. Mix the herbs with a pinch of salt in a small bowl.

4. Take the peppers out of the plastic bag and remove the skins, stems, and seeds. Remove any white pith inside the peppers. Do not rinse them, or you'll wash away flavor. Cut the peppers into thin strips 1½ to 2 inches long.

5. Add about 2 tablespoons salt to the boiling water, put in the fusilli, and stir well. Cook until al dente.

6. While the pasta is cooking, put the herbs, olive oil, and pepper strips in a small skillet over medium heat. As soon as the peppers begin sizzling, remove the pan from the heat.

7. When the pasta is done, drain it well and toss it with the sauce. Mix in the grated cheese and serve at once.

Note: You can roast the peppers up to 1 day ahead and keep them in the refrigerator.

FUSILLI WITH EGGPLANT AND PEPPERS

Fusilli ai Peperoni e Melanzane

Total time: 45 minutes

Serves 4 as a main course or 6 as part of a multicourse Italian meal

10 ounces eggplant
1 red bell pepper
1 yellow bell pepper
1 medium clove garlic
1 to 2 sprigs fresh marjoram
3 tablespoons extra virgin olive oil
Salt
1 pound ripe tomatoes
1 pound short or long fusilli
12 Kalamata olives

1. Peel the eggplant and cut into ½-inch dice (about 3 cups). Core, seed, and peel the peppers (pages 31–32). Cut away any white pith inside the peppers and cut into 1-inch squares.

2. Fill a pot for the pasta with at least 6 quarts water, place over high heat, and bring to a boil.

3. Peel and thinly slice the garlic. Coarsely chop enough of the marjoram leaves to measure 1 teaspoon. Put the garlic and marjoram in a 10-inch skillet with the olive oil. Place over medium-high heat and sauté until the garlic begins to sizzle, 1 to 2 minutes. Add the peppers and sauté for another few minutes. Add the eggplant and season with salt. Lower the heat to medium, cover the pan, and cook until the eggplant is tender, 6 to 8 minutes.

4. While the eggplant is cooking, peel the tomatoes (pages 30–31) and coarsely chop. When the eggplant is done, add the tomato, season lightly

with salt, and cook, uncovered, until the tomatoes are reduced and the liquid they release is evaporated, 10 to 15 minutes.

5. Add about 2 tablespoons salt to the boiling water, put in the fusilli, and stir well. Cook until al dente.

6. While the tomatoes are cooking, slice the flesh of the olives away from the pits. When the tomatoes are done, add the olives, cook for 2 more minutes, and remove from the heat.

7. When the pasta is done, drain it well, toss with the sauce, and serve at once.

Note: You can make the sauce up to 1 day ahead and refrigerate it. Wait to add the olives until you are ready to cook the pasta.

FUSILLI WITH EGGPLANT AND RICOTTA

Fusilli con Melanzane e Ricotta

In this Sicilian pasta dish, ricotta makes the sauce creamy without cream.

Total time: 40 minutes

Serves 4 as a main course or 6 as part of a multicourse Italian meal

½ small yellow onion
2 tablespoons extra virgin olive oil
1 pound eggplants
1 small clove garlic
Salt
1½ pounds ripe tomatoes
1 pound long fusilli
12 medium basil leaves
½ cup whole-milk ricotta

1. Peel and finely chop the onion. Put it in a 10-inch skillet with the olive oil. Place over medium-high heat and sauté, stirring occasionally, until the onion turns a rich golden color, about 5 minutes.

2. While the onion is sautéing, peel the eggplants and cut into ½-inch dice. Peel and finely chop the garlic. When the onion is ready, add the garlic and sauté for about 1 minute. Add the eggplant and season with salt. Lower the heat to medium, cover the pan, and cook until the eggplant is tender, about 10 minutes.

3. Fill a pot for the pasta with at least 6 quarts of water, place over high heat, and bring to a boil.

4. While the eggplant is cooking, peel the tomatoes (pages 30–31) and coarsely chop. When the eggplant is tender, add the tomatoes, season lightly with salt, and cook, uncovered, until they are no longer watery, 10 to 15 minutes.

5. Add about 2 tablespoons salt to the boiling water, put in the fusilli, and stir until all the strands are submerged. Cook until al dente.

6. When the tomatoes are done, coarsely shred the basil leaves and add them to the pan. Cook for about 1 minute, then remove from the heat.

7. When the pasta is done, drain it well, toss it with the sauce and ricotta, and serve at once.

Note: You can make the sauce up to 1 day ahead and refrigerate it. Wait to add the basil until you are ready to cook the pasta.

FUSILLI WITH SAVOY CABBAGE AND PANCETTA

Fusilli alla Verza e Pancetta

Sweet Savoy cabbage, bitter curly endive, and pancetta complement each other perfectly in this savory pasta sauce.

Preparation time: 20 minutes
Total time from start to finish: 45 minutes

Serves 4 as a main course or 6 as part of a multicourse Italian meal

> ½ medium yellow onion
> 3 tablespoons extra virgin olive oil, plus extra for serving
> 2 ounces pancetta, sliced about ¼ inch thick
> ½ medium Savoy cabbage, about 12 ounces
> Salt
> 8 ounces curly endive
> Freshly ground black pepper
> 1 pound short or long fusilli

1. Peel and chop the onion. Put it with the olive oil in a 12-inch skillet. Place over medium-high heat and sauté, stirring occasionally, until the onion turns a rich golden color, about 5 minutes.

2. While the onion is sautéing, unravel the pancetta and cut it into thin strips. When the onion is done, add the pancetta and cook until it just begins to brown, 2 to 3 minutes.

3. Finely shred the Savoy cabbage and, when the pancetta is done, add it to the pan. Season with salt, cover the pan, and lower the heat to medium. Cook until the cabbage is wilted, about 10 minutes.

4. While the cabbage is cooking, finely shred the curly endive. After the cabbage is wilted, add the endive to the pan. Season lightly with salt and fairly generously with pepper. Cover the pan and cook until the vegetables are very tender, about 30 minutes. Check them from time to time and, if they begin to stick to the pan, add a little water. It's fine if they brown a little. Remove from the heat.

5. Fill a pot for the pasta with at least 6 quarts water, place over high heat, and bring to a boil.

6. When the vegetables are done, add about 2 tablespoons salt to the boiling water, put in the fusilli, and stir well. Cook until al dente. Drain the pasta well and toss it with the sauce. If it seems a little dry, add a little olive oil. Serve at once.

Note: You can make the sauce up to 2 hours ahead of time but do not refrigerate.

FUSILLI WITH LAMB
AND PEPPER SAUCE

Fusilli col Sugo di Agnello e Peperoni

Preparation time: 45 minutes
Total time from start to finish: 2¾ hours

Serves 4 as a main course or 6 as part of a multicourse Italian meal

> ½ small yellow onion
> 12 ounces boneless lamb shoulder or shank
> 3 tablespoons extra virgin olive oil
> 1 sprig fresh rosemary
> ¼ cup dry white wine
> 1½ cups canned whole peeled tomatoes with their juice
> Salt
> 1 yellow bell pepper
> 1 pound short or long fusilli

1. Peel and finely chop the onion. Cut the lamb into ¼-inch dice. Put the olive oil and onion in a heavy-bottomed saucepan and place over medium-high heat. Sauté, stirring occasionally, until the onion turns a rich golden color, about 5 minutes.

2. Chop enough rosemary leaves to measure 1 teaspoon and add it to the onion. Stir well, then add the lamb. Sauté until the lamb has lost its raw red color. Add the wine and let it bubble away until it is reduced by about half. While the wine is reducing, coarsely chop the tomatoes. Add them to the pan and season with salt. Adjust the heat so that the tomatoes simmer gently. Cook, uncovered, until the meat is very tender, at least 2 hours. If the liquid in the pan evaporates, add a little water.

3. While the sauce is cooking, core, seed, and peel the pepper (pages 31–32). Cut away any white pith inside the pepper and cut it into narrow strips 1 to 1½ inches long.

4. Fill a pot for the pasta with at least 6 quarts water, place over high heat, and bring to a boil.

5. Add the pepper to the sauce and cook, covered, until it is quite tender, 15 to 20 minutes.

6. Add about 2 tablespoons salt to the boiling water, put in the fusilli, and stir well. Cook until al dente. When the pasta is done, drain it well, toss with the sauce, and serve at once.

Note: You can make the sauce up to 2 days ahead and refrigerate it. Wait to add the bell pepper until you are ready to cook the pasta.

SMALL MACCHERONI WITH SWORDFISH

Maccheroncini al Pesce Spada

This dish epitomizes what I have found true Sicilian cooking to be: fresh tasting, light, and fragrant.

Total time: 30 minutes

Serves 4 as a main course or 6 as part of a multicourse Italian meal

> ½ medium yellow onion
> ¼ cup extra virgin olive oil
> 1½ pounds ripe tomatoes
> Salt
> 1 pound maccheroncini
> 1 pound swordfish
> 6 to 8 sprigs flat-leaf Italian parsley
> Freshly ground black pepper

1. Fill a pot for the pasta with at least 6 quarts water, place over high heat, and bring to a boil.

2. Peel and finely chop the onion. Put it in a 12-inch skillet with the olive oil. Place over medium-high heat and sauté, stirring occasionally, until the onion turns a rich golden color, about 5 minutes.

3. While the onion is sautéing, peel the tomatoes (pages 30–31) and coarsely chop. When the onion is done, add the tomatoes, season with salt, and cook until the tomatoes are no longer watery, 10 to 15 minutes.

4. Add about 2 tablespoons salt to the boiling water, put in the pasta, and stir well. Cook until al dente.

5. While the tomatoes are cooking, remove the swordfish skin and cut the fish into ¼-inch dice. Finely chop enough of the parsley leaves to measure 2 tablespoons. When the tomatoes are done, add the swordfish, season with salt and pepper, and cook briefly until the fish is cooked through, 2 to 3 minutes. Add the parsley, cook for another minute, and remove from the heat.

6. When the pasta is done, drain it well, toss with the sauce, and serve at once.

SMALL MACCHERONI WITH PEAS AND PANCETTA

Maccheroncini ai Piselli e Pancetta

Fresh peas will give the best flavor to this sauce, but when they are not in season, substitute premium frozen peas.

Total time: 40 minutes

Serves 4 as a main course or 6 as part of a multicourse Italian meal

> 1½ pounds fresh peas in the pod *or* 8 ounces frozen peas
> ½ medium yellow onion
> 2 tablespoons butter
> 3 ounces pancetta, sliced ¼ inch thick
> Salt
> Freshly ground black pepper
> 1 pound maccheroncini
> ¾ cup heavy cream
> ½ cup freshly grated Parmigiano-Reggiano

1. If using fresh peas, shell them.

2. Peel and finely chop the onion. Put it with the butter in a 10-inch skillet. Place over medium-high heat and sauté, stirring occasionally, until it turns a rich golden color, about 5 minutes.

3. Fill a pot for the pasta with at least 6 quarts water, place over high heat, and bring to a boil.

4. While the onion is sautéing, unravel the pancetta and cut into thin strips about 1 inch long. When the onion is done, add the pancetta and cook until it begins to brown, 2 to 3 minutes. Add the peas, season with salt and pepper, and stir until well coated. If using fresh peas, add just enough water to cover the peas. Lower the heat to medium and cook, uncovered, until the

peas are tender, about 20 minutes if using fresh or 10 minutes if using frozen. If the pan dries out before the peas are tender, add a little water. When the peas are done, there should not be any liquid left in the pan.

5. Add about 2 tablespoons salt to the boiling water, put in the pasta, and stir well. Cook until al dente.

6. Add the cream to the peas and cook until the cream is thick enough to coat a spoon, 1 to 2 minutes. Remove from the heat.

7. When the pasta is done, drain it well, toss with the sauce and the Parmigiano, and serve at once.

"MACARONI AND CHEESE"

Pasta al Burro e Formaggio

Although this bears little resemblance to the macaroni and cheese typically served in the States, it is certainly as universally loved by children (and adults) in Italy. The cheese, Parmigiano-Reggiano, makes it a nutritious meal as well as a delicious one. It is an easily digestible cheese rich in protein, vitamins, calcium, and phosphorus. In fact pediatricians in Italy recommend introducing it to a baby's diet as soon as the child begins eating solid food. It is best to use a sturdy flour-and-water pasta such as spaghetti, rigatoni, maccheroni, or conchiglie.

Total time: 25 minutes

Serves 4 as a main course or 6 as part of a multicourse Italian meal

> **Salt**
> **1 pound dried pasta**
> **3 tablespoons butter**
> **1 cup freshly grated Parmigiano-Reggiano**
> **¼ cup heavy cream**

1. Fill a pot for the pasta with at least 6 quarts of water, place over high heat, and bring to a boil. Add about 3 tablespoons salt to the boiling water, put in the pasta, and stir. Cook until al dente.

2. While the pasta is cooking, cut the butter into 3 or 4 pieces and place it at the bottom of a serving bowl.

3. When the pasta is done, drain it well and put it in the bowl with the butter. Add half of the grated cheese and mix very thoroughly. Add the heavy cream and mix again. Add the remaining cheese, mix well, and serve at once.

MACCHERONI
WITH ASIAGO CHEESE

Maccheroni all'Asiago

Fresh Asiago is one of several cheeses that can be used in this recipe. Fontina, Taleggio, Gorgonzola, or a young mild pecorino are also good. Or you can do a combination.

Total time: 25 minutes

Serves 4 as a main course or 6 as part of a multicourse Italian meal

> 6 ounces Asiago fresco (not the sharper aged variety)
> 1 tablespoon butter
> 2 tablespoons whole milk
> 2 tablespoons heavy cream
> Salt
> Freshly ground black pepper
> 1 pound maccheroni
> ¼ cup freshly grated Parmigiano-Reggiano

1. Fill a pot for the pasta with at least 6 quarts water, place over high heat, and bring to a boil.

2. Remove the rind from the Asiago and cut the cheese into small pieces. Put the butter, milk, and cream in a medium saucepan and place over medium heat. When the butter is melted, add the Asiago. Cook, stirring occasionally, until the cheese is completely melted, about 5 minutes. Season with salt and pepper and set aside.

3. Add about 2 tablespoons salt to the boiling water, put in the pasta, and stir well. Cook until al dente.

4. Just before the pasta is done, reheat the sauce over medium heat. When the pasta is done, drain it well, toss with the sauce and the Parmigiano, and serve at once.

MACCHERONI WITH OLIVES, ANCHOVIES, AND BREAD CRUMBS

Maccheroni alle Olive, Acciughe, e Pane

I discovered this dish in Taormina, a gem of a town on the eastern coast of Sicily. Fresh bread crumbs soften the robust flavors of anchovies and olives while adding substance. This technique is often used in Sicily.

Total time: 30 minutes

Serves 4 as a main course or 6 as part of a multicourse Italian meal

> ½ medium yellow onion
> 6 tablespoons extra virgin olive oil
> 6 anchovy fillets
> 1 small handful green feathery fennel tops
> 12 Kalamata olives
> Salt
> ½ cup fresh bread crumbs (page 42)
> 1 pound maccheroni

1. Peel and finely chop the onion. Put it in a 10-inch skillet with 4 tablespoons of the olive oil and place over medium-high heat. Sauté, stirring occasionally, until it turns a rich golden color, about 5 minutes.

2. While the onion is sautéing, chop the anchovy fillets. Coarsely chop enough of the fennel tops to measure ½ cup. Cut the olive flesh away from the pits and finely chop it.

3. Fill a pot for the pasta with at least 6 quarts water, place over high heat, and bring to a boil.

4. When the onion is ready, add the anchovies and cook until they are dissolved, 1 to 2 minutes. Add the fennel tops, season lightly with salt, and cook for about 10 minutes.

5. Make the bread crumbs.

6. Add about 2 tablespoons salt to the boiling water, put in the pasta, and stir well. Cook until al dente.

7. While the pasta is cooking, add the olives to the skillet and cook for about 1 minute. Add the bread crumbs, cook for 2 minutes, and remove from the heat.

8. When the pasta is done, drain it well and toss with the sauce and remaining 2 tablespoons olive oil. Serve at once.

MACCHERONI
WITH NEAPOLITAN PORK RAGÙ

Maccheroni al Ragù Napoletano

As you travel in Italy, you will find a number of different ragùs including the classic Bolognese meat sauce (page 108). This ragù is similar to one I had in Naples, where pork ribs are cooked in tomatoes until very tender. The meat is removed from the bone and mixed with the tomatoes to form a sauce. In this version I've added peas, which add a sweet, mellow flavor.

Preparation time: 15 minutes
Total time from start to finish: 2½ hours

Serves 4 as a single-course meal or 6 as part of a multicourse meal

> 1½ pounds pork spareribs
> 2 tablespoons extra virgin olive oil
> Salt
> Freshly ground black pepper
> ½ medium yellow onion
> ¼ cup dry white wine
> 2 cups canned whole peeled tomatoes with their juice
> 1 pound fresh peas in the pod *or* 6 ounces frozen peas
> 1 pound maccheroni

1. Cut the ribs into pieces that will easily fit into a medium braising pan.

2. Put the olive oil in the braising pan and place over medium-high heat. When the oil is hot, add the ribs and brown on both sides. Remove the pan from the heat, put the ribs on a platter, and season them with salt and pepper.

3. While the ribs are browning, finely chop the onion. Once you've taken the ribs out of the pan, put the onion in, return the pan to medium heat, and sauté, stirring occasionally, until the onion turns a dark golden color, 2 to 3 minutes.

4. Raise the heat to high, add the wine, and let it bubble for about 30 seconds to allow the alcohol to evaporate. Add the tomatoes, season lightly with salt, and break them up into small pieces with a spoon.

5. Put the ribs back in the pan. Once the tomatoes begin bubbling, lower the heat to medium-low and cover the pan with the lid slightly askew. Cook until the meat is very tender and separates easily from the bone, about 1¾ hours.

6. While the ribs are cooking, shell the fresh peas if using. When the meat is very tender, remove all the ribs from the pot, separate the meat from the bone, and cut it into bite-size pieces. Return the meat to the sauce and add the peas. If using fresh peas, add about ½ cup water. Cook, uncovered, until the peas are tender and the sauce is not watery, about 10 minutes if using frozen peas or 20 minutes if using fresh.

7. While the peas are cooking, fill a pot for the pasta with at least 6 quarts water, place over high heat, and bring to a boil.

8. When the peas are done, add about 2 tablespoons salt to the boiling water, put in the pasta, and stir well. Cook until al dente. Drain the pasta well, toss it with the sauce, and serve at once.

Note: The sauce can be prepared through step 5 up to 2 days ahead of time. Store, covered, in the refrigerator. When ready to serve, bring the sauce back to a simmer, cook the peas in it, and toss with the pasta.

BAKED MACCHERONI

Pasticcio di Maccheroni al Forno

Pasticcio literally means "a mess" and this is a particularly delicious one. The pasta is tossed with Bolognese sauce and béchamel, then baked. If you have Bolognese already made, it will take just over an hour to make from start to finish. An ideal dish for a buffet, it is good even when only lukewarm and can easily be prepared ahead of time (see note below).

Preparation time: 1 hour 20 minutes
Total time from start to finish: 4¾ hours

Serves 4 as a single-course meal or 6 as part of a multicourse meal

> Classic Bolognese Meat Sauce (page 108)
> Béchamel sauce (page 43) made with 1½ cups milk, 3 table-
>   spoons butter, and 3 tablespoons flour
> Salt
> 1 pound maccheroni
> 2 tablespoons butter
> ¼ cup freshly grated Parmigiano-Reggiano

1. Make the Bolognese sauce and the béchamel.

2. Preheat the oven, on convection heat, preferably to 400° or 425° on regular bake.

3. Fill a pot for the pasta with at least 6 quarts water, place over high heat, and bring to a boil. Add about 2 tablespoons salt, put in the maccheroni, and stir well. When the pasta is almost done, a little firmer than al dente, drain it well and toss it with the Bolognese and the béchamel sauces.

4. Transfer the maccheroni to a shallow baking dish, dot with the butter, and sprinkle the Parmigiano on top. Bake until a golden crust forms on top, about 20 minutes. Remove from the oven and let rest for 5 minutes before serving.

Note: You can easily prepare this dish the day before up to the point it goes in the oven. Wrap well and refrigerate. Add an extra 5 minutes to the baking time if the dish is coming straight from the refrigerator.

FARFALLE WITH PEAS, SAUSAGE, AND TOMATO

Farfalle alla Salsiccia e Piselli

Total time: 40 minutes (1 hour if using fresh peas)

Serves 4 as a main course or 6 as part of a multicourse Italian meal

> 1 pound fresh peas in the pod *or* 6 ounces frozen peas
> ½ small yellow onion
> 1 pound ripe tomatoes
> 2 tablespoons butter
> 4 ounces plain mild sausage (use breakfast links or ¼ recipe homemade sausage, page 45)
> Salt
> Freshly ground black pepper
> 1 pound farfalle
> ¼ cup freshly grated Parmigiano-Reggiano

1. If using fresh peas, shell them. Peel and finely chop the onion. Peel the tomatoes (pages 30–31) and coarsely chop.

2. Put the butter and onion in a 10-inch skillet and place over medium heat. Sauté, stirring occasionally, until the onion turns a rich golden color, about 5 minutes.

3. Fill a pot for the pasta with at least 6 quarts water, place over high heat, and bring to a boil.

4. While the onion is sautéing, remove the casing from the sausage if using links. When the onion is done, add the sausage and break it up with a spoon. Sauté until the sausage is nicely browned, 3 to 4 minutes. Add the tomatoes and peas. If using fresh peas, cover the pan and cook, covered, over medium heat for 15 minutes. If using frozen peas, proceed to the next step.

5. Season with salt and pepper and cook, uncovered, until the tomatoes are reduced and no longer watery, about 15 minutes. Set aside.

6. Add about 2 tablespoons salt to the boiling water, put in the pasta, and stir well. Cook until al dente. When the pasta is done, drain it well, toss with the sauce and Parmigiano, and serve at once.

FARFALLE
WITH SAUTÉED VEGETABLES

Farfalle all'Ortolana

The key to making this sauce is to sauté the vegetables long enough for them to develop a rich, sweet, intense flavor.

Preparation time: 15 minutes
Total time from start to finish: 1 hour

Serves 4 as a main course or 6 as part of a multicourse Italian meal

> 4 medium carrots
> 6 ounces broccoli florets
> 6 ounces cauliflower florets
> 1 medium clove garlic
> ½ medium yellow onion
> 3 tablespoons extra virgin olive oil
> Salt

Freshly ground black pepper
1 pound farfalle

1. Peel the carrots and cut them into ¼-inch dice. Rinse the broccoli and cauliflower and cut the florets into ½-inch pieces. Peel and finely chop the garlic.

2. Peel and finely chop the onion. Put it with the olive oil in a 12-inch skillet. Place over medium-high heat and sauté, stirring occasionally, until the onion turns a rich golden color, about 5 minutes. Add the garlic and sauté for about 1 minute. Add the carrots, broccoli, and cauliflower and lower the heat to medium. Season with salt and pepper and add about ½ cup water. Cook until all the water is evaporated, then add another ½ cup water. Continue this routine until the vegetables are tender, 25 to 30 minutes. Sauté the vegetables, stirring occasionally, without adding any more water, until they are lightly browned, 15 to 20 minutes.

3. After the vegetables have cooked for about 30 minutes, fill a pot for the pasta with at least 6 quarts water, place over high heat, and bring to a boil. Add about 2 tablespoons salt to the boiling water, put in the pasta, and stir well. Cook until al dente.

4. While the pasta is cooking and after the vegetables have browned, add 2 to 3 tablespoons of the pasta water to the sauce to moisten it. When the pasta is done, drain it well, toss it with the sauce, and serve at once.

Note: You can make the sauce up to 2 hours ahead of time. Do not refrigerate.

ORECCHIETTE
WITH BROCCOLI RABE

Orecchiette ai Broccoletti

This is the dish most often associated with Apulia, the region of Italy where the spur and the heel of the boot are. Factory-made orecchiette can be very good and are fairly easily available. Broccoli rabe (sometimes called rapini) with olive oil, garlic, and anchovies is the classic sauce served with orecchiette. The broccoli rabe is cooked with the pasta, which absorbs some of the its flavor.

Preparation time: 25 minutes

Serves 4 as a main course or 6 as part of a multicourse Italian meal

> 4 medium cloves garlic
> 5 tablespoons extra virgin olive oil
> Pinch crushed red pepper flakes
> 6 anchovy fillets
> Salt
> 1 pound orecchiette
> 12 ounces broccoli rabe (rapini)

1. Fill a pot for the pasta with at least 6 quarts water, place over high heat, and bring to a boil.

2. Lightly crush and peel the garlic cloves. Put them in a small skillet with 4 tablespoons of the olive oil and the crushed red pepper. Place over medium-high heat and sauté the garlic cloves until they are lightly browned all over. Take out the garlic and discard.

3. While the garlic is sautéing, coarsely chop the anchovies. After removing the garlic, put the anchovies in the pan and cook, stirring occasionally, until they dissolve, 1 to 2 minutes. Keep hot over very low heat.

4. Add about 2 tablespoons salt to the boiling water, put in the pasta, and stir well. Cook until al dente.

5. While the pasta is cooking, rinse the broccoli rabe under cold water, trim the stems, and coarsely chop. When the pasta is about halfway done, after about 4 minutes, add the broccoli rabe. When the pasta is done, drain everything well, transfer to a serving bowl, and add the anchovy sauce. Add the remaining 1 tablespoon olive oil, toss well, and serve at once.

EGG PASTA
OF EMILIA ROMAGNA

Pasta all'Uovo

Making pasta dough by hand is simple. Do not be discouraged by the length of my instructions. With a little practice it will easily become second nature, and you will have finished dough in less than 15 minutes. Rolling the dough out by hand with a rolling pin undoubtedly makes better pasta than using a machine with rollers, but it is a difficult skill to master. Fortunately, machine-rolled pasta is almost as good as hand-rolled and certainly far superior to store-bought. If you must buy pasta, look for dried egg noodles in boxes rather than the so-called "fresh pasta" in the refrigerated case. Pasta cooked while still fresh is not superior to pasta that dried completely. Pasta that is not allowed to dry spoils unless some kind of preservative is used, which is why you should avoid commercial "fresh pasta."

The region that is best known for egg pasta is Emilia Romagna, of which Bologna is the capital. There are other regions that have an egg pasta tradition and each makes it differently. In Tuscany a little olive oil and salt is often added to the dough. In Liguria they use fewer eggs and add water. In Piedmont and the Veneto, a very rich pasta is made using mostly egg yolks and very few whites. The egg pasta from Emilia Romagna is made simply with whole eggs and flour. My family is from Emilia Romagna, so perhaps I am biased, but I find this egg pasta the most satisfying.

It is impossible to give a precise measurement for the flour. Depending on the size of the eggs, the humidity, and even the temperature in the room, you may need more or less. When making pasta, it is important to avoid cold, so use room-temperature eggs. Also, do not work on a naturally cold surface, such as marble or stainless steel. Wood is best; otherwise Corian or linoleum will work. If you do not make perfect pasta dough the first time, don't be discouraged. All you need is a little practice. Just have some store-bought pasta on hand for dinner the first time around.

Preparation time: 20 minutes
Total time from start to finish: approximately 45 minutes

Makes enough pasta for 4 as a main course
or 6 as part of a multicourse meal

2¼ cups all-purpose unbleached flour
3 large eggs

1. Pour the flour in a mound in the center of your work counter. With your fingers make a well, pushing the sides out to make it large enough for the eggs to fit comfortably. It is better to make the well too wide than too small to avoid the possibility that the eggs will overflow.

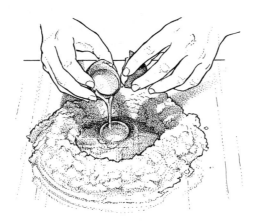

2. Break the eggs into the center of the well. Using a fork, beat the eggs as if you were making scrambled eggs until the yolks and whites are thoroughly blended. Use the fork to mix a little flour into the eggs by taking it from the bottom of the inside walls of the well. Continue until the mixture is thick enough to cling to the fork. Use your fingers to squeeze the dough attached to the fork back into the well and set the fork aside. Push about ¼ cup flour to the side, then use your hands to bring the rest into the center of the well. Mix together with your hands to begin forming a dough. If the dough feels sticky when you plunge a finger into it, add a little more flour. The dough should feel moist but not sticky. Wrap the dough in plastic, because the surface of the dough can

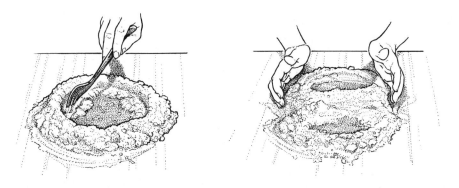

begin to dry out in as little as a minute, while you scrape off any bits of dough that have stuck to the counter. Reserve any remaining flour to the side.

3. Unwrap the dough and begin kneading it. Think of stretching the dough rather than compressing it by using the heel of your palm and pushing away from you. Knead until the dough feels homogeneous and smooth. If it sticks to your hand or to the counter, add a little more flour. On the other hand, if it feels too hard to knead, you may have added too much flour. Try wetting your hands and kneading the moisture in. If that does not seem to help, it's probably easier and faster to start over. If you don't need to add any more flour while kneading, it should take only 5 to 6 minutes. Adding flour during the kneading process will increase the time since the further along you are, the longer it takes for the flour to get incorporated. When you have kneaded the dough sufficiently, wrap it in plastic again and let it rest for at least 15 minutes and up to 3 hours. As the dough rests, the gluten in the flour will relax, making it much easier to roll the dough. Never refrigerate or freeze pasta dough.

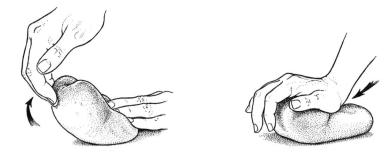

4. Unwrap the pasta dough and knead it a few times to incorporate the moisture that inevitably rises to the surface. The surface of the dough at this

point should feel silky smooth (a baby's bottom is what it is traditionally compared to).

If rolling the dough by hand:

a. Flatten the dough by pressing it down on the counter with your hands, making an even, round disk. Use a rolling pin at least 30 inches in length if possible, place it on the bottom third of the disk, and roll away from you, stopping just short of the edge. Turn the dough 90° and repeat. Continue until the dough is about ¼ inch thick.

b. Roll the top edge of the dough onto the rolling pin. Hold the dough in place with one hand and place your other hand on top of the rolling pin. Gently stretch the dough by rolling the pin back and forth. While the dough is still on the rolling pin, turn it 90°, unroll it, and again roll the top edge onto the rolling pin.

c. After you've done this at least four times and the dough is no more than ⅛ inch thick, begin rolling more of the dough onto the rolling pin and use both

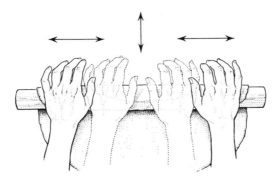

hands on the pin, sliding them together and apart while rolling forward and back. Continue until the pasta is very thin, almost transparent.

5. If making noodles, let the pasta dry on a cloth until it is leathery in consistency, dry enough so that the cut noodles will not stick together but will still be pliable enough to keep from cracking. It will take between 5 and 25 minutes, depending on the temperature and humidity in the room. To cut pasta using the machine, cut the pasta sheets into 12- to 15-inch lengths. Put each piece through the desired cutting attachment of the pasta machine. Loosely fold the noodles into nests. Once the noodles are completely dry, they will be easier to pick up. If cutting the pasta by hand, roll the dough loosely and use a chef's knife or cleaver to cut the pasta into noodles of the desired width. After every 5 or 6 cuts, unravel the noodles, then loosely fold them into nests.

To make filled pasta: You need to keep the pasta moist in order to seal it. Work on just a portion of the pasta at a time and cover the rest with plastic wrap so it won't dry out. If using the machine, roll out only one piece, while keeping the rest of the dough wrapped in plastic. Cut the pasta sheet in half before putting it through the rollers the last time. For filled pasta squares, such as tortelloni or tortelli, lay the pasta flat on a cutting board. Place tablespoon-

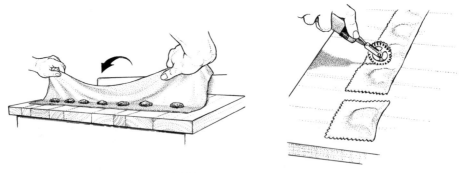

size dollops of filling at 1-inch intervals along the bottom half of the pasta sheet. Fold the top half of the pasta sheet over the filling and gently press down with your fingers between the dollops to squeeze out excess air. Use a pastry cutting wheel to trim the bottom and sides and cut between the dollops of filling, forming approximately 1½-inch squares. The edges will be sealed by the cutting action of the pastry wheel. Place the filled pasta in a single layer on a dry cloth. Continue the process until all the pasta and/or the filling is used up.

6. Noodles can be cooked right away or dried and stored in a cool dry place (not the refrigerator) almost indefinitely. Noodles that are cooked right away will be done by the time the water comes back to a boil. Dried noodles will be done in about 3 minutes. Filled pasta needs to be cooked within a couple of hours or the pasta that is in contact with the filling will get too wet and eventually dissolve. Filled pasta is best when served as soon as it is cooked, but it is possible to make it up to 2 days ahead if necessary. Cook it partially, about 1 minute, then toss with some vegetable oil, cool, and store in resealable plastic bags in the refrigerator (do not freeze). When ready to serve, drop into salted boiling water and cook until done, 1 to 2 minutes.

Green pasta variation: Cook 8 ounces frozen spinach or 12 ounces fresh spinach in salted boiling water until tender. Drain and set aside to cool. Using your hands, squeeze out as much water as possible. Finely chop by hand or in a food processor. Proceed as for Egg Pasta of Emilia Romagna (above), adding the spinach to the eggs and increasing the flour by ½ cup.

If using a pasta machine to roll out the dough:
a. Cut the dough in as many pieces as you used eggs, in this case three. Wrap two of the pieces in plastic wrap. Flatten the remaining piece of dough

as best you can with your hands, then put it through the rollers of the machine set at the widest setting. Fold the dough in thirds and put it through the rollers again with the folds perpendicular to the rollers. Fold the dough in half and put it through one more time, again with the folds perpendicular to the rollers. Lay the dough on a towel and repeat the procedure with the other two pieces.

b. When all the pieces have been through the machine at the widest setting, adjust the rollers down one notch and put each piece of dough through once more. Repeat, going down one notch at time, until you reach the next-to-last setting. Cut each sheet of pasta in half, then put each piece through the machine at the thinnest setting.

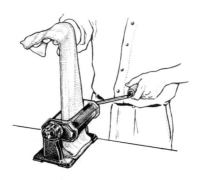

FETTUCCINE WITH GORGONZOLA

Fettuccine al Gorgonzola

This is the classic Gorgonzola sauce found in northern Italy. It is also often paired with potato gnocchi (page 198). The type of Gorgonzola required is the creamy, almost runny, cheese called *dolce,* not the drier sharper variety.

Total time: 20 minutes

Serves 4 as a main course or 6 as part of a multicourse Italian meal

> 4 ounces Gorgonzola dolce
> ½ cup milk
> 2 tablespoons butter
> Salt
> ⅓ cup heavy cream
> Egg Pasta of Emilia Romagna (pages 170–176), cut into fettuccine,
>   or 9 ounces dried egg fettuccine
> ⅓ cup freshly grated Parmigiano-Reggiano

1. Fill a pot for the pasta with at least 6 quarts water, place over high heat, and bring to a boil.

2. Put the Gorgonzola, milk, and butter in a 12-inch skillet and place over low heat. Season with salt. Break up the cheese with a wooden spoon and cook until it is melted completely, 3 to 4 minutes. Add the cream and raise the heat to medium-high. Cook, stirring often, until the cream is reduced by a third, 2 to 3 minutes. Remove from the heat.

3. Add about 2 tablespoons salt to the boiling water, put in the fettuccine, and stir until all the strands are submerged. Cook until al dente. Drain the pasta well and put it in the pan with the sauce. Place over low heat, add the Parmigiano, and toss well for about 30 seconds. Serve at once.

FETTUCCINE WITH WALNUT PESTO

Fettuccine al Pesto di Noci

Pesto is not only made with basil. In fact, it can be any ingredient ground fine, traditionally with a mortar and pestle, though most people use a food processor or blender now. The most famous pesto in Liguria is basil pesto, but almost equally popular in the region is one made with walnuts and ricotta.

Total time: 20 minutes

Serves 4 as a single-course meal or 6 as part of a multicourse meal

> 1 small clove garlic
> 4 ounces shelled walnuts
> 1 tablespoon extra virgin olive oil
> ¼ cup whole-milk ricotta
> Salt
> Freshly ground black pepper
> ¼ cup heavy cream
> Egg Pasta of Emilia Romagna (pages 170–176), cut into fettuccine,
>   or 9 ounces dried egg fettuccine
> ¼ cup freshly grated Parmigiano-Reggiano

1. Fill a pot for the pasta with at least 6 quarts water, place over high heat, and bring to a boil.

2. Peel and finely chop the garlic and put it with the walnuts and olive oil in a food processor. Run the processor until the mixture is smooth. Add the ricotta and run the processor to mix it in thoroughly. Transfer to a serving bowl. Season with salt and pepper and stir in the heavy cream.

3. When the water for the pasta has come to a boil, add 2 tablespoons of salt, put in the fettuccine, and stir until all the strands are submerged. Cook until al dente.

4. While the pasta is cooking, mix 3 tablespoons of the pasta water into the walnut pesto. When the pasta is done, drain it well, toss it with the sauce, and serve at once, sprinkling a little Parmigiano over each serving.

FETTUCCINE WITH ARTICHOKES

Fettuccine ai Carciofi

I used to avoid making artichoke pasta sauces because I found artichokes to be too mild to adequately season pasta. Then I discovered the trick to more intensely flavor artichoke sauces: Simmer the artichoke trimmings and use the resulting water to make the sauce.

Preparation time: 40 minutes

Serves 4 as a main course or 6 as part of a multicourse Italian meal

> 1 lemon
> 3 large or 4 small to medium artichokes
> Salt
> ½ medium yellow onion
> 3 tablespoons butter
> 10 to 12 sprigs flat-leaf Italian parsley
> Egg Pasta of Emilia Romagna (pages 170–176), cut into fettuccine,
>   or 9 ounces dried egg fettuccine
> 1 cup heavy cream

1. Cut the lemon in half. Trim the artichokes (pages 34–35), rubbing the cut parts with a lemon half. Save the artichoke tops. Squeeze the juice from the remaining lemon half into a medium bowl and fill the bowl halfway with water. Cut the trimmed artichokes lengthwise in half, thinly slice, and put them in the lemon water. Put the reserved artichoke tops in a saucepan with just enough water to cover. Place over medium-high heat, season with salt, and bring to

a boil. Cook for 15 minutes. Strain, discard the artichoke trimmings, and save the water.

2. Peel and finely chop the onion. Place it with the butter in a 12-inch skillet over medium heat and sauté, stirring occasionally, until the onion turns a rich golden color, about 5 minutes.

3. While the onion is sautéing, fill a pot for the pasta with at least 6 quarts water, place over high heat, and bring to a boil.

4. Drain the sliced artichokes and add them to the onion. Season with salt and sauté, stirring, for about 1 minute to coat the artichokes with butter. Add the artichoke water to the pan and cook until all the liquid is evaporated. The artichoke slices should be very tender; if not, add some water and continue cooking.

5. While the artichokes are cooking, finely chop enough of the parsley leaves to measure 3 tablespoons.

6. Add about 2 tablespoons salt to the boiling water, put in the fettuccine, and stir until all the strands are submerged. Cook until al dente.

7. Raise the heat under the artichokes to medium-high and add the cream and parsley. Cook for 1 to 2 minutes until the cream thickens a bit. Remove from the heat. When the pasta is done, drain it well, toss with the sauce, and serve at once.

CLASSIC TORTELLONI OF EMILIA ROMAGNA WITH A SIMPLE TOMATO SAUCE

Tortelloni di Biete al Pomodoro

If I were hard pressed to choose a favorite dish, something I usually avoid, this would have to be the one. My first encounter with these tortelloni was at age three when my grandmother prepared them for me in my mother's hometown of Cesenatico. I apparently put away quite a hefty portion, then closed my eyes and plopped my head down on the table. Terrified, my grandmother called the doctor who pronounced me "very happily sleeping." They are good simply tossed with butter, sage, and Parmigiano-Reggiano, but the ultimate complement for me is the simple tomato sauce with just a splash of cream.

Total time: 1¾ hours

Serves 4 as a main course or 6 as part of a multicourse Italian meal

Simple Butter and Tomato Sauce (page 106)
2 pounds Swiss chard
½ cup water
Salt
Egg Pasta of Emilia Romagna (pages 170–176), made with 2 eggs
    and 1½ cups flour
½ medium yellow onion
3 tablespoons butter
2 ounces prosciutto, thinly sliced
1 cup whole-milk ricotta
¾ cup freshly grated Parmigiano-Reggiano
1 large egg yolk
⅛ teaspoon freshly grated nutmeg
Freshly ground black pepper
¼ cup heavy cream

1. Make the tomato sauce. It can cook on its own while you work on the rest of the recipe; just remember to stir it once in a while.

2. Remove the stalks from the Swiss chard. Rinse the leaves in several changes of cold water and put them in a pot with ½ cup water and 1 teaspoon salt. Place the pot over medium-high heat, cover, and cook until the leaves are tender, 5 to 6 minutes. Drain in a colander and squeeze out as much water as possible by pressing on the leaves with a spoon. Transfer the chard to a cutting board and finely chop it.

3. Make the pasta dough.

4. Peel and finely chop the onion and put it in a 10-inch skillet with the butter. Place over medium-high heat and sauté, stirring occasionally, until the onion turns a rich golden color, about 5 minutes.

5. Finely chop the prosciutto. When the onion is ready, add the prosciutto and sauté until it loses its raw pink color and begins to brown. Add the Swiss chard, lower the heat to medium, and sauté for 5 minutes, stirring periodically. Transfer the chard to a medium bowl and set aside to cool slightly, about 10 minutes.

6. Add the ricotta, ½ cup of the Parmigiano, the egg yolk, and nutmeg to the chard. Season with salt and pepper and stir very thoroughly. Taste the filling and adjust the seasoning if necessary.

7. Fill a pot for the pasta with at least 6 quarts water, place over high heat, and bring to a boil.

8. Roll and fill the pasta dough as described on pages 173–174.

9. Add 2 tablespoons salt to the boiling water. Collect all the filled pasta on one towel and slide them into the boiling water. Cook until the edges are tender but al dente, about 3 minutes, then drain or lift them out with a skimmer. Transfer to a shallow serving bowl and gently toss with the sauce and cream. Sprinkle with the remaining Parmigiano over each serving.

SPINACH AND RICOTTA TORTELLONI IN A PORCINI CREAM SAUCE

Tortelloni di Ricotta e Spinaci al Sugo di Porcini

Although similar, the filling here is more delicate than the classic tortelloni from Emilia Romagna in the previous recipe. There is no prosciutto and more ricotta than spinach. The result I find is perfectly suited to the porcini sauce.

Total time: 1¾ hours

Serves 4 as a main course or 6 as part of a multicourse Italian meal

> 1 ounce dried porcini mushrooms
> Egg Pasta of Emilia Romagna (pages 170–176), made with 2 eggs
>   and 1½ cups flour
> 6 ounces fresh spinach, preferably baby spinach
> ½ cup water
> Salt
> 1 medium yellow onion
> 2½ tablespoons butter
> ¾ cup whole-milk ricotta
> 1 large egg yolk
> ¾ cup freshly grated Parmigiano-Reggiano
> ⅛ teaspoon freshly grated nutmeg
> 2 ounces pancetta, sliced ¼ inch thick
> 8 ounces white mushrooms
> Freshly ground black pepper
> ¾ cup heavy cream

1. Put the dried porcini in a bowl, cover with water, and soak for at least 15 minutes.

2. Make the pasta dough.

3. Rinse the spinach and remove any thick stems. Put the spinach in a pot with ½ cup water and 1 teaspoon salt. Cover the pot and place over medium heat. Cook until the spinach is quite tender, 5 to 6 minutes (longer if using mature spinach). Drain in a colander and squeeze out as much water as possible by pressing on the spinach with a spoon.

4. Peel and finely chop the onion and put half in a small skillet with 1 tablespoon butter. Place over medium-high heat and sauté, stirring occasionally, until the onion turns a rich golden color, about 5 minutes.

5. While the onion is sautéing, finely chop the spinach. When the onion is ready, add the spinach, lower the heat to medium, and sauté for 5 minutes.

6. Transfer the spinach to a medium bowl. Add the ricotta, egg yolk, ½ cup of the Parmigiano, and the nutmeg. Season with salt and mix thoroughly.

7. Put the remaining onion and 1½ tablespoons butter in a 10-inch skillet and place over medium-high heat. Sauté, stirring occasionally, until the onion turns a rich golden color, about 5 minutes.

8. While the onion is sautéing, unravel the pancetta and cut it into thin strips. When the onion is done, add the pancetta and sauté until it begins to brown, 3 to 4 minutes.

9. While the pancetta is sautéing, lift the porcini out of the water and squeeze the excess back into the bowl; do not discard the water. Rinse the porcini under running water, then coarsely chop them. Add the porcini to the skillet along with the soaking water. Be aware that there may be some sand at the bottom of the bowl, so pour carefully or strain through a paper towel. Cook, uncovered, until all the liquid is evaporated.

10. Meanwhile, thinly slice the white mushrooms. When the liquid in the pan is evaporated, add the mushrooms. Season with salt and pepper and continue cooking until the mushrooms are tender and all the liquid they release is evaporated, 15 to 20 minutes. Remove from the heat and set aside.

11. Fill a pot for the pasta with at least 6 quarts water, place over high heat, and bring to a boil.

12. Roll out and fill the pasta as described on pages 173–175.

13. Return the pan with the mushrooms to a medium-high heat and as soon as the sauce begins bubbling, add the cream. Cook until the cream is reduced by half, 1 to 2 minutes, then remove from the heat.

14. Add 2 tablespoons salt to the boiling water. Collect all the filled pasta on one towel and slide them into the boiling water. Cook until the edges are tender but al dente, about 3 minutes, then drain or lift them out with a skimmer. Transfer to a shallow serving bowl and gently toss with the sauce. Sprinkle some of the remaining ¼ cup Parmigiano over each serving.

Note: You can make the sauce up to 1 day ahead and refrigerate it. Wait to add the cream until you are ready to serve.

TORTELLONI FILLED WITH RADICCHIO

Tortelloni di Radicchio

Total time: 1¾ hours

Serves 4 as a main course or 6 as part of a multicourse Italian meal

> ½ recipe Simple Butter and Tomato Sauce (page 106)
> ½ medium yellow onion
> 2 tablespoons butter
> 1½ ounces pancetta, thinly sliced
> 12 ounces radicchio
> Salt
> Freshly ground black pepper
> Egg Pasta of Emilia Romagna (pages 170–176), made with 2 eggs
> and 1½ cups flour

¾ cup freshly grated Parmigiano-Reggiano
¾ cup whole-milk ricotta
1 large egg yolk
¾ cup heavy cream

1. Make the tomato sauce.

2. Peel and finely chop the onion. Put it with the butter in a 10-inch skillet and place over medium-high heat. Sauté, stirring occasionally, until the onion turns a rich golden color, about 5 minutes.

3. While the onion is sautéing, chop the pancetta and finely shred the radicchio. When the onion is ready, add the pancetta and cook, stirring, until it loses its raw pink color. Lower the heat to medium-low and add the radicchio. Season with salt and pepper and cover the pan. Cook, stirring occasionally, until the radicchio is wilted and quite tender, 10 to 15 minutes.

4. Make the pasta dough.

5. Transfer the radicchio to a medium bowl and add ½ cup of the Parmigiano, the ricotta, and egg yolk. Mix thoroughly and season with salt if needed.

6. Fill a pot for the pasta with at least 6 quarts water, place over high heat, and bring to a boil.

7. Roll out and fill the pasta as described on pages 173–175.

8. Put the pot with the tomato sauce over low heat and bring to a simmer. Add the cream, mix it in well, and after about a minute remove the sauce from the heat.

9. Add 2 tablespoons salt to the boiling water. Collect all the filled pasta on one towel and slide them into the boiling water. Cook until the edges are tender but al dente, about 3 minutes, then drain or lift them out with a skimmer. Transfer to a shallow serving bowl and gently toss with the sauce. Sprinkle some of the remaining ¼ cup Parmigiano over each serving.

RICOTTA-AND-PARSLEY-FILLED TORTELLONI WITH A PINK TOMATO SAUCE

Tortelloni di Ricotta al Sugo Rosa

When my daughter Gabriella was four years old, we invited her preschool class over for a cooking class. Although I am quite comfortable teaching adults, I was a little concerned about holding the attention of a group of four-year-olds. I decided, in the words of Ms. Frizzle of *The Magic School Bus,* to take chances, make mistakes, and get messy by having everyone make pasta. Well, we did get a little messy, and some mistakes were made, but in the end a lunch of delicious homemade tortelloni filled with ricotta was enjoyed by all.

These tortelloni are shaped differently from those in the preceding recipes. A specialty of Bologna, they are a larger version of the city's famous tortellini.

Total time: 1½ hours

Serves 4 as a main course or 6 as part of a multicourse Italian meal

> ½ recipe Simple Butter and Tomato Sauce (page 106)
> Egg Pasta of Emilia Romagna (pages 170–176), made with 2 eggs
>   and 1½ cups flour
> ½ small bunch flat-leaf Italian parsley
> 1½ cups whole-milk ricotta cheese
> 1¼ cups freshly grated Parmigiano-Reggiano
> 1 large egg yolk
> ⅛ teaspoon freshly grated nutmeg
> Salt
> Freshly ground black pepper
> ¾ cup heavy cream

1. Make the tomato sauce.

2. Make the pasta dough.

3. Finely chop enough of the parsley leaves to measure ½ cup. Put the parsley, ricotta, 1 cup of the Parmigiano, the egg yolk, and nutmeg in a medium bowl. Season with salt and pepper and mix thoroughly.

4. Roll out the pasta dough as described on pages 173–174. Lay the pasta flat on a cutting board and cut it into 2-inch squares. Place 1 tablespoon of the filling in the center of each square. Fold the pasta square in half forming a triangle, then wrap the 2 opposite points around the tip of your index finger forming the shape of a bishop's hat. Place the tortelloni on a dry cloth in a single layer. Continue the process until all the pasta and/or filling are used up.

5. Fill a pot for the pasta with at least 6 quarts water, place over high heat, and bring to a boil.

6. Put the pot with the tomato sauce over low heat to reheat it gently. After it begins to simmer, add the cream, mix it in well, and after about a minute remove the sauce from the heat.

7. Add 2 tablespoons of salt to the boiling water. Collect all the filled pasta on one towel and slide them into the boiling water. Cook until the edges are tender but al dente, about 3 minutes, then drain or lift them out with a skimmer. Transfer to a shallow serving bowl and gently toss with the sauce. Sprinkle with the remaining ¼ cup Parmigiano and serve at once.

"PUMPKIN"-FILLED TORTELLI
WITH BUTTER AND SAGE

Tortelli di Zucca al Burro e Salvia

The pumpkin used in Italy for this delicious filled pasta is a rich and sweet squash called *zucca barucca*. In the States, I use sweet potato instead of pumpkin because the flavor of *zucca barucca* most closely approximates the orange-fleshed sweet potatoes (sometimes called yams), more than the pumpkin available here. The shape is identical to the tortelloni in the previous recipes, but they are a specialty of Mantova and Ferrara, where they are called *tortelli*. Some make them with ground amaretti cookies and sometimes with the sweet and spicy preserved fruit known as *mostarda*. I personally prefer the ones without amaretti because I find them cloyingly sweet. The recipe below includes prosciutto, which admittedly is rarely used, but my mother makes them with it and I like the way it balances the sweetness of the filling.

Preparation time: 1 hour
Total time from start to finish: 1 hour 35 minutes

Serves 4 as a main course or 6 as part of a multicourse Italian meal

> 1 large orange-fleshed sweet potato, weighing at least 12 ounces
> Vegetable oil
> Egg Pasta of Emilia Romagna (pages 170–176), made with 2 eggs
> and 1½ cups flour
> 6 to 8 sprigs flat-leaf Italian parsley
> 1 ounce prosciutto, thinly sliced
> 1½ cups freshly grated Parmigiano-Reggiano
> 1 egg yolk
> ⅛ teaspoon freshly grated nutmeg
> Salt
> Freshly ground black pepper
> 2 large sprigs fresh sage
> 4 tablespoons butter

1. Preheat the oven to 400°.

2. Brush the sweet potato with vegetable oil, pierce the skin in several places, and put it on a baking sheet. Bake the sweet potato until tender when pierced, about 1 hour. Weigh 12 ounces of the sweet potato and set aside the excess.

3. While the potato is baking, make the pasta dough.

4. Finely chop enough of the parsley leaves to measure 2 tablespoons. Finely chop the prosciutto.

5. When the potato is cool enough to handle, remove the skin, cut the flesh into chunks, and purée in a food mill or food processor. Put the purée into a medium bowl and add the parsley, prosciutto, 1 cup of the Parmigiano, the egg yolk, and nutmeg. Season generously with salt and pepper and mix thoroughly.

6. Fill a pot for the pasta with at least 6 quarts of water, place over high heat, and bring to a boil.

7. Roll out and fill the pasta as described on pages 173–175.

8. Finely shred enough of the sage leaves to measure 2 tablespoons. Put it in a small saucepan with the butter and place over medium heat. When the butter just begins to turn color, remove from the heat and set aside.

9. Add 2 tablespoons salt to the boiling water. Collect all the tortelli on one towel and slide them into the boiling water. Cook until the edges are tender but al dente, about 3 minutes, then drain or lift them out with a skimmer. Transfer to a shallow serving bowl, add the butter and sage, and gently toss the tortelli. Sprinkle some of the remaining ½ cup Parmigiano over each serving.

TORTELLINI/CAPPELLETTI

Cappelletti are shaped somewhat like a bishop's hat; hence the name, which comes from the Italian word for hat, *cappello*. In Bologna they are also called tortellini; but in Romagna tortellini are made from little disks instead of little squares making them look more like a belly button than a hat. In fact, there is a legend about how the first round tortellino was created. Once upon a time there was a baker and pasta maker who was secretly and madly in love with a girl who worked for him. Before she started work she would change her clothes in the back room, and one day the owner could not resist the temptation to peek through the keyhole. All he could see was her navel, but he found it so beautiful that he picked up a small round disk of pasta and shaped it like her belly button. The first tortellino was born.

The classic way to serve tortellini is in homemade meat broth. Do not substitute store bought. It would be a shame to take the time to make tortellini and then use store-bought broth. Tortellini are also excellent with heavy cream and Parmigiano-Reggiano cheese.

Total time: 1 hour 20 minutes

Serves 4 as a main course or 6 as part of a multicourse Italian meal

> Egg Pasta of Emilia Romagna (pages 170–176), made with 2 eggs
> and 1½ cups flour
> 2 ounces lean boneless pork loin
> 3 ounces boneless, skinless chicken breast
> 1 tablespoon butter
> 1 tablespoon vegetable oil
> Salt
> Freshly ground black pepper
> 2 ounces mortadella
> ¾ cup whole-milk ricotta
> 1 large egg yolk
> ¾ cup freshly grated Parmigiano-Reggiano
> ⅛ teaspoon freshly grated nutmeg

1. Make the pasta dough.

2. Cut the pork and chicken into ½-inch chunks. Put the butter and the vegetable oil in a small skillet and place over medium heat. Add the pork and cook, turning as needed, until cooked through, 2 to 3 minutes. Use a slotted spoon to lift the meat out of the pan and set it aside on a plate. Put the chicken cubes in the pan and cook, turning as needed, until cooked through, 1 to 2 minutes. Use the slotted spoon to remove them from the pan and set aside with the pork. Season the pork and chicken with salt and pepper.

3. Coarsely chop the mortadella and put it with the pork and chicken in a food processor. Chop to a fine consistency but do not purée. Transfer to a medium bowl and add the ricotta, egg yolk, Parmigiano, and nutmeg. Mix thoroughly. Taste and season with salt if needed. Set aside.

4. Roll out the pasta dough as described on pages 173–174. Cut the sheets into 1½-inch squares. Put just over ¼ teaspoon of the filling in the center of each square. Fold the pasta square in half, forming a triangle, then wrap the 2 opposite points around the tip of your index finger forming the shape of a bishop's hat. Pinch the ends together to seal. As you make them, set the tortellini on a clean dry cloth. Continue the process until all the pasta and filling are used up.

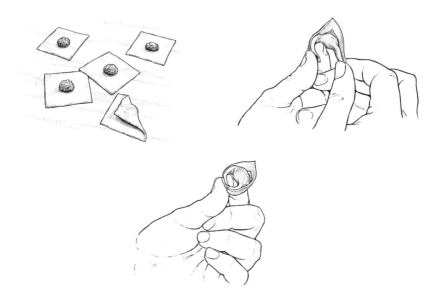

Note: Do not refrigerate and plan on cooking the tortellini within 2 to 3 hours. Otherwise, cook them partially, about 1 minute, then toss with a little vegetable oil, cool, and store in resealable plastic bags in the refrigerator (do not freeze).

TORTELLINI IN BROTH

6 cups homemade meat broth (page 46)
Tortellini (page 191)
⅓ cup freshly grated Parmigiano-Reggiano

Bring the broth to a boil in a large pot. Collect all the tortellini on one towel, slide them into the broth, and cook until the part where they are sealed is al dente, 6 to 8 minutes. Ladle the broth and tortellini into bowls and sprinkle some of the Parmigiano over each serving.

TORTELLINI WITH CREAM

Tortellini (page 191)
2 tablespoons butter
1 cup heavy cream
Salt
⅓ cup freshly grated Parmigiano-Reggiano

1. Fill a pot for the pasta with at least 6 quarts water, place over high heat, and bring to a boil. Collect all the tortellini on one towel, slide them into the boiling water, and cook until the part where they are sealed is al dente, 6 to 8 minutes.

2. While the tortellini are cooking, put the butter in a 12-inch skillet and place over medium-high heat. Once the butter is melted completely, add the cream and season lightly with salt. Cook until the cream is reduced by half, then remove from the heat.

3. When the tortellini are done, drain them, transfer them to the pan with the sauce, toss with the Parmigiano, and serve at once.

LASAGNE WITH BOLOGNESE MEAT SAUCE

Lasagne alla Bolognese

This is the classic lasagne of Emilia Romagna. Its ultimate rendition is with green spinach pasta, but it is unquestionably delicious with regular egg pasta as well. Homemade pasta is essential, however. Take the extra 25 minutes to make your own pasta instead of using the thick, store-bought lasagne sheets. You will be rewarded with an extraordinarily fine and memorable dish.

Preparation time: 1 hour 25 minutes
Total time from start to finish: 5 hours

Serves 6 as a main course or 8 as part of a multicourse Italian meal

> Classic Bolognese Meat Sauce (page 108)
> Green or regular Egg Pasta of Emilia Romagna (pages 170–176),
>   made with 2 eggs and 1½ cups flour
> Béchamel sauce (page 43)
> Salt
> ¾ cup freshly grated Parmigiano-Reggiano
> 1 tablespoon butter

1. Make the Bolognese sauce.

2. Make the pasta dough, wrap it in plastic, and set aside to rest.

3. Make the béchamel sauce.

4. Fill a pot for the pasta with at least 6 quarts water, place over high heat, and bring to a boil.

5. Roll out the pasta dough as described on pages 173–174. Cut the pasta sheets so you have a total of 8 sheets. Fill a medium bowl halfway with ice water and keep it close to the pot of water on the stove.

6. Add 2 tablespoons of salt to the boiling water and put in 4 of the pasta sheets. Cook for 1 minute, then lift the pasta out of the water with tongs and place it in the ice water. Swish the pasta sheets in the water, then lay them flat on dry towels. Repeat with the remaining 4 pasta sheets.

7. Preheat the oven to 425°.

8. Coat the bottom of an 11½ x 8-inch baking pan with some béchamel, then mix the rest with the Bolognese sauce and ½ cup of the Parmigiano. Place a sheet of pasta on the bottom of the pan, trimming any excess so it fits. Spread a thin coating of the sauce over the pasta sheet, then cover with another sheet of pasta. Continue until you have 7 layers of pasta and sauce, saving a little sauce to cover the top layer. Do not worry if the sheets of pasta do not fit perfectly; it's all right to patch as necessary. Place the remaining sheet of pasta on top, coat with the remaining sauce, sprinkle with the remaining ¼ cup Parmigiano, and dot with the butter.

9. Bake until the top is lightly browned, about 25 minutes. Take the lasagne out of the oven and let rest for 10 minutes before serving.

> *Note:* The lasagne can be assembled completely up to 1 day in advance. Store, well wrapped, in the refrigerator. Take it out of the refrigerator 1 hour before baking. It will also keep in the refrigerator after it is baked for up to 2 days.

LEEK AND PORCINI LASAGNE

Lasagne ai Porri e Porcini

Preparation time: 1 hour 25 minutes
Total time from start to finish: 2 hours

Serves 6 as a main course or 8 as part of a multicourse Italian meal

> 1 ounce dried porcini mushrooms
> 4 or 5 medium leeks (about 2 pounds)
> 2½ tablespoons butter
> ½ cup water
> Salt
> Freshly ground black pepper
> Egg Pasta of Emilia Romagna (pages 170–176), made with 2 eggs
>   and 1½ cups flour
> Béchamel sauce (page 43)
> ¾ cup freshly grated Parmigiano-Reggiano

1. Put the dried porcini in a bowl, cover with water, and soak for at least 15 minutes.

2. Trim the root ends and dark green tops from the leeks (page 35). Cut the leeks lengthwise in half (or in quarters if they are more than ¾ inch thick), then slice them crosswise into ½-inch chunks. Place the leeks in a large bowl, cover with cold water, and swish them around to loosen any dirt that is clinging to them. Lift the leeks out of the water and put them in a deep skillet. Place over medium heat and add 2 tablespoons of the butter and ½ cup water. Season with salt and pepper, cover the pan, and cook until the leeks are wilted, about 10 minutes.

3. Lift the porcini out of the water and squeeze the excess back into the bowl; do not discard the water. Rinse the mushrooms under running water, then coarsely chop them. Add the porcini to the leeks along with the soaking water. Be aware that there may be some sand at the bottom of the bowl, so pour

carefully or strain through a paper towel. Season lightly with salt and cook, uncovered, over medium heat until all the liquid in the pan is evaporated.

4. Make the pasta dough.

5. Make the béchamel sauce.

6. Fill a pot for the pasta with at least 6 quarts water, place over high heat, and bring to a boil.

7. Roll out the pasta dough as described on pages 173–174. Cut the pasta sheets so you have a total of 8 pieces. Fill a medium bowl halfway with ice water and keep it close to the pot of water on the stove.

8. Add 2 tablespoons salt to the boiling water and put in 4 of the pasta sheets. Cook for 1 minute, then lift the pasta out of the water with tongs and place it in the ice water. Swish the pasta sheets in the water, then lay them flat on dry towels. Repeat with the remaining 4 pasta sheets.

8. Preheat the oven to 425°.

9. Coat the bottom of an 11½ x 8-inch baking pan with some of the béchamel, then mix the rest into the leek and porcini mixture along with ½ cup of the Parmigiano. Place a sheet of pasta on the bottom of the pan, trimming any excess so it fits. Spread a thin coating of the filling over the pasta sheet, then cover with another sheet of pasta. Continue until you have 7 layers of pasta and filling, saving a little filling to cover the top layer. Do not worry if the sheets of pasta do not fit perfectly; it's all right to patch as necessary. Place the remaining sheet of pasta on top, coat with the remaining filling, sprinkle the remaining ¼ cup Parmigiano, and dot with the remaining ½ tablespoon butter.

10. Bake until the top is lightly browned, about 25 minutes. Take the lasagne out of the oven and let rest for 10 minutes before serving.

Note: The lasagne can be assembled completely up to 1 day in advance. Store, well wrapped, in the refrigerator. Take it out of the refrigerator 1 hour before baking. It will also keep in the refrigerator after it is baked for up to 2 days.

POTATO GNOCCHI

Gnocchi di Patate

Making potato gnocchi is simple. What can cause them to be too gluey, tough, or heavy is often simply using the wrong potato or too much flour. Use a potato that is neither too waxy, such as the small red "creamers," or floury, such as Idaho baking potatoes. I find Yukon Gold potatoes work best. Stop adding flour when the potato dough is smooth and only slightly sticky.

Gnocchi can be served with many pasta sauces. The classic pairings are with pesto (page 107), Gorgonzola (page 177), and Simple Butter and Tomato Sauce (page 106). Gnocchi are best with smooth sauces, so I recommend puréeing the tomato sauce through the coarse disk of a food mill.

Preparation time: 15 minutes
Total time from start to finish: 45 minutes

Serves 4 as a main course or 6 as part of a multicourse Italian meal

> 1½ pounds Yukon Gold potatoes
> 1½ cups all-purpose flour
> Salt

1. Scrub the potatoes and put them in a saucepan. Cover with water, place over high heat, and cover with a lid. Once the water comes to a boil, adjust the heat so that the water simmers. Cook until the potatoes are tender when pierced, about 30 minutes. Try not to test them too often or they may become waterlogged.

2. Drain the potatoes and peel as soon as possible. Sprinkle some of the flour on a counter and mash the potatoes through the medium disk of a food mill or a potato ricer onto the floured counter. Add half of the flour and work it with your hands into the potato to form a dough. Continue adding flour a little at a time until the mixture is smooth and only slightly sticky. You will probably have a little flour left over.

3. Divide the dough in half. Take one piece and roll it to form a long snake about ¾ inch thick. Cut the snake into 1-inch dumplings. One by one, place a dumpling on the front of the tines of a dinner fork. Push your index finger in the center of the dumpling and roll it down along the tines of the fork, letting it fall on the counter at the end. The finished gnocchi will have a cavity on one side and convex ridges on the other. Collect them in a single layer (do not let them touch each other) on a clean kitchen towel. Gnocchi are best when they are cooked within a couple of hours of being made. Do not refrigerate.

4. Fill a pot with at least 4 quarts water, place over high heat, and bring to a boil. Add 2 tablespoons salt and use the towel to slide half of the gnocchi into the boiling water. Once they rise to the surface, cook for 10 seconds. Scoop them up with a strainer and put them in a warm serving bowl with half of the sauce you are serving them with. Slide the remaining gnocchi in the boiling water and cook the same way. Scoop them up and add them to the serving bowl with the rest of the sauce. Serve at once.

RICE AND RISOTTO

- **Risotto with Butter and Parmigiano**
- **Risotto with Lemon**
- **Risotto with Rosemary**
- **Risotto with Amarone Wine**
- **Risotto with Porcini**
- **Risotto with Asparagus**
- **Risotto with Artichokes**
- **Risotto with Artichokes and Leeks**
- **Risotto with Zucchini**
- **Risotto with Red and Yellow Peppers**
- **Risotto with Clams**
- **Risotto with Squid and Peas**
- **Risotto with Saffron**
- **Risotto with Chicken**
- **Risotto with Sausage and Radicchio**
- **Risotto with Pork and Smoked Mozzarella**
- **Rice with Peas and Radicchio**
- **Nonna Mary's White Rice**

Risotto is made with a particular type of rice, a short grain characterized by an opaque center surrounded by a translucent "shell," both different types of starches. The center swells as the rice cooks, increasing its volume threefold. The outer translucent starch melts away and makes it creamy. Risotto's characteristic creaminess does not come from anything added to the dish but from the rice itself. Risotto made with olive oil and no butter or cheese should be just as creamy as a butter-based risotto. Making perfect risotto takes a little practice but is not difficult, nor is it a dish that takes a long time. In fact, my five-year-old daughter, Gabriella, has gotten quite good at it, with supervision, of course. Often when I have not planned anything for dinner, I make a risotto with whatever vegetable is in the refrigerator, or perhaps with dried porcini, or simply Parmigiano-Reggiano.

The basic steps in making a risotto are as follows:

1. Prepare the base, whether it is vegetable, seafood, or meat, or simply sautéed onions.

2. Heat the liquid that will be used, usually either a meat broth or water.

3. Add the rice to the base and stir until the rice is well coated and begins to absorb some of the moisture. It is not necessary or even desirable to "toast" the rice as it may damage the outer translucent starch.

4. Add just enough hot liquid to attain a thick soupy consistency. Too much liquid at once may cause the outer starch to solidify and permanently attach to the rice kernel, which is what happens if you cook this kind of rice in boiling water.

5. Stir constantly, not only to prevent the rice from sticking to the bottom of the pan but also to create friction which helps the outside starch melt and become creamy.

6. Only add more liquid when you can see the bottom of the pan clearly as you stir.

7. Cook over as high a heat as possible without the rice sticking to the pan.

8. Risotto is done when it is al dente, which means tender yet firm, not mushy, but not crunchy either. You may find that you need more or less liquid than the recipe calls for. If all the broth is used up and the rice is not done yet, continue with water.

9. The base for a risotto can often be prepared 1 to 2 hours ahead of time, but the rice must be cooked from start to finish just before serving. And it's imperative to serve it at once, or it will become gluey rather than creamy because the rice will continue to absorb liquid, even off the heat.

RISOTTO WITH BUTTER AND PARMIGIANO

Risotto alla Parmigiana

This is the most basic of risotti, although that hardly makes it less delectable. It is an ideal base for a generous amount of shaved fresh white truffle.

Total time: 40 minutes

Serves 4 as a main course or 6 as part of a multicourse Italian meal

> 6 cups homemade meat broth (page 46) *or* ½ each beef and chicken bouillon cube dissolved in 6 cups water
> ½ medium yellow onion
> 3 tablespoons butter
> 1¾ cups rice for risotto (Arborio, Carnaroli, or Vialone Nano)
> Salt
> ½ cup freshly grated Parmigiano-Reggiano

1. Put the broth in a pot over high heat and bring to a boil. Lower the heat to maintain a very gentle simmer.

2. Peel and finely chop the onion. Put it in a heavy-bottomed braising pan with 2 tablespoons of the butter. Place over medium-high heat and sauté, stirring occasionally, until it turns a rich golden color, about 5 minutes.

3. Add the rice and stir until it is well coated. Add about 1 cup of the hot broth and continue stirring. Add only enough broth to produce the consistency of a rather thick soup and wait until all the liquid is absorbed before adding more. Season with salt and continue until the rice is al dente, 20 to 25 minutes.

4. Remove the risotto from the heat and stir in the remaining 1 tablespoon butter and the Parmigiano. Serve at once.

RISOTTO WITH LEMON

Risotto al Limone

When my mother-in-law, Jackie, comes to visit around Thanksgiving, she usually brings wonderfully fragrant, sweet Meyer lemons that she grows in her California backyard. When I made this typical Italian risotto with them, it was superb.

Total time: 40 minutes

Serves 4 as a main course or 6 as part of a multicourse Italian meal

> 6 cups homemade meat broth (page 46) *or* ½ each beef
> and chicken bouillon cube dissolved in 6 cups water
> ½ medium yellow onion
> 3 tablespoons butter
> 2 lemons
> 1¾ cups rice for risotto (Arborio, Carnaroli, or Vialone Nano)
> Salt
> ⅓ cup freshly grated Parmigiano-Reggiano

1. Put the broth in a pot over high heat and bring to a boil. Lower the heat to maintain a very gentle simmer.

2. Peel and finely chop the onion. Put it in a heavy-bottomed braising pan with 2 tablespoons of the butter. Place over medium-high heat and sauté until it turns a rich golden color, about 5 minutes.

3. While the onion is sautéing, grate the zest from the lemons, then juice them.

4. Add the rice to the onion and stir until it is well coated. Add about 1 cup of the hot broth and continue stirring. Add only enough broth to produce the consistency of a rather thick soup and wait until all the liquid is absorbed before adding more. After the rice has cooked for 15 minutes, season with

salt and add half the grated lemon zest and 3 tablespoons of the lemon juice. Continue cooking until the rice is al dente, 5 to 10 minutes more.

5. Remove the risotto from the heat and stir in the remaining 1 tablespoon butter and the Parmigiano. Serve at once, sprinkling the remaining lemon zest over each portion.

RISOTTO WITH ROSEMARY

Risotto al Rosmarino

This is a simple risotto with the fresh, fragrant aroma of rosemary.

Total time: 30 minutes

Serves 4 as a main course or 6 as part of a multicourse Italian meal

> ½ small yellow onion
> 3 tablespoons butter
> 3 to 4 sprigs fresh rosemary
> 1 large beef bouillon cube
> 1¾ cups rice for risotto (Arborio, Carnaroli, or Vialone Nano)
> Salt
> ⅓ cup freshly grated Parmigiano-Reggiano

1. Put a pot with about 2 quarts water over high heat and bring to a boil. Lower the heat to maintain a very gentle simmer.

2. Peel and finely chop the onion. Put it in a heavy-bottomed braising pan with 2 tablespoons of the butter. Place over medium-high heat and sauté until it turns a rich golden color, about 5 minutes.

3. While the onion is sautéing, finely chop enough of the rosemary leaves to measure 3 teaspoons. When the onion is ready, add 1 teaspoon of the rosemary and the bouillon cube to the onion and stir until the cube is completely dissolved, about 1 minute.

4. Add the rice and stir until it is well coated. Add about 1 cup of the hot water and continue stirring. Add only enough water to produce the consistency of a rather thick soup and wait until all the liquid is absorbed before adding more. Season with salt and continue until the rice is al dente, 20 to 25 minutes. Add the remaining 2 teaspoons rosemary and 1 tablespoon butter and stir well.

5. Remove from the heat and stir in the Parmigiano. Serve at once.

RISOTTO WITH AMARONE WINE

Risotto all'Amarone

This is Verona's classic dish, made with Amarone from the neighboring Valpolicella wine region. Amarone is a rich, full-bodied red made entirely from dried grapes. A good bottle of Amarone can be rather expensive and, although not quite the same, a very good version of this dish can be made with a good Valpolicella di Ripasso, a less expensive wine sometimes referred to as "baby" Amarone. Ripasso wine is made using both fresh and dried grapes. In any case, use a well-made wine; I would certainly choose a good Ripasso wine over a mediocre Amarone.

Total time: 35 minutes

Serves 4 as a main course or 6 as part of a multicourse Italian meal

> 2 cups Amarone wine
> 2 bay leaves
> 5 cups homemade meat broth (page 46) *or* ½ each beef
>   and chicken bouillon cube dissolved in 5 cups water
> ½ medium yellow onion
> 2 tablespoons extra virgin olive oil
> 1¾ cups rice for risotto (Arborio, Carnaroli, or Vialone Nano)
> Salt
> 1 tablespoon butter

1. Put 1¾ cups of the wine and the bay leaves in a small saucepan. Place over medium-high heat and bring to a boil. Lower the heat to maintain a very gentle simmer.

2. Put the broth in a pot over high heat and bring to a boil. Lower the heat to maintain a very gentle simmer.

3. Peel and finely chop the onion. Put it in a heavy-bottomed braising pan with the olive oil. Place over medium-high heat and sauté until it turns a rich golden color, about 5 minutes.

4. Add the rice and stir until it is well coated. Add about 1 cup of the hot wine and continue stirring. Add only enough wine to produce the consistency of a rather thick soup and wait until it is all absorbed before adding more. When you have used all the wine in the pot, begin adding the broth. After the rice has cooked for about 15 minutes, add the remaining ¼ cup wine and season with salt. Continue cooking and adding the broth until the rice is al dente, 5 to 10 minutes more.

5. Remove the risotto from the heat and stir in the butter. Serve at once.

RISOTTO WITH PORCINI

Risotto ai Porcini

Total time: 45 minutes

Serves 4 as a main course or 6 as part of a multicourse Italian meal

> 1 ounce dried porcini mushrooms
> 5 cups homemade meat broth (page 46) *or* ½ each beef
>   and chicken bouillon cube dissolved in 5 cups water
> ½ medium yellow onion
> 3 tablespoons butter
> Salt
> 1¾ cups rice for risotto (Arborio, Carnaroli, or Vialone Nano)
> ⅓ cup freshly grated Parmigiano-Reggiano

1. Put the dried porcini in a bowl, cover with water, and soak for at least 15 minutes.

2. Put the broth in a pot over high heat and bring to a boil. Lower the heat to maintain a very gentle simmer.

3. While the porcini are soaking, peel and finely chop the onion.

4. When the porcini are ready, put the onion and 2 tablespoons of the butter in a heavy-bottomed braising pan and place over medium-high heat. Sauté, stirring occasionally, until the onion turns a rich golden color, about 5 minutes.

5. While the onion is sautéing, lift the porcini out of the water and squeeze the excess back into the bowl; do not discard the water. Rinse the mushrooms under running water, then coarsely chop them. Pour the soaking water into a small pot. Be aware that there may be some sand at the bottom of the bowl, so pour carefully or strain through a paper towel. Place over high heat and bring to a boil. Lower the heat to maintain a very gentle simmer.

6. Add the chopped porcini to the onion, season with salt, and stir a few times. Add the rice and stir until it is well coated. Add about 1 cup of the hot broth and continue stirring. Add only enough broth to produce the consistency of a rather thick soup and wait until all the liquid is absorbed before adding more. As soon as the porcini water is hot, add that until you've used it all up, then go back to using the broth. Continue until the rice is al dente, 20 to 25 minutes.

7. Remove the risotto from the heat and stir in the remaining 1 tablespoon butter and the Parmigiano. Serve at once.

RISOTTO WITH ASPARAGUS

Risotto agli Asparagi

To give this risotto a rich asparagus flavor, use the water the asparagus is cooked in as part of the liquid to cook the rice.

Total time: 45 minutes

Serves 4 as a main course or 6 as part of a multicourse Italian meal

> 3 cups water
> 1 pound asparagus
> Salt
> 4 cups homemade meat broth (page 46) *or* ½ each beef
>   and chicken bouillon cube dissolved in 4 cups water
> ½ small yellow onion
> 3 tablespoons butter
> Freshly ground black pepper
> 1¾ cups rice for risotto (Arborio, Carnaroli, or Vialone Nano)
> ¼ cup freshly grated Parmigiano-Reggiano

1. Put 3 cups water in a deep skillet, place over high heat, and bring to a boil.

2. Cut off the woody bottom part of the asparagus spears, then peel the remaining bottom third. Add 1 teaspoon salt to the boiling water, then gently slide in the asparagus. Cook until the asparagus are tender, 5 to 6 minutes, then lift them out, saving the water. Keep the asparagus water over low heat to maintain a very gentle simmer.

3. Put the broth in a pot over high heat and bring to a boil. Lower the heat to maintain a very gentle simmer.

4. Peel and finely chop the onion. Put it in a heavy-bottomed braising pan with 2 tablespoons of the butter. Place over medium-high heat and sauté until it turns a rich golden color, about 5 minutes.

5. Cut the asparagus into 1-inch lengths. Add the asparagus to the onion, season with salt and pepper (go easy with the salt because there is already salt in the asparagus water), and sauté for 3 to 4 minutes. Add the rice and stir until it is well coated. Add about 1 cup of the hot asparagus water and continue stirring. When all the asparagus water has been used, begin adding the broth. Add only enough liquid to produce the consistency of a rather thick soup and wait until all the liquid is absorbed before adding more. Continue until the rice is al dente, 20 to 25 minutes.

6. Remove the risotto from the heat and stir in the remaining 1 tablespoon butter and the Parmigiano. Serve at once.

RISOTTO WITH ARTICHOKES

Risotto ai Carciofi

Total time: 1 hour

Serves 4 as a main course or 6 as part of a multicourse Italian meal

> 1 lemon
> 4 large artichokes
> ½ small yellow onion
> 3 tablespoons extra virgin olive oil
> 1 medium clove garlic
> ½ small bunch flat-leaf Italian parsley
> Salt
> Freshly ground black pepper
> 6 cups homemade meat broth (page 46) *or* ½ each beef
>   and chicken bouillon cube dissolved in 6 cups water
> 1¾ cups rice for risotto (Arborio, Carnaroli, or Vialone Nano)

1. Cut the lemon in half. Squeeze the juice from half the lemon into a medium bowl and fill the bowl halfway with cold water. Trim the artichokes as described on pages 34–35. Cut them into wedges about ¼ inch thick and put them in the bowl of lemon water to prevent them from discoloring.

2. Peel and finely chop the onion. Put it in a heavy-bottomed braising pan with 2 tablespoons of the olive oil. Place over medium-high heat and sauté until it turns a rich golden color, about 5 minutes.

3. While the onion is sautéing, peel and chop the garlic. Finely chop enough of the parsley leaves to measure ¼ cup. When the onion is ready, add the garlic and parsley. Cook for about 1 minute, then add the drained artichokes. Stir until the artichokes are well coated, then season with salt and pepper. Add about ½ cup water, cover the pan, and turn the heat down to medium. Cook until the artichokes are tender, 10 to 15 minutes, by which time all the water should be evaporated. If all the liquid evaporates before the artichokes are tender, add a little more water.

4. While the artichokes are cooking, put the broth in a pot over high heat and bring to a boil. Lower the heat to maintain a very gentle simmer.

5. Raise the heat under the artichokes to medium-high. Add the rice and stir until it is well coated. Add about 1 cup of the hot broth and continue stirring. Add only enough broth to produce the consistency of a rather thick soup and wait until all the liquid is absorbed before adding more. Season with salt and continue until the rice is al dente, 20 to 25 minutes.

6. Remove the risotto from the heat, stir in the remaining 1 tablespoon olive oil, and serve at once.

RISOTTO WITH ARTICHOKES
AND LEEKS

Risotto ai Carciofi e Porri

This is similar to the preceding artichoke risotto, but the leeks add a richness and sweetness that gives this risotto a distinctively different personality.

Total time: 1 hour

Serves 4 as a main course or 6 as part of a multicourse Italian meal

> 2 large or 3 medium leeks
> 1 medium clove garlic
> ½ small bunch flat-leaf Italian parsley
> 3 tablespoons extra virgin olive oil
> Salt
> 1 lemon
> 3 large artichokes
> Freshly ground black pepper
> 6 cups homemade meat broth (page 46) *or* ½ each beef
>   and chicken bouillon cube dissolved in 6 cups water
> 1¾ cups rice for risotto (Arborio, Carnaroli, or Vialone Nano)

1. Trim the root ends and dark green tops from the leeks (page 35). Cut the leeks lengthwise in quarters, then slice them crosswise in ½-inch chunks. Place the cut leeks in a large bowl of cold water and swish them around to loosen any dirt that is clinging to them.

2. Peel and finely chop the garlic. Finely chop enough of the parsley leaves to measure 4 tablespoons. Put the garlic and half of the parsley in a heavy-bottomed braising pan with 2 tablespoons of the olive oil. Place over medium-high heat and sauté until the garlic begins to sizzle. Lift the leeks out of the water and put them in the pan with ½ cup water. Season lightly with salt and cook, stirring occasionally, until the leeks are wilted, about 10 minutes.

3. Cut the lemon in half. Squeeze the juice from half the lemon into a medium bowl and fill the bowl halfway with cold water. Trim the artichokes as described on pages 34–35. Cut them into wedges about ¼ inch thick and put them in the bowl of lemon water to prevent them from discoloring.

4. When the leeks are done, add the artichokes. Season with salt and pepper and add another ½ cup water. Cover the pan, lower the heat to medium, and cook until the artichokes are tender, 10 to 15 minutes, by which time all the water should be evaporated. If all the liquid evaporates before the artichokes are tender, add a little more water.

5. While the artichokes are cooking, put the broth in a pot over high heat and bring to a boil. Lower the heat to maintain a very gentle simmer.

6. Raise the heat under the artichokes to medium-high. Add the rice and stir until it is well coated. Add about 1 cup of the hot broth and continue stirring. Add only enough broth to produce the consistency of a rather thick soup and wait until all the liquid is absorbed before adding more. Season with salt and continue until the rice is al dente, 20 to 25 minutes.

7. Remove the risotto from the heat and stir in the remaining 2 tablespoons parsley and 1 tablespoon olive oil. Serve at once.

RISOTTO WITH ZUCCHINI

Risotto alle Zucchine

Total time: 50 minutes

Serves 4 as a main course or 6 as part of a multicourse Italian meal

    1 pound small zucchini
    ½ small yellow onion
    3 tablespoons butter
    Salt
    Freshly ground black pepper
    6 cups homemade meat broth (page 46) *or* ½ each beef
        and chicken bouillon cube dissolved in 6 cups water
    3 to 4 sprigs flat-leaf Italian parsley
    1¾ cups rice for risotto (Arborio, Carnaroli, or Vialone Nano)
    ¼ cup freshly grated Parmigiano-Reggiano

1. Cut the zucchini into ½-inch chunks.

2. Peel and finely chop the onion. Put it in a heavy-bottomed braising pan with 2 tablespoons of the butter. Place over medium-high heat and sauté until it turns a rich golden color, about 5 minutes.

3. Add the zucchini, season with salt and pepper, and cook until they are tender and lightly browned, 10 to 15 minutes.

4. While the zucchini are cooking, put the broth in a pot over high heat and bring to a boil. Lower the heat to maintain a very gentle simmer. Finely chop enough of the parsley leaves to measure 1 tablespoon.

5. Add the rice to the zucchini and stir until it is well coated. Add about 1 cup of the hot broth and continue stirring. Add only enough broth to produce the consistency of a rather thick soup and wait until all the liquid is absorbed before adding more. Season with salt and continue until the rice is al dente, 20 to 25 minutes.

6. Remove the risotto from the heat and add the remaining 1 tablespoon butter, the parsley, and Parmigiano. Stir well and serve at once.

RISOTTO WITH RED AND YELLOW PEPPERS

Risotto coi Peperoni alla Napoletana

A classic Neapolitan dish is penne with sautéed peppers, garlic, and basil. This risotto is made with peppers that are cooked almost exactly the same way.

Total time: 50 minutes

Serves 4 as a main course or 6 as part of a multicourse Italian meal

> 2 red bell peppers
> 2 yellow bell peppers
> 3 medium cloves garlic
> 2 tablespoons extra virgin olive oil
> Salt
> 6 cups homemade meat broth (page 46) *or* ½ each beef
>   and chicken bouillon cube dissolved in 5 cups water
> 1¾ cups rice for risotto (Arborio, Carnaroli, or Vialone Nano)
> 12 fresh basil leaves
> 1 tablespoon butter
> ¼ cup freshly grated Parmigiano-Reggiano

1. Peel the peppers (pages 31–32) and seed them. Cut away any white pith inside the peppers and cut into ¾-inch squares.

2. Lightly crush and peel the garlic cloves and put them in a heavy-bottomed braising pan with the olive oil. Place over medium-high heat and

sauté until the garlic is lightly browned on all sides, 1 to 2 minutes. Remove the garlic and discard. Add the peppers to the oil and season with salt. Sauté until the peppers are tender and lightly browned, 10 to 15 minutes.

3. While the peppers are sautéing, put the broth in a pot over high heat and bring to a boil. Lower the heat to maintain a very gentle simmer.

4. When the peppers are done, add the rice and stir until it is well coated. Add about 1 cup of the hot broth and continue stirring. Add only enough broth to produce the consistency of a rather thick soup and wait until all the liquid is absorbed before adding more. Season with salt. When the rice has cooked about 10 minutes, tear the basil leaves into fairly wide strips and add them to the risotto. Continue adding broth and stirring until the rice is al dente, 20 to 25 minutes.

5. Remove the risotto from the heat and stir in the butter and Parmigiano. Serve at once.

RISOTTO WITH CLAMS

Risotto alle Vongole

Clams in Italy are as small as a large pea and so flavorful they hardly need any seasoning. Here I add a little hot red pepper to compensate for the mild flavor of American clams. Use the juice the clams release when you steam them open as part of the liquid to cook the rice; it imbues the risotto with clam flavor.

Total time: 40 minutes

Serves 4 as a main course or 6 as part of a multicourse Italian meal

> 3 dozen littleneck, Manila, or mahogany clams
> 1 small clove garlic

Pinch crushed red pepper flakes
6 to 8 sprigs flat-leaf Italian parsley
3 tablespoons extra virgin olive oil
1¾ cups rice for risotto (Arborio, Carnaroli, or Vialone Nano)
Salt
Freshly ground black pepper

1. Rinse the clams in several changes of cold water until you do not see any sand at the bottom of the bowl. Put the clams in a deep skillet or sauté pan with about ½ cup water. Cover and place over high heat. Cook until all the clams are open, 3 to 5 minutes. Don't be concerned if some clams take longer to open; they are the freshest ones. When the clams are open, take them out of the pan and set aside. Transfer the liquid remaining in the pan to a small pot and place it over low heat to keep it hot. Remove the clams from the shells and set aside.

2. Put about 2 quarts water in a pot over high heat and bring to a boil. Lower the heat to maintain a very gentle simmer.

3. Peel and finely chop the garlic. Finely chop enough of the parsley leaves to measure 2 tablespoons. Put the garlic, hot red pepper, and 2 tablespoons of the olive oil in a large heavy-bottomed braising pan over medium-high heat. Sauté until the garlic begins to sizzle, 1 to 2 minutes. Stir in the parsley.

4. Add the rice and stir until it is well coated. Add the hot clam juice and stir with a wooden spoon. Season with salt and continue stirring until all the liquid in the pan is absorbed. Add about 1 cup of the hot water and continue stirring. Add only enough water to produce the consistency of a rather thick soup and wait until all the liquid is absorbed before adding more. Continue until the rice is almost al dente, 20 to 25 minutes, then stir in the clams.

6. Remove the risotto from the heat, season with pepper, and drizzle with the remaining 1 tablespoon olive oil. Serve at once.

RISOTTO WITH SQUID AND PEAS

Risotto ai Calamari e Piselli

Preparation time: 40 minutes
Total time from start to finish: 1 hour 40 minutes

Serves 4 as a main course or 6 as part of a multicourse Italian meal

> 12 ounces ripe tomatoes
> ½ medium yellow onion
> 3 tablespoons extra virgin olive oil
> 1 pound cleaned squid tubes and tentacles
> ⅓ cup dry white wine
> Salt
> Freshly ground black pepper
> 6 to 8 sprigs flat-leaf Italian parsley
> 1 pound fresh peas in the pod *or* 6 ounces frozen peas
> 1¾ cups rice for risotto (Arborio, Carnaroli, or Vialone Nano)

1. Peel the tomatoes (pages 30–31) and coarsely chop.

2. Peel and finely chop the onion. Put it in a heavy-bottomed braising pan with 2 tablespoons of the olive oil. Place over medium-high heat and sauté until it turns a rich golden color, about 5 minutes.

3. While the onion is sautéing, rinse the squid and cut the tubes into rings about ¼ inch thick. When the onion is done, raise the heat to high and add the squid. Stir for about 1 minute, then add the wine. Let the wine boil for about 30 seconds to let the alcohol evaporate, then add the tomatoes. Season with salt and pepper and adjust the heat so that the liquid simmers. Cover the pan and cook, stirring occasionally, until the squid is very tender, about 45 minutes.

4. While the squid is cooking, finely chop enough of the parsley leaves to measure 2 tablespoons. If using fresh peas, shell them. Put about 2 quarts

water in a pot over high heat and bring to a boil. Lower the heat to maintain a very gentle simmer.

5. When the squid is done, add the peas. Cook until the peas are tender, 20 minutes for fresh or 10 for frozen. Add the rice and stir until it is well coated. Add about 1 cup of the hot water and continue stirring. Add only enough water to produce the consistency of a rather thick soup and wait until all the liquid is absorbed before adding more. Season with salt and continue until the rice is al dente, 20 to 25 minutes.

6. Remove the risotto from the heat and add the parsley and the remaining 1 tablespoon olive oil. Serve at once.

RISOTTO WITH SAFFRON

Risotto alla Milanese

It is rare that risotto is served with the meat course instead of by itself as a first course. This risotto, however, is traditionally paired with the *ossobuchi* on page 283. If you do serve them together, have the *ossobuchi* ready before you start the risotto so that you can serve as soon as the risotto is ready. An essential ingredient, which gives it its characteristic richness, is beef marrow. Ask your butcher or meat department for beef marrow bones.

Total time: 35 minutes

Serves 4 as a main course or 6 served with ossobuchi

> 6 cups homemade meat broth (page 46) *or* ½ each beef
> and chicken bouillon cube dissolved in 6 cups water
> ½ teaspoon saffron strands or powder
> ½ small yellow onion
> 3 tablespoons butter
> 2 ounces beef marrow, from about 3 1½-inch marrow bones
> 1¾ cups rice for risotto (Arborio, Carnaroli, or Vialone Nano)
> Salt
> Freshly ground black pepper
> ¼ cup freshly grated Parmigiano-Reggiano

1. Put the broth in a pot over high heat and bring to a boil. Lower the heat to maintain a very gentle simmer. If using saffron strands, finely chop them and put them in a small bowl with ½ cup of the hot broth; set aside.

2. Peel and finely chop the onion. Put it in a heavy-bottomed braising pan with 2 tablespoons of the butter. Place over medium-high heat and sauté until it turns a dark golden color, about 5 minutes.

3. While the onion is sautéing, scoop the marrow from the bones and cut it into ¼-inch dice. When the onion is done, add the chopped marrow and sauté for 1 minute.

4. Add the rice and stir until it is well coated. Add about 1 cup of the hot broth and continue stirring. Add only enough broth to produce the consistency of a rather thick soup and wait until all the liquid is absorbed before adding more. After the rice has cooked for 15 minutes, add the saffron and season with salt and pepper. Continue cooking until the rice is al dente, 5 to 10 minutes more.

5. Remove the risotto from the heat and stir in the remaining 1 tablespoon butter and the Parmigiano. Serve at once.

RISOTTO WITH CHICKEN

Risotto al Pollo

Using chicken for a pasta sauce or risotto base is challenging because chicken has a mild flavor and a sauce or risotto base must be flavorful enough to season the pasta or rice. In this recipe I use only the more flavorful dark meat, which also allows me to cook the chicken longer to concentrate flavors without drying out the meat.

Preparation time: 50 minutes
Total time from start to finish: 1½ hours

Serves 4 as a main course or 6 as part of a multicourse Italian meal

> 1½ pounds bone-in chicken thighs *or* 1 pound boneless thighs
> ½ small yellow onion
> 1 medium carrot
> 3 tablespoons extra virgin olive oil
> 2 ounces pancetta, thinly sliced
> ⅓ cup dry white wine
> 1½ cups canned whole peeled tomatoes with their juice
> Salt
> Freshly ground black pepper
> 6 cups homemade meat broth (page 46) *or* ½ each beef
>   and chicken bouillon cube dissolved in 6 cups water
> 1¾ cups rice for risotto (Arborio, Carnaroli, or Vialone Nano)

1. If you have chicken thighs on the bone, remove the skin and cut the flesh away from the bone. Cut the chicken into ½-inch pieces.

2. Peel and finely chop the onion. Peel and dice the carrot. Put the olive oil with the onion and carrot in a large heavy-bottomed braising pan. Place over medium-high heat and sauté, stirring occasionally, until the onion and carrot begin to brown lightly, 5 to 8 minutes.

3. Finely chop the pancetta and add it to the pan. Sauté until it loses its raw pink color, 1 to 2 minutes. Add the chicken and cook until it is lightly browned, about 3 minutes.

4. Raise the heat to high and add the wine. Let the wine boil for about 30 seconds to let the alcohol evaporate. Add the tomatoes, season with salt and pepper, and break them up with a spoon. Lower the heat so that the tomatoes simmer and cover the pan with the lid slightly askew. Cook, stirring occasionally, until the chicken is tender and the tomatoes are reduced and form a thick sauce, about 45 minutes. If all the liquid evaporates before the chicken is done, add a little water.

5. Put the broth in a pot over high heat and bring to a boil. Lower the heat to maintain a very gentle simmer.

6. Raise the heat under the chicken to medium-high, add the rice, and stir until it is well coated. Add about 1 cup of the hot broth and continue stirring. Add only enough broth to produce the consistency of a rather thick soup and wait until all the liquid is absorbed before adding more. Season with salt and continue until the rice is al dente, 20 to 25 minutes. Remove from the heat and serve at once.

RISOTTO WITH SAUSAGE AND RADICCHIO

Risotto alla Salsiccia e Radicchio

I have found that bitter and salty flavors go well together, each complementing the other. In this dish the saltiness of the sausage takes the edge off the radicchio's bitterness and makes a rich and satisfying risotto easily served as a single-course meal.

Total time: 45 minutes

Serves 4 as a main course or 6 as part of a multicourse Italian meal

> ½ medium yellow onion
> 3 tablespoons butter
> 12 ounces plain mild sausage (use breakfast links or ¾ recipe
>   homemade sausage, page 45)
> 1 medium to large radicchio, about 12 ounces
> Salt
> Freshly ground black pepper
> 6 cups homemade meat broth (page 46) *or* ½ each beef
>   and chicken bouillon cube dissolved in 6 cups water
> 6 to 8 sprigs flat-leaf Italian parsley
> 1¾ cups rice for risotto (Arborio, Carnaroli, or Vialone Nano)
> ½ cup freshly grated Parmigiano-Reggiano

1. Peel and finely chop the onion. Put it in a heavy-bottomed braising pan with 2 tablespoons of the butter. Place over medium-high heat and sauté until it turns a rich golden color, about 5 minutes.

2. If using sausage links, cut the sausage into ¼-inch rounds. When the onion is ready, add the sausage and cook until it is lightly browned, 2 to 3 minutes. If using homemade sausage, break it up with a spoon as it cooks.

3. While the sausage is cooking, remove any bruised or wilted leaves from the radicchio, trim the root end, and thinly shred the leaves. When the sausage is done, add the radicchio to the pan and season with salt and pepper. Lower the heat to medium, cover the pan, and cook until the radicchio is wilted and tender, about 10 minutes.

4. Put the broth in a pot over high heat and bring to a boil. Lower the heat to maintain a very gentle simmer.

5. While the radicchio is cooking, finely chop enough of the parsley leaves to measure 2 tablespoons.

6. Uncover the radicchio, raise the heat to medium-high, and add the rice. Stir until it is well coated. Add about 1 cup of the hot broth and continue stirring. Add only enough broth to produce the consistency of a rather thick soup and wait until all the liquid is absorbed before adding more. Season with salt and continue until the rice is al dente, 20 to 25 minutes.

7. Remove the risotto from the heat and add the parsley, the remaining 1 tablespoon butter, and the Parmigiano. Stir well and serve at once.

RISOTTO WITH PORK
AND SMOKED MOZZARELLA

Risotto al Ragù di Maiale e Mozzarella Affumicata

Total time: 50 minutes

Serves 4 as a main course or 6 as part of a multicourse Italian meal

> ½ small yellow onion
> 3 tablespoons butter
> 3 to 4 sprigs fresh marjoram
> 8 ounces ground pork
> 1 pound ripe tomatoes
> Salt
> Freshly ground black pepper
> 3 ounces smoked mozzarella
> 6 cups homemade meat broth (page 46) *or* ½ each beef
>   and chicken bouillon cube dissolved in 6 cups water
> 1¾ cups rice for risotto (Arborio, Carnaroli, or Vialone Nano)

1. Peel and finely chop the onion. Put it in a heavy-bottomed braising pan with 2 tablespoons of the butter. Place over medium-high heat and sauté until it turns a dark golden color, about 5 minutes.

2. While the onion is sautéing, chop enough of the marjoram leaves to measure 2 teaspoons. When the onion is done, add the marjoram along with the ground pork. Break up the meat with a spoon and cook, stirring occasionally, until it browns lightly, 3 to 4 minutes.

3. Peel the tomatoes (pages 30–31) and coarsely chop them. Add them to the pork and season with salt and pepper. Lower the heat to medium and cook until the tomatoes are reduced and no longer watery, about 15 minutes.

4. While the tomatoes are cooking, grate the smoked mozzarella.

5. Put the broth in a pot over high heat and bring to a boil. Lower the heat to maintain a very gentle simmer.

6. Add the rice to the tomatoes and stir until it is well coated. Add about 1 cup of the hot broth and continue stirring. Add only enough broth to produce the consistency of a rather thick soup and wait until all the liquid is absorbed before adding more. Season with salt and continue until the rice is al dente, 20 to 25 minutes.

7. Remove from the heat and stir in the remaining 1 tablespoon butter and the mozzarella. Serve at once.

RICE WITH PEAS AND RADICCHIO

Risi e Bisi al Radicchio

Risi e bisi is Venetian for "rice and peas." In its simplest and most classic form, it is a thick soup of rice and peas, traditionally served in the spring when fresh peas are at their peak. This varies the original with the addition of radicchio and pancetta. It is meant to be thick enough to eat with a fork, so that it almost resembles a risotto. It does not have the creamy texture of risotto, however, but a more rustic personality.

Preparation time: 20 minutes (40 minutes if using fresh peas)
Total time from start to finish: 50 minutes (1 hour 10 minutes if using fresh
peas)

Serves 4 as a main course or 6 as part of a multicourse Italian meal

> 2 pounds fresh peas in the pod *or* 12 ounces frozen peas
> 6 to 8 sprigs flat-leaf Italian parsley
> ½ medium yellow onion
> 4 tablespoons butter
> 3 ounces pancetta, thinly sliced
> Salt
> Freshly ground black pepper
> 1 medium to large radicchio, about 12 ounces
> 6 cups homemade meat broth (page 46) *or* ½ each beef
>   and chicken bouillon cube dissolved in 6 cups water
> 1½ cups rice for risotto (Arborio, Carnaroli, or Vialone Nano)
> ½ cup freshly grated Parmigiano-Reggiano

1. If using fresh peas, shell them. Finely chop enough of the parsley leaves to measure 2 tablespoons.

2. Peel and finely chop the onion. Put it in a heavy-bottomed braising pan with 2 tablespoons of the butter. Place over medium-high heat and sauté until it turns a rich golden color, about 5 minutes.

3. While the onion is sautéing, chop the pancetta. When the onion is done, add the pancetta and sauté until the pancetta begins to brown, 1 to 2 minutes. Add the parsley and peas. Season with salt and pepper and cover the pot. If using frozen peas, cook over medium heat for 5 minutes. If using fresh peas, add about ¼ cup water and cook for 15 minutes.

4. While the peas are cooking, remove any wilted leaves from the radicchio, trim the root end, and thinly shred the leaves. When the peas are done, add the radicchio, a little salt, and the broth. Cover the pan and bring to a boil. Lower the heat and simmer for 10 minutes.

5. Add the rice and cook, uncovered, until tender, 15 to 20 minutes. Stir occasionally but not constantly. When the rice is done, the liquid should be mostly absorbed. Stir in the remaining 2 tablespoons butter and the Parmigiano. Serve at once.

NONNA MARY'S WHITE RICE

Il Riso di Nonna Mary

This is how my grandmother used to cook rice, and it's a foolproof easy recipe. I use the same rice I use for risotto, which comes out slightly sticky but I love its starchy flavor. It's also good with basmati rice or good plain white rice.

Preparation time: 25 minutes
Total time from start to finish: 45 minutes

Serves 6 as a side dish

> 2 tablespoons butter
> 1½ cups rice
> 2¼ cups water
> Salt

1. Preheat the oven to 350°.

2. Put the butter in an ovenproof pot and melt over medium-high heat. Add the rice and stir until it is well coated. Add the water and season with salt. When the water begins to bubble, cover the pot and place in the oven. Bake for 20 minutes. Remove from the oven and let stand, covered, for 3 to 5 minutes before serving.

FISH AND SEAFOOD

- Grilled Swordfish with Oregano Sauce
- Grilled Salmon with Thyme and Parsley Sauce
- Boiled Lobster with Marjoram and Parsley Sauce
- Poached Fish with Herb Sauce
- Sturgeon with Saffron Sauce
- Aromatic Salmon in a Pouch
- Tuna Steaks in a Pouch
- Tuna Marinated with Onions and Capers
- Pan-Seared Tuna with Fresh Tomato and Bay Leaves
- Pan-Roasted Mahi Mahi with Garlic and Vinegar
- Savory Baked Chilean Sea Bass
- Baked Cod with Tomatoes and Red Onions
- Fish Fillets with Tomatoes and Capers
- Red Snapper with Mussels
- Baked Swordfish Rolls
- Grilled Shrimp Adriatic Style
- Shrimp with Red and Yellow Peppers
- Sea Scallops with Tomato and Basil

Fish and shellfish dishes are the hardest to replicate in the States because the varieties of seafood in Italy are so different from what is available here. I use a similar approach to how fish is prepared in Italy and apply it to what I can buy in U.S. markets. When seafood is very fresh, it's best to do as little as possible. The simple, light-handed Italian approach is best exemplified by fresh fish served with a simple sauce. Poaching and grilling are my favorite ways to prepare fresh seafood. In Italy, grilled or poached fish is served with either extra virgin olive oil and lemon, or a simple, uncooked herb sauce, such as the Sicilian *salmoriglio* sauce served with swordfish. For poached fish, the classic Italian sauce is *salsa verde,* literally "green sauce," a savory parsley-based sauce with a deep green color.

GRILLED SWORDFISH
WITH OREGANO SAUCE

Pesce Spada al Salmoriglio

Total time: 20 minutes

Serves 4 as a main course or 6 as part of a multicourse Italian meal

> 2 tablespoons fresh lemon juice
> Salt
> 1 to 2 sprigs fresh oregano
> ¼ cup extra virgin olive oil
> 2 pounds swordfish steaks, about ¾ inch thick
> Freshly ground black pepper

1. Preheat a charcoal or gas grill.

2. Put the lemon juice with 1 teaspoon salt in a small bowl. Mix together thoroughly with a small whisk or fork until the salt is dissolved. Chop enough of the oregano leaves to measure 2 teaspoons and add it to the bowl. Whisk in the olive oil until emulsified.

3. Season the swordfish on both sides with salt and pepper and place it on the grill. Cook for 2 to 3 minutes on each side until barely pink in the center. Transfer to a serving platter, pour the sauce over it, and serve at once.

GRILLED SALMON WITH THYME AND PARSLEY SAUCE

Salmone alla Griglia con Salsa al Timo

Total time: 25 minutes

Serves 4 as a main course or 6 as part of a multicourse Italian meal

2 tablespoons fresh lemon juice
Salt
6 to 8 sprigs flat-leaf Italian parsley
3 to 4 sprigs fresh thyme
5 tablespoons extra virgin olive oil
2 pounds salmon fillets
Freshly ground black pepper
2 to 3 tablespoons fine dry bread crumbs

1. Preheat a charcoal or gas grill.

2. Put the lemon juice with 1 teaspoon salt in a small bowl. Mix together thoroughly with a small whisk or fork until the salt is dissolved. Chop enough of the parsley leaves to measure 2 tablespoons and enough of the thyme leaves to measure 2 teaspoons. Add the herbs to the bowl. Whisk in 4 tablespoons of the olive oil until emulsified.

3. Season the fish with salt and pepper and coat it with the bread crumbs. Drizzle the remaining 1 tablespoon olive oil on the salmon and place it on the grill. Cook the fish for about 5 minutes per inch of thickness, turning the fillets halfway through the cooking time. When salmon is done, it should flake but still be somewhat pink in the center. Transfer to a serving platter, pour the sauce over it, and serve at once.

BOILED LOBSTER WITH MARJORAM AND PARSLEY SAUCE

Astice con Salsa di Maggiorana

This is a typical New England specialty served in an unmistakably Italian way. A tip I learned from Maine lobster fishermen is to cook lobsters in very salty water, in essence recreating their tradition of cooking them in sea water.

Total time: 30 minutes

Serves 4

> Salt
> 4 live Maine lobsters, about 1½ pounds each
> 3 tablespoons fresh lemon juice
> 6 to 8 sprigs flat-leaf Italian parsley
> 3 to 4 sprigs fresh marjoram
> 6 tablespoons extra virgin olive oil

1. Put at least 8 quarts water in a large, wide pot that will accommodate the lobsters, place over high heat, and bring to a boil. (If you do not have a large enough pot, use two pots.) Add at least ¼ cup salt to the water and put in the lobsters. Cook them 12 minutes per pound (18 minutes for 1½-pound lobsters), then take them out of the pot.

2. While the lobsters are cooking, make the sauce. Put the lemon juice with 1 teaspoon salt in a small bowl. Mix together thoroughly with a small whisk or fork until the salt is dissolved. Chop enough of the parsley leaves to measure 2 tablespoons and enough of the marjoram leaves to measure 2 teaspoons. Add the herbs to the bowl. Whisk in the olive oil until emulsified. Divide the sauce among 4 dipping bowls and serve with the lobsters.

POACHED FISH WITH HERB SAUCE

Pesce Lesso con Salsa Verde

This is a classic Italian *salsa verde* traditionally served with poached fish. Both the Marjoram and Parsley Sauce (page 237) and the Thyme and Parsley Sauce (page 236) would also be very good here.

Total time: 30 minutes

Serves 4 as a main course or 6 as part of a multicourse Italian meal

> 2 pounds striped bass, halibut, or other fine, firm white
>   fish fillets
> 1 medium yellow onion
> 2 carrots
> 1 rib celery
> Salt
> 4 tablespoons red wine vinegar
> 1 large egg
> ½ small bunch flat-leaf Italian parsley
> ¼ cup capers
> 8 anchovies
> 6 tablespoons extra virgin olive oil

1. Choose a pot large enough to hold the fish comfortably. Fill halfway with water and place over high heat. Peel and quarter the onion. Peel the carrots and celery. Add the vegetables to the pot and cover it. When the water comes to a boil, add 1 tablespoon salt and 2 tablespoons red wine vinegar. Carefully slide in the fish and when the water returns to a boil, adjust the heat so that the water simmers gently. Cook for about 10 minutes per inch of thickness. Lift the fillets out carefully with 2 spatulas or large spoons and transfer to a platter. The fish is done if it flakes easily. Discard the vegetables.

2. While the fish is cooking, make the sauce. Put the egg in a small pot, cover with water, and place over medium-high heat. After the water comes to a boil, cook for 10 minutes.

3. While the egg is cooking, chop enough of the parsley leaves to measure ¼ cup. Put the parsley, capers, anchovies, olive oil, and remaining 2 table-spoons vinegar in a food processor. Run the processor until everything is very finely chopped. When the egg is done, rinse it in cold water to cool, then remove the shell and egg white. Add only the yolk to the processor and run the processor again until the sauce is smooth and creamy.

4. Serve the fish warm or at room temperature with the sauce on the side.

STURGEON WITH SAFFRON SAUCE

Storione allo Zafferrano

Total time: 30 minutes

Serves 4 as a main course or 6 as part of a multicourse Italian meal

> 3 to 4 sprigs flat-leaf Italian parsley
> ½ medium yellow onion
> 3 tablespoons extra virgin olive oil
> 1 small clove garlic
> ⅛ teaspoon saffron strands
> ¼ cup dry white wine
> 1 teaspoon Dijon mustard
> 1½ pounds skinless sturgeon, grouper, or other delicate,
>   firm white fish fillets
> Salt
> Freshly ground black pepper

1. Finely chop enough of the parsley leaves to measure 1 tablespoon.

2. Peel and finely chop the onion. Put it in a 12-inch skillet with the olive oil. Place over medium-high heat and sauté, stirring occasionally, until it turns to a rich golden color.

3. While the onion is sautéing, peel and finely chop the garlic. Chop the saffron and mix it with the white wine. When the onion is ready, add the garlic and sauté for another minute. Add the wine and let it bubble away for about 30 seconds to let the alcohol evaporate. Add the mustard and parsley and stir until all the ingredients are well mixed.

4. Add the fish fillets, season with salt and pepper, and cover the pan. Cook for 5 minutes, then turn the fillets. Continue cooking until the fish flakes easily with a fork, about 5 minutes more. The fish should cook for about 10 minutes per inch of thickness. When the fish is done, the sauce should be quite thick. If it is not, transfer the fish to a warm platter, uncover the pan, turn the heat up, and simmer until the sauce reduces. Pour the sauce over the fish and serve hot.

AROMATIC SALMON IN A POUCH

Salmone Aromatico al Cartoccio

Cooking in a pouch is one of the best ways to prepare fish because it keeps the fish moist while delicately infusing it with the flavors of other ingredients in the pouch. Using aluminum foil makes it easy to create a well-sealed pouch.

Preparation time: 25 minutes
Total time from start to finish: 1 hour

Serves 4 as a main course or 6 as part of a multicourse Italian meal

12 ounces ripe tomatoes
1 medium clove garlic
10 to 12 sprigs flat-leaf Italian parsley
1 to 2 sprigs fresh oregano
3 tablespoons extra virgin olive oil

Salt
Freshly ground black pepper
2 pounds skinless salmon fillet
2 tablespoons dry white wine

1. Preheat the oven to 400° on convection heat or 425° on regular bake.

2. Peel the tomatoes (pages 30–31), remove the seeds, and cut into ½-inch dice.

3. Peel and finely chop the garlic. Finely chop enough of the parsley leaves to measure 3 tablespoons. Coarsely chop enough of the oregano leaves to measure 2 teaspoons. Mix the garlic, 2 tablespoons of the parsley, the oregano, and 2 tablespoons of the olive oil. Season with salt and pepper.

4. Butterfly the salmon fillet by slicing horizontally along its thicker side so that the fillet opens like a book. Do not cut all the way through to the other side.

5. Tear a sheet of extra-wide heavy-duty aluminum foil large enough to wrap around the fish completely leaving enough room for the steam to circulate around the fish as it cooks. Put the remaining 1 tablespoon olive oil in the center of the foil and place the fish over it. Spread the herb mixture on the inside and outside of the salmon fillet, then close it like a book. Sprinkle with the white wine. Spread the tomatoes over the fish and sprinkle the remaining 1 tablespoon parsley on top. Season with salt and pepper and seal the pouch, making sure not to leave any openings.

6. Place the pouch on a baking sheet and put it in the oven. Bake for 25 to 30 minutes, depending on how thick the fish is. If you are unsure whether the fish is cooked or not, partially open the pouch and check with a fork. It should be slightly pink in the center and flake easily. When it is done, remove the baking sheet from the oven. Gently open the foil, taking care not to spill the juices. Slide the contents onto a serving dish. Serve at once.

TUNA STEAKS IN A POUCH

Tonno al Cartoccio

One of the challenges in preparing tuna is keeping it moist. Cooking tuna in a pouch ensures it will not dry out and also infuses the tuna with flavor, making it both delicate and fragrant. Do not discard the lemon slices. They are delicious and should be eaten along with the tuna. As in the salmon recipe on page 240, using aluminum foil makes it easy to create a well-sealed pouch.

Preparation time: 10 minutes
Total time from start to finish: 25 minutes

Serves 4

> About ¼ cup extra virgin olive oil
> 4 tuna steaks, 6 to 8 ounces each, about ¾ inch thick
> Salt
> Freshly ground black pepper
> 2 teaspoons red wine vinegar
> 1 lemon
> ½ cup small bunch flat-leaf Italian parsley
> 4 teaspoons capers

1. Preheat the oven to 400° on convection heat or 425° on regular bake.

2. Cut 4 sheets of heavy-duty aluminum foil large enough to wrap around each tuna steak, leaving enough room for the steam to circulate around the fish as it cooks. Drizzle a little olive oil in the center of each sheet of foil and place a tuna steak on it. Season the fish with salt and pepper and pour ½ teaspoon vinegar over each steak. Cut the lemon crosswise into 8 very thin slices. Finely chop enough of the parsley leaves to measure 4 tablespoons. On each tuna steak place 2 lemon slices, 1 tablespoon parsley, ½ teaspoon capers, and 1 tablespoon olive oil.

3. Seal each pouch, making sure not to leave any openings. Place the pouches on a baking sheet and place in the oven. Bake for 15 minutes. Open the pouches and slide the tuna steaks onto dinner plates, pouring all the juices from the pouch over the fish. Serve at once.

TUNA MARINATED
WITH ONIONS AND CAPERS

Tonno Marinato

One time I found myself with quite a bit of leftover grilled tuna. I didn't want to reheat it since it would inevitably overcook. Recalling that Venetians marinate fried sole in sweet-and-sour onions, and leftover boiled beef is often served with smothered onions, I decided to marinate the tuna with caramelized onions and capers and serve it the next day. It was so good that now I grill tuna expressly to marinate it this way.

Preparation time: 25 minutes
Total time from start to finish: 12½ or more hours

Serves 4 as a main course or 6 as part of a multicourse Italian meal

> 2 medium sweet yellow onions
> 5 tablespoons extra virgin olive oil
> Salt
> Freshly ground black pepper
> 1½ pounds fresh tuna steaks, about ¾ inch thick
> 2 tablespoons capers

1. Preheat a charcoal or gas grill.

2. Peel, halve, and thinly slice the onions crosswise. Put them in a skillet with 4 tablespoons of the olive oil. Place over medium-high heat and season

with salt and pepper. When the onions begin to brown, reduce the heat to low and cook, stirring occasionally, until the onions become very soft, 15 to 20 minutes.

3. While the onions are cooking, drizzle both sides of the tuna steaks with the remaining 1 tablespoon olive oil and season with salt and pepper. Grill for 2 to 3 minutes on each side for medium-rare tuna. Remove from the grill and place in a deep platter.

4. When the onions are done, add the capers and cook for another minute. Pour the contents of the pan over the tuna. When it is cool, cover with plastic wrap and refrigerate for at least 12 hours. Serve at room temperature.

PAN-SEARED TUNA WITH FRESH TOMATO AND BAY LEAVES

Tonno Fresco al Pomodoro e Alloro

Total time from start to finish: 45 minutes

Serves 4

> 1 large yellow onion
> 4 tablespoons extra virgin olive oil
> 1½ pounds tuna steaks, about ¾ inch thick
> Salt
> Freshly ground black pepper
> 3 to 4 sprigs flat-leaf Italian parsley
> 12 ounces ripe tomatoes
> 3 tablespoons dry white wine
> 1 tablespoon red wine vinegar
> 2 bay leaves

1. Peel, halve, and thinly slice the onion crosswise.

2. Put 2 tablespoons of the olive oil in a skillet large enough to hold the tuna in a single layer and place it over medium-high heat. Season the tuna on both sides with salt and pepper. When the oil is very hot, put the tuna in the pan and cook just long enough to brown the tuna on both sides, about 1 minute each side. Remove the tuna from the pan and set aside on a platter. Turn the heat under the pan down to medium and add the remaining 2 tablespoons olive oil and the onion. Season lightly with salt and sauté, stirring occasionally, until the onion softens and turns a rich golden color, 10 to 15 minutes.

3. While the onion is sautéing, finely chop enough of the parsley leaves to measure 1 tablespoon. Peel the tomatoes (pages 30–31) and coarsely chop.

4. When the onion is done, raise the heat to medium-high and add the wine and the vinegar. Let them bubble away for 2 to 3 minutes to allow the alcohol and some of the vinegar's acidity to evaporate. Add the tomatoes, bay leaves, and parsley, season lightly with salt, and cook until the tomatoes are reduced and form a thick sauce, 15 to 20 minutes.

5. Return the tuna to the pan and cover. Cook until the tuna is heated through and medium-rare, 2 to 3 minutes. Serve at once.

PAN-ROASTED MAHI MAHI WITH GARLIC AND VINEGAR

La Buridda dei Pescatori Friulani

I had a version of this dish at a restaurant in the picturesque town of Grado, which juts into the Adriatic just west of Trieste in Friuli. Our host explained how fishermen prepared imperfect or damaged (but very fresh) fish that could not be sold. The acidity of the red wine vinegar is just barely noticeable, but its fragrance comes through, making this a fine dish. Bluefish and mackerel are excellent alternatives to mahi mahi.

Total time: 20 minutes

Serves 4 as a main course or 6 as part of a multicourse Italian meal

>4 medium cloves garlic
>3 tablespoons extra virgin olive oil
>2 pounds skinless mahi mahi fillet
>2 tablespoons all-purpose flour
>Salt
>Freshly ground black pepper
>3 tablespoons red wine vinegar
>¼ cup water

1. Peel and lightly crush the garlic cloves and put them in a 12-inch skillet with the olive oil. Place over medium-high heat and lightly brown the cloves on all sides, then remove and discard them.

2. While the garlic is browning, dust both sides of the fish with the flour and shake off the excess. After removing the garlic cloves, put the fish in the pan and season with salt and pepper. When the fillet is browned, turn it, season with salt and pepper, and brown the other side. It should take 2 to 3 minutes to brown each side.

3. Add the vinegar and let it bubble away for about 30 seconds to allow most of the acidity to evaporate. Add ¼ cup water, lower the heat to medium, and cover the pan. Cook until the fish flakes easily, about 10 minutes.

4. When the fish is done, the liquid in the pan should have mostly evaporated. If not, transfer the fish to a warm platter, raise the heat under the pan, and cook the sauce until it is thick enough to coat a spoon. Remove the pan from the heat, return the fish, and coat it with the sauce. Serve at once.

SAVORY BAKED CHILEAN SEA BASS

Pesce al Forno Saporito

The sweet flavor of Chilean sea bass is particularly well suited to this recipe, but those who would prefer not to support the overfishing of this precious fish could use halibut, black cod, or even grouper with excellent results.

Preparation time: 20 minutes
Total time from start to finish: 35 minutes

Serves 4 as a main course or 6 as part of a multicourse Italian meal

> 1 medium clove garlic
> 6 to 8 sprigs flat-leaf Italian parsley
> 2 tablespoons fine dry bread crumbs
> ¼ teaspoon dried oregano
> Salt
> 2 anchovy fillets
> 1 tablespoon fresh lemon juice
> 3 tablespoons extra virgin olive oil
> 1¾ pounds skinless Chilean sea bass fillet

1. Preheat the oven to 375° on convection heat, or 400° on regular bake.

2. Peel and finely chop the garlic. Finely chop enough of the parsley leaves to measure 2 tablespoons. Put the garlic and parsley in a small bowl with the bread crumbs, oregano, and a pinch of salt. Finely chop the anchovies, add them to the bowl, and mix well. Transfer the mixture to a small plate.

3. In a shallow bowl large enough to accommodate the fish, whisk together the lemon juice, olive oil, and some salt until emulsified. Dip the fish in the lemon and olive oil mixture, coat it well on all sides, then roll it in the bread crumb mixture. Try to get as much of it as possible to cling to the fish, then put the fish in a baking dish. Drizzle the remaining lemon and olive oil mixture over the fish. Bake for approximately 10 minutes per inch of thickness of the fillet. The fish is done when it flakes easily when prodded with a fork. Serve hot.

BAKED COD WITH TOMATOES
AND RED ONIONS

Spatola al Forno

Spatola is a fish found in Sicily that most closely resembles the ling cod of the Pacific coast. On the Atlantic coast cod or scrod are good substitutes. As is the case with many Sicilian dishes, fresh, rather than dry, bread crumbs are used to absorb the flavors and make a delicious crispy topping.

Preparation time: 30 minutes
Total time from start to finish: 45 minutes

Serves 4 as a main course or 6 as part of a multicourse Italian meal

> ½ cup fresh bread crumbs (page 42)
> ½ medium red onion
> 3 tablespoons extra virgin olive oil
> 1 pound ripe tomatoes
> Salt
> 6 to 8 sprigs flat-leaf Italian parsley
> 1½ pounds skinless cod, scrod, or ling cod fillets
> Freshly ground black pepper

1. Make the fresh bread crumbs.

2. Peel and finely chop the red onion. Put it in a 10-inch skillet with 2 tablespoons of the olive oil. Place over medium heat and sauté, stirring occasionally, until it begins to brown, about 5 minutes.

3. Preheat the oven to 375° on convection heat or 400° on regular bake.

4. While the onion is sautéing, peel the tomatoes (pages 30–31), remove the seeds, and cut into ¼-inch dice. When the onion is ready, add the tomato, season with salt, and cook for 2 to 3 minutes.

5. Chop enough of the parsley leaves to measure 2 tablespoons. Lay the fish fillets in a baking dish and season with salt and pepper. Spread the tomato mixture over the fish. Top with the parsley and bread crumbs and drizzle the remaining 1 tablespoon olive oil on top. Bake until the fish flakes easily when prodded with a fork, about 15 minutes. Serve hot.

FISH FILLETS WITH TOMATOES AND CAPERS

Pesce in Umido ai Capperi

We are fortunate to have a friend who is an avid fisherman. When he catches more than he can use, we are sometimes the lucky recipients of some wonderfully fresh fish. I usually either grill it or prepare it in a pan with fresh tomatoes and capers. I have used this recipe for a variety of snapper (red snapper, yellow snapper, mangrove snapper) and grouper. Any very fresh, mild-flavored fish works well.

Total time: 30 minutes

Serves 4 as a main course or 6 as part of a multicourse Italian meal

> 2 pounds ripe tomatoes
> 1 medium clove garlic
> 3 tablespoons extra virgin olive oil
> Salt
> 2 tablespoons capers
> 2 pounds fish fillets
> Freshly ground black pepper

1. Peel the tomatoes (pages 30–31) and coarsely chop.

2. Peel and thinly slice the garlic. Put the garlic and olive oil in a skillet large enough to accommodate the fish in a single layer. Place over medium-high heat. As soon as the garlic begins to sizzle, add the tomatoes; season lightly with salt, and cook until all the liquid the tomatoes release is evaporated, about 10 minutes.

3. Add the capers and put in the fish fillets. Season the fish with salt and pepper, lower the heat to medium-low, and cover the pan. After about 5 minutes, turn over the fillets and cook, covered, until the fish flakes easily when prodded with a fork, about 5 minutes more. If the fish is done but the sauce is too watery, transfer the fish to a warm platter, raise the heat under the pan, and cook the sauce until it thickens. Put the fish back in the pan, turn it in the sauce, and serve.

RED SNAPPER WITH MUSSELS

Pagello Stufato con le Cozze

When I was living in Oregon for a brief period, I discovered that Pacific red snapper bears little resemblance to the delicate, fine Atlantic snapper I was accustomed to on the East Coast. If I were making this dish on the West Coast, I would use perch, halibut, or other firm, delicate, white-fleshed fish.

Preparation time: 15 minutes
Total time from start to finish: 25 minutes

Serves 4 as a main course or 6 as part of a multicourse Italian meal

>   2 pounds ripe tomatoes
>   ½ medium yellow onion
>   3 tablespoons extra virgin olive oil
>   Pinch crushed red pepper flakes
>   1 small clove garlic

6 to 8 sprigs flat-leaf Italian parsley
Salt
2 pounds mussels
2 pounds red snapper fillet

1. Peel the tomatoes (pages 30–31) and coarsely chop.

2. Peel and finely chop the onion. Put the onion with the olive oil and hot red pepper in a large deep skillet over medium-high heat. Sauté, stirring occasionally, until the onion turns a rich golden color, about 5 minutes.

3. While the onion is sautéing, peel and finely chop the garlic. Finely chop enough of the parsley leaves to measure 2 tablespoons. When the onion is done, add the garlic and parsley and stir for about 1 minute.

4. Add the tomatoes, season with salt, and cook until they begin to break down and form a sauce, about 5 minutes.

5. While the tomatoes are cooking, rinse the mussels in several changes of water until you do not see any more sand at the bottom of the bowl.

6. Put the red snapper fillets with the skin side up in the pan. After 2 to 3 minutes, turn the fish over and season with salt. Add the mussels to the pan and cover. Cook until the mussels open, 2 to 3 minutes. Remove the mussels from the pan as they open and remove them from the shell. Cook the fish until the flesh flakes easily when prodded with a fork, 1 to 2 minutes more. Return the mussels to the pan and let them heat through for about 30 seconds. Serve at once with some good crusty bread.

BAKED SWORDFISH ROLLS

Involtini di Pesce Spada

Swordfish is a local fish in Sicily and a favorite on the island. This Sicilian preparation is moist, flavorful, and absolutely delicious.

Preparation time: 40 minutes
Total time from start to finish: 55 minutes

Serves 4 as a main course or 6 as part of a multicourse Italian meal

> 1½ cups fresh bread crumbs (page 42)
> 3 to 4 sprigs fresh oregano
> 1½ pounds swordfish steaks, sliced ¼ inch thick
> Salt
> 2 tablespoons capers
> 2 tablespoons extra virgin olive oil, plus extra for the
>   baking sheet

1. Make the fresh bread crumbs.

2. Preheat the oven to 400°.

3. Chop enough of the oregano leaves to measure 1 tablespoon.

4. Remove the skin from the swordfish. Lightly season each slice with salt. Sprinkle with the bread crumbs, capers, and oregano, then drizzle the olive oil on top. Roll up the fish slices loosely so that the ends just overlap and secure with a toothpick.

5. Coat a rimmed baking sheet with a little olive oil and place all the rolls on it. Bake until the swordfish is cooked, about 15 minutes. Serve at once.

GRILLED SHRIMP ADRIATIC STYLE

Spiedini di Gamberi all'Adriatica

I remember this dish from childhood summer vacations spent with my grand-mother in Cesenatico, on the Adriatic coast. I can think of no better way to grill shrimp. The seasoned bread crumb coating makes them lightly crispy on the outside and moist and sweet inside.

Preparation time: 30 minutes
Total time from start to finish: 1 hour

Serves 4 as a main course or 6 as part of a multicourse Italian meal

> 2 pounds large (16 to 20 count) shrimp
> 1 small clove garlic
> 3 to 4 sprigs flat-leaf Italian parsley
> Salt
> Freshly ground black pepper
> About ½ cup extra virgin olive oil
> About ⅔ cup fine dry bread crumbs
> 2 tablespoons fresh lemon juice

1. Shell and devein the shrimp (page 36).

2. Peel and finely chop the garlic. Finely chop enough of the parsley leaves to measure 1 tablespoon. Place the shrimp in a large shallow bowl. Add the garlic and parsley, season with salt and pepper, and toss to coat. Add the olive oil and bread crumbs a little at a time until the shrimp are nicely coated with the mixture but not drenched. Depending on the size of the shrimp, you may need a little more or less olive oil and bread crumbs. The bread crumbs should cling to the shrimp but not so heavily that they form a thick crust. Let the shrimp marinate for 20 to 30 minutes.

3. Preheat a charcoal or gas grill.

4. Thread the shrimp onto skewers. Cook the shrimp on a very hot grill until pink, about 2 minutes on each side. After turning the skewers, sprinkle with the lemon juice. Serve at once.

SHRIMP WITH RED AND YELLOW PEPPERS

Gamberi ai Peperoni

If you would like this dish a little spicy, you can add a pinch of crushed red pepper when you sauté the garlic. Serve these shrimp with good crusty bread or Nonna Mary's White Rice (page 232).

Total time: 35 minutes

Serves 4 as a main course or 6 as part of a multicourse Italian meal

> 1 red bell pepper
> 1 yellow bell pepper
> 1 medium clove garlic
> 3 tablespoons extra virgin olive oil
> Salt
> 1 pound ripe tomatoes
> 2 pounds large (16 to 20 count) shrimp
> 1 sprig fresh oregano
> 1 tablespoon capers

1. Peel the peppers (pages 31–32) and seed them. Cut away any white pith inside the peppers and cut them into narrow 1½-inch strips.

2. Peel and thinly slice the garlic. Put it with the olive oil in a 12-inch skillet and place over medium-high heat. As soon as the garlic begins to sizzle, add the

peppers. Season lightly with salt and cook until the peppers are tender, about 10 minutes. Do not stir too often so that the peppers have a chance to brown lightly.

3. While the peppers are cooking, peel the tomatoes (pages 30–31) and coarsely chop. When the peppers are done, add the tomatoes to the pan. Season them lightly with salt and cook until the tomatoes are reduced and no longer watery, about 10 minutes.

4. While the tomatoes are cooking, peel and devein the shrimp (page 36).

5. Chop enough of the oregano leaves to measure 1 teaspoon and add it to the tomatoes along with the capers. Cook for about 30 seconds. Add the shrimp and season with salt before stirring them in. Cook the shrimp just until they are pink through and through, 2 to 3 minutes.

SEA SCALLOPS
WITH TOMATO AND BASIL

Cappe Sante al Pomodoro e Basilico

Total time: 35 minutes

Serves 4 as a main course or 6 as part of a multicourse Italian meal

> 1 medium clove garlic
> 1 pound ripe tomatoes
> 3 tablespoons extra virgin olive oil
> 2 pounds large sea scallops
> Salt
> Freshly ground black pepper
> 12 fresh basil leaves

1. Peel and finely chop the garlic. Peel the tomatoes (pages 30–31) and coarsely chop.

2. Put the olive oil in a 10-inch skillet and place over medium-high heat. When the oil is hot, add half the scallops and lightly brown on both sides, 1 to 2 minutes for each side. Set aside on a platter and repeat with the remaining scallops. When all the scallops are done, season them with salt and pepper.

3. Add the garlic to the skillet and sauté for less than 1 minute. As soon as the garlic begins to color, add the tomatoes and season lightly with salt. Cook until the tomatoes are reduced and no longer watery, 10 to 15 minutes.

4. While the tomatoes are cooking, shred the basil with a knife. After the tomatoes have cooked for 5 minutes, add the basil. When the tomatoes are done, return all the scallops to the pan and turn them in the sauce for about 1 minute, just long enough for them to reheat. Serve at once.

MEATS

Chicken and Fowl

- **Chicken Breast Fillets with Lemon**
- **Chicken Braised with Tomato and Chickpeas**
- **Braised Chicken with Peppers and Eggplant**
- **Chicken Braised with Porcini Mushrooms**
- **Chicken Cacciatora**
- **Roast Chicken**
- **Grilled Chicken Marinated with Lemon**
- **Crispy Stuffed Grilled Duck**

Veal

- **Veal Medallions with Porcini**
- **Veal Slices Topped with Prosciutto and Sage**
- **Veal Scaloppine with Marsala**
- **Veal Scaloppine with Mushrooms**
- **Veal Marinated in Tuna Sauce**
- **Pan-Roasted Veal with Pancetta and Sage**
- **Pan-Roasted Veal with Vegetables**
- **Braised Veal Shanks, Milanese Style**
- **Veal Shanks Braised with Tomatoes and Peas**
- **Milanese Veal Chops**

- Veal Chops with Prosciutto and Fontina
- Veal Stew with Wild Mushrooms
- Calf's Liver Sautéed with Onions

Pork

- Pork Chops with Balsamic Vinegar
- Oven-Roasted Pork Shoulder with Fennel Tops
- Pork Loin Braised in Milk
- Pan-Roasted Pork Loin with Fresh Leeks
- Pork Loin with Apples and Plums
- Pan-Roasted Pork Loin with Radicchio
- Sweet-and-Sour Pork Stew
- Pork and Porcini "Burgers"
- Fava Beans with Sausage

Lamb

- Oven-Roasted Lamb with Fresh Mint
- Pan-Roasted Lamb with Artichokes
- Braised Lamb Shanks
- Lamb Stew with Olives
- Lamb Rib Chops Grilled Italian Style

Beef

- Beef Tenderloin with Balsamic, Arugula, and Parmigiano
- Beef Tenderloin with Cherries

- **Beef Tenderloin with Tomato, Pancetta, and Thyme**
- **Sliced Steak with Olive Oil, Garlic, and Rosemary**
- **Sliced Steak with Arugula and Pecorino**
- **Savory Beef Steaks with Tomatoes and Olives**
- **Beef Rolls Filled with Cheese, Capers, and Olives**
- **Beef Braised with Anchovies**
- **Beef Braised with Lemon**
- **Slow-Cooked Beef, "Pastisada" Style**
- **Beef Short Ribs Braised with Tomatoes and Potatoes**
- **Meatballs with Tomatoes and Peas**
- **Meatloaf with Mushrooms**
- **Mixed Boiled Meats (and Homemade Meat Broth)**

In a classic Italian meal, meats are the second course, following a pasta, risotto, or soup. Since the appetite has been somewhat subdued by the first course, a smaller portion of meat is served than we are used to in America. Italian meat dishes are rarely just a slab of meat. Most dishes involve vegetables or a tasty sauce to soak up with bread, also reducing the amount of meat required.

The kind of meat served varies regionally in Italy. Veal is primarily found in northern Italian cooking. In central and southern Italy, you'll find lamb and goat, usually either braised or grilled. Beef, pork, and chicken are found more or less throughout. Although historically beef has not been predominant in Italian cooking, it is now more common. Tuscany is famous for a particular kind of beef called Chianina. Wonderfully tender and flavorful, it is what makes the classic *fiorentina,* the famous Florentine grilled T-bone steak, memorable.

CHICKEN BREAST FILLETS
WITH LEMON

Petti di Pollo al Limone

This simple, classic preparation is as good with chicken breast fillets as it is with veal scaloppine. Serve it with a vegetable dish, such as Green Beans with Parmigiano (page 365) or Fried Portobello Mushrooms (page 354).

Total time: 30 minutes

Serves 4 as a main course or 6 as part of a multicourse Italian meal

> 1½ pounds boneless, skinless chicken breasts
> 2 lemons
> 3 to 4 sprigs flat-leaf Italian parsley
> 3 tablespoons butter
> 1 tablespoon vegetable oil
> ¼ cup all-purpose flour
> Salt
> Freshly ground black pepper

1. Trim any fat from the chicken breasts and slice them horizontally in half.

2. Grate the zest from one of the lemons and juice both lemons. You need about ¼ cup juice. Finely chop enough of the parsley leaves to measure 1 tablespoon.

3. Put 2 tablespoons of the butter and the vegetable oil in a large skillet and place over medium-high heat.

4. Spread the flour on a small plate. Coat the chicken fillets with flour, shaking off the excess. When the butter in the pan is no longer foamy and the chicken sizzles when a corner is placed in the pan, carefully slide the chicken into the pan. Put in only as many fillets as will comfortably fit in the pan at once. When one side is lightly browned, turn the fillets and brown the second

side. The chicken should take 3 to 4 minutes to cook, depending on the thickness of the fillet. When done, the chicken will feel firm when prodded with tongs. Transfer to a platter and continue until all the chicken is cooked. Season the fillets with salt and pepper.

5. Lower the heat to medium-low and add the lemon juice and zest. Season lightly with salt and cook until the sauce is thick enough to coat a spoon, 1 to 2 minutes. Swirl in the remaining 1 tablespoon butter and add the parsley. Return the chicken to the pan and turn the fillets in the sauce. Serve at once.

CHICKEN BRAISED
WITH TOMATO AND CHICKPEAS

Pollo in Umido con i Ceci

One of the tricky things about cooking chicken is that breast pieces cook faster than dark meat and will dry out if overcooked. Holding back the breast and putting it in after the rest of the chicken has cooked for about 20 minutes ensures moist, perfectly cooked breast pieces.

Preparation time: 20 minutes
Total time from start to finish: 1 hour

Serves 4 as a main course or 6 as part of a multicourse Italian meal

> 1 chicken, about 3½ pounds
> 1½ cups canned whole peeled tomatoes with their juice
> 3 medium garlic cloves
> 2 tablespoons extra virgin olive oil
> Salt
> Freshly ground black pepper
> 1 sprig fresh rosemary
> 1½ cups drained canned chickpeas

1. Cut the chicken into 12 pieces as described on pages 37–38. Coarsely chop the canned tomatoes.

2. Lightly crush and peel the garlic cloves and put them in a 12-inch skillet with the olive oil. Place over medium heat and sauté until they brown lightly, then remove and discard them. Pat the chicken dry with paper towels and put half of the chicken pieces in the pan. Brown them lightly on both sides, then set them aside on a platter. Repeat with the remaining chicken pieces. Once all the chicken is done, season with salt and pepper.

3. Chop enough of the rosemary leaves to measure 1 teaspoon. Add the rosemary, tomatoes, and chickpeas to the pan and season with salt and pepper. When the tomatoes start bubbling, adjust the heat so that the tomatoes simmer. Add all the chicken pieces except for the breasts. Cover the pan with the lid slightly askew and cook for 20 minutes, turning the chicken once during that time.

4. Put the breast pieces in the pan and cook, turning the chicken occasionally, until the dark meat is tender and begins to fall off the bone, 20 to 25 minutes more. If all of the liquid in the pan evaporates before the chicken is done, add a little water. If the chicken is almost done and there is still a lot of liquid in the pan, raise the heat, and finish cooking uncovered to allow the excess liquid to evaporate.

5. Scoop out about one-quarter of the chickpeas and purée them in a food mill or food processor. Stir the puréed chick peas into the sauce. Serve hot.

Note: This dish will keep well for a couple of days in the refrigerator. Add a couple tablespoons water when reheating it.

BRAISED CHICKEN
WITH PEPPERS AND EGGPLANT

Pollo in Umido con Peperoni e Melanzane

Preparation time: 30 minutes
Total time from start to finish: 1¼ hours

Serves 4 as a main course or 6 as part of a multicourse Italian meal

> 1 yellow bell pepper
> 6 ounces eggplant (about ½ medium eggplant)
> 8 ounces ripe tomatoes
> 6 ounces cipolline or pearl onions
> 1 chicken, about 3½ pounds
> 2 medium cloves garlic
> 2 tablespoons extra virgin olive oil
> Salt
> Freshly ground black pepper
> 1 sprig fresh rosemary

1. Core, seed, and peel the pepper (pages 31–32). Cut away any white pith inside the pepper and cut it into 1 x ½-inch strips. Peel the eggplant and cut it into ½-inch dice. Peel the tomatoes (pages 30–31) and coarsely chop. Peel the onions; if using cipolline, quarter them.

2. Cut the chicken into 12 pieces as described on pages 37–38.

3. Peel and lightly crush the garlic cloves. Put them in a 12-inch skillet with the olive oil and place over medium-high heat. When the garlic has turned a golden brown, remove and discard it. Pat the chicken dry with paper towels and put half of the chicken pieces in the pan. Brown them lightly on both sides, then set them aside on a platter. Repeat with the remaining chicken pieces. Once all the chicken is done, season with salt and pepper.

4. Put the yellow pepper, eggplant, and onions in the pan and sauté for a couple of minutes. Chop enough of the rosemary leaves to measure ½ teaspoon and add it to the pan. Add the tomatoes and season lightly with salt. When the tomatoes start bubbling, adjust the heat so that the tomatoes simmer. Add all the chicken pieces except for the breasts. Cover the pan with the lid slightly askew and cook for 20 minutes, turning the chicken once during that time.

4. Put the breast pieces in the pan and cook, turning the chicken occasionally, until the dark meat is tender and begins to fall off the bone, 20 to 25 minutes more. If all of the liquid in the pan evaporates before the chicken is done, add a little water. If the chicken is almost done and there is still a lot of liquid in the pan, raise the heat and finish cooking uncovered to allow the excess liquid to evaporate. Serve hot.

Note: This dish will keep well for a couple of days in the refrigerator. Add a couple tablespoons water when reheating it.

CHICKEN BRAISED WITH PORCINI MUSHROOMS

Pollo ai Funghi Porcini

Preparation time: 50 minutes
Total time from start to finish: 1 hour 10 minutes

Serves 4 as a main course or 6 as part of a multicourse Italian meal

1 ounce dried porcini mushrooms
1 chicken, about 3½ pounds
2 tablespoons extra virgin olive oil
Salt
Freshly ground black pepper

½ **medium sweet onion**
8 ounces cremini or white mushrooms

1. Put the dried porcini in a bowl, cover with water, and soak for at least 15 minutes.

2. Cut the chicken into 12 pieces as described on pages 37–38. Put the olive oil in a sauté pan large enough to accommodate the chicken snugly and place over medium-high heat. When the oil is hot, pat the chicken dry with paper towels and put half of the chicken pieces in the pan. Brown them lightly on both sides, then set them aside on a platter. Repeat with the remaining chicken pieces. Once all the chicken is done, season with salt and pepper.

3. While the chicken is browning, slice the onion. When all the chicken is done, lower the heat to medium-low and add the onion to the pan. Sauté, stirring occasionally, until the onions soften and turns a rich golden color, 5 to 10 minutes.

4. While the onion is sautéing, thinly slice the fresh mushrooms.

5. Lift the porcini out of the water and squeeze the excess back into the bowl; do not discard the water. Rinse the mushrooms under running water, then coarsely chop them.

6. When the onion is done, add the porcini and fresh mushrooms to the pan. Season with salt and cook, stirring occasionally, until the mushrooms are tender, about 10 minutes.

7. Add the porcini water. Be aware that there may be some sand at the bottom of the bowl, so pour carefully or strain through a paper towel. When the liquid in the pan starts bubbling, adjust the heat so that it simmers and put all the chicken pieces in except for the breasts. Cover the pan with the lid slightly askew and cook for 20 minutes, turning the chicken once during that time.

8. Put the breast pieces in the pan and cook, turning the chicken occasionally, until the dark meat is tender and begins to fall off the bone, 20 to 25 minutes more. If all of the liquid in the pan evaporates before the chicken is done, add a little water. If the chicken is almost done and there is still a lot of liquid

in the pan, raise the heat and finish cooking uncovered to allow the excess liquid to evaporate. Serve hot.

Note: This dish will keep well for a couple of days in the refrigerator. Add a couple tablespoons water when reheating it.

CHICKEN CACCIATORA

Pollo alla Cacciatora

Literally "hunter's chicken," there are probably as many permutations of this dish as there are hunters in Italy. Probably it began as a preparation for whatever game was brought home. Basically the meat is braised with tomatoes and sometimes other vegetables until very tender. The recipe below is the way I like to make it.

Preparation time: 25 minutes
Total time from start to finish: 1 hour

Serves 4 as a main course or 6 as part of a multicourse Italian meal

> 3 medium carrots
> ½ yellow bell pepper
> 12 ounces ripe tomatoes
> 1 chicken, about 3½ pounds
> 2 tablespoons extra virgin olive oil
> Salt
> 1 medium yellow onion
> Pinch crushed red pepper flakes

1. Peel the carrots and cut into 1½ x ¼-inch sticks. Core, seed, and peel the pepper (pages 31–32). Cut away any white pith inside the pepper and cut it into 1 x ½-inch sticks. Peel the tomatoes (pages 30–31) and coarsely chop.

2. Cut the chicken into 12 pieces as described on pages 37–38. Put the olive oil in a sauté pan large enough to accommodate the chicken snugly and place over high heat. When the oil is hot, pat the chicken dry with paper towels and put half of the chicken pieces in the pan. Brown them lightly on both sides, then set them aside on a platter. Repeat with the remaining chicken pieces. Once all the chicken is done, season with salt.

3. While the chicken is browning, peel, halve, and thinly slice the onion crosswise. When all the chicken is browned, turn the heat down to medium-low and add the onion and red pepper flakes. Sauté, stirring occasionally, until the onion is soft and turns a rich golden color, 5 to 10 minutes.

4. Add the carrots and yellow pepper to the pan and sauté for about 1 minute. Add the tomatoes and lightly season with salt. When the tomatoes start bubbling, adjust the heat so that the tomatoes simmer. Add all the chicken pieces except for the breasts. Cover the pan with the lid slightly askew and cook for 20 minutes, turning the chicken once during that time.

5. Put the breast pieces in the pan and cook, turning the chicken occasionally, until the dark meat is tender and begins to fall off the bone, 20 to 25 minutes more. If all of the liquid in the pan evaporates before the chicken is done, add a little water. If the chicken is almost done and there is still a lot of liquid in the pan, raise the heat and finish cooking uncovered to allow the excess liquid to evaporate.

Note: This dish will keep well for a couple of days in the refrigerator. Add a couple tablespoons water when reheating it.

ROAST CHICKEN

Pollo Arrosto

Julia Child once said that being able to make a good roast chicken is the mark of an accomplished cook. Here is a recipe that will make it easy for you to do just that. Rosemary and garlic flavor this distinctively Italian roast chicken. Begin roasting with the breast down to keep the meat moister.

Preparation time: 15 minutes
Total time from start to finish: 1¾ hours

Serves 4 as a main course or 6 as part of a multicourse Italian meal

> 1 chicken, about 3½ pounds
> Salt
> Freshly ground black pepper
> 3 medium cloves garlic
> 2 sprigs fresh rosemary
> 1 tablespoon extra virgin olive oil

1. Preheat the oven to 375° on regular bake.

2. Pat the chicken dry with paper towels. Sprinkle some salt and pepper inside the cavity. Lightly crush and peel the garlic cloves and place them inside along with one of the rosemary sprigs. Close the cavity on both ends with toothpicks.

3. Rub the olive oil over the skin of the chicken. Chop the remaining rosemary leaves and sprinkle it all over the chicken along with some salt and pepper. Put the chicken breast down in a roasting pan and place in the oven. Calculate approximately 25 minutes cooking time per pound (1½ hours for a 3½-pound chicken). After roasting for one third of the cooking time, turn the chicken so the breast is facing up. After the chicken has roasted for two thirds of the total cooking time, switch the oven setting to convection heat and raise the temperature to 400°. If your oven does not have convection heat, simply raise the temperature to 425°.

4. To check if the chicken is done, pierce the flesh near the leg joint to see if the juices run clear. If they do not, roast for another 10 minutes and test again. Remove from the oven and let the chicken rest for 5 minutes before carving and serving.

Note: Roast chicken will keep in the refrigerator for 1 to 2 days. Serve leftovers cold or reheat in the oven at 350° or in the microwave.

GRILLED CHICKEN MARINATED WITH LEMON

Pollo Marinato ai Ferri

People marvel at how moist and flavorful this grilled chicken is. The trick is in the lemon-based marinade that actually starts cooking the chicken long before it hits the grill. When it is time to grill, it takes less time to cook so the chicken stays moister.

Preparation time: 30 minutes
Total time from start to finish: 2½ hours

Serves 4 as a main course or 6 as part of a multicourse Italian meal

> 1 chicken, about 3½ pounds
> Salt
> Freshly ground black pepper
> 3 medium cloves garlic
> 3 to 4 sprigs fresh rosemary
> ¼ cup fresh lemon juice
> 2 tablespoons extra virgin olive oil

1. Cut the chicken into 12 pieces as described on pages 37–38. Put the chicken in a baking dish where the pieces fit snugly in a single layer. Season

generously with salt and pepper. Lightly crush and peel the garlic cloves and add them to the dish. Add the rosemary sprigs, lemon juice, and olive oil to the dish. Turn the chicken pieces a few times to coat, cover the dish, and marinate in the refrigerator for at least 2 hours and up to 12 hours.

2. Preheat a charcoal or gas grill.

3. Place the chicken skin side down on the grill. When the chicken pieces have browned well, after 6 to 8 minutes, turn them over. Brush some of the marinade on the chicken, cover, and continue cooking until the juices run clear when a piece is pierced at its thickest point. Most pieces will be done in 15 to 20 minutes total cooking time. Serve hot.

CRISPY STUFFED GRILLED DUCK

Anatra Ripiena ai Ferri

This preparation is from Da Nanni, a country restaurant on the way from Verona to Lake Garda. Run by the same family for generations, the restaurant's signature dish is a stuffed duck that is first boiled, then finished on the grill. The duck loses most of its fat while boiling, so that, once grilled, the meat is very moist with a wonderfully crispy skin. It is one of the most delicious preparations for duck I've tasted.

Preparation time: 1 hour
Total time from start to finish: at least 5 hours

Serves 4 as a main course or 6 as part of a multicourse Italian meal

> ½ small yellow onion
> 1 small carrot
> 1 rib celery
> 4 tablespoons butter

1 duck, about 6 to 7 pounds
3 to 4 leaves fresh sage
Salt
¼ recipe homemade sausage (page 45) *or* 4 ounces plain
    mild sausage
1 ounce pancetta, thinly sliced
¼ cup freshly grated Parmigiano-Reggiano
¼ cup fine dry bread crumbs

1. Peel and finely chop the onion. Peel the carrot and celery and cut into ¼-inch dice. Put the onion, carrot, and celery with the butter in a medium skillet over medium-high heat. Sauté, stirring occasionally, until the vegetables begin to brown, 8 to 10 minutes.

2. While the vegetables are browning, remove the liver, heart, and gizzard from the duck's cavity, rinse them, and pat dry with a paper towel. Chop them with a knife (not in a food processor, which would chop them too fine). Coarsely chop enough of the sage to measure 2 teaspoons. When the vegetables are ready, add the sage and chopped duck organs. Season lightly with salt and cook until they begin to brown, 5 to 10 minutes. Transfer the contents of the pan to a medium bowl.

3. Finely chop the pancetta and add it to the bowl along with the sausage, Parmigiano, and bread crumbs. Thoroughly mix everything together with your hands.

4. Put the duck in a large pot and cover with water. Remove the duck, place the pot over high heat, and bring to a boil.

5. Rinse the duck inside and out and pat it dry with a paper towel. Put as much of the stuffing into the cavity as will fit comfortably. Use a trussing needle and kitchen string to sew the opening of the cavity closed.

6. Add about 2 tablespoons salt to the boiling water, then gently lower the duck into the water. Cover the pot and return the water to a boil. Lower the heat so that it simmers gently and cook for 1¾ hours. Lift the duck out of the water and let it cool. Refrigerate until it is completely chilled, at least 2 hours or overnight.

7. Preheat a charcoal or gas grill and preheat the oven to 325°.

8. Remove the string from the duck and scoop out the stuffing. Put the stuffing in a baking dish and bake until hot, about 10 minutes. (The stuffing can also be heated in a microwave.)

9. While the stuffing is heating, cut the duck into pieces and season with salt. Grill about 5 to 6 minutes on each side until nicely browned and crisp. Serve at once, accompanied by the stuffing.

> **Note:** This is an ideal dish for a dinner party because the boiled duck can be refrigerated for 2 to 3 days. The duck can then be grilled and served in 15 to 20 minutes.

VEAL MEDALLIONS WITH PORCINI

Filetto di Vitello ai Porcini

Total time: 40 minutes

Serves 4

1 ounce dried porcini mushrooms
2 tablespoons butter
1 tablespoon vegetable oil
4 veal loin medallions, 5 to 6 ounces each, about 1 inch thick
Salt
Freshly ground black pepper
8 ounces white mushrooms
5 to 6 fresh sage leaves
⅓ cup dry white wine
6 to 8 sprigs flat-leaf Italian parsley

1. Put the dried porcini in a bowl, cover with water, and soak for at least 15 minutes.

2. Put 1 tablespoon of the butter and the vegetable oil in a skillet and place over medium-high heat. When the oil and butter are hot and the butter is just beginning to turn color, put in the veal medallions. Cook for 4 to 5 minutes on each side for medium doneness. Transfer to a platter and season with salt and pepper.

3. While the veal is cooking, thinly slice the white mushrooms.

4. After transferring the veal, coarsely chop the sage and add it to the skillet. Add the wine and let it boil for about 30 seconds to let the alcohol evaporate. Remove the pan from the heat.

5. Lift the porcini out of the water and squeeze the excess back into the bowl; do not discard the water. Rinse the mushrooms under running water, then coarsely chop them. Put the skillet back over medium-high heat and add the porcini along with the soaking water. Be aware that there may be some sand at the bottom of the bowl, so pour carefully or strain through a paper towel. Cook until the porcini water is almost completely evaporated. Add the fresh mushrooms, season with salt and pepper, and cook until the mushrooms are tender and all the liquid they release is evaporated, 10 to 15 minutes.

6. While the mushrooms are cooking, finely chop enough of the parsley leaves to measure 2 tablespoons. When the mushrooms are done, add the parsley and the remaining 1 tablespoon butter. Return the medallions to the pan and turn them in the sauce to heat them through. Serve at once.

Note: This recipe is also very good with loin chops. To ensure they are done near the bone, let them cook in the sauce, covered, for 3 to 5 minutes before serving.

VEAL SLICES TOPPED WITH PROSCIUTTO AND SAGE

Saltinbocca alla Romana

Salta in bocca in Italian means "jump in the mouth," because that is exactly what you want these tasty veal slices to do. This is the classic Roman rendition. In Sorrento, they add a slice of mozzarella, which is also very good. Since you can't turn these over while cooking, put a lid over the pan for about a minute to let the cheese melt.

Total time: 30 minutes

Serves 4 as a main course or 6 as part of a multicourse Italian meal

> 1 pound veal scaloppine
> 4 ounces prosciutto, thinly sliced
> 1 sage leaf for each slice of veal
> 2 tablespoons vegetable oil
> 2 tablespoons butter
> ¼ cup all-purpose flour
> Salt
> ¼ cup dry white wine

1. Pound the veal as described on pages 38–39. Cover each slice with a layer of prosciutto and a sage leaf. Use a toothpick to skewer the sage, prosciutto, and meat together, while keeping it flat.

2. Put the vegetable oil and 1 tablespoon of the butter in a 12-inch skillet and place over medium-high heat. Put the flour on a small plate. When the oil and butter are hot and the butter is just beginning to turn color, coat the veal with the flour on both sides, making sure to shake off the excess. Slide as many slices into the skillet, veal side down, as will fit comfortably. Cook briefly until the meat loses its pink raw color, less than 1 minute on each side. Transfer the slices to a warm platter with the prosciutto side down. Cook the remaining veal in the same manner, then season very lightly with salt.

*Frittata with Leeks
and Red Peppers, page 62*

Orecchiette with Broccoli Rabe, page 168

Fresh Beet Salad, page 381

Risotto with Amarone Wine, page 208

Eggplant Parmigiana, page 350

Aromatic Salmon in a Pouch, page 240

Pappardelle, page 105,
with Classic Bolognese Meat Sauce, page 108

Yellow Squash with Grape Tomatoes, page 358

Seafood Salad with Cannellini Beans, page 51

*Oven-Roasted Pork Shoulder
with Fennel Tops, page 296*

Baked Stuffed Red and Yellow Peppers, page 355

Pan-Seared Tuna with Fresh Tomato and Bay Leaves, page 244

Shrimp and Zucchini Soup, page 93

Berry Salad, page 410

Grandma's Custard Pie, page 398

Raisin, Pine Nut, and Cornmeal Cookies, page 408, with White Nectarine Ice Cream, page 413

3. Add the wine to the skillet and pour in any juices the veal has released on the platter. Scrape the cooking residue from the bottom of the pan with a wooden spoon and let the wine bubble away until it is reduced and thickened, 1 to 2 minutes. Add the remaining 1 tablespoon butter and, as soon as it melts, remove the pan from the heat. Turn each *saltinbocca* in the sauce to coat, then place prosciutto side up on a serving platter. Pour any remaining sauce from the pan over the meat and serve at once.

VEAL SCALOPPINE WITH MARSALA

Scaloppine di Vitello al Marsala

One of the most loved Italian classics, it is at its best when the ingredients are kept to a minimum and it is simply prepared and served immediately.

Total time: 20 minutes

Serves 4 as a main course or 6 as part of a multicourse Italian meal

> 1 pound veal scaloppine
> About ½ cup all-purpose flour
> 1 tablespoon vegetable oil
> 2 tablespoons butter
> Salt
> Freshly ground black pepper
> ½ cup dry Marsala

1. Pound the veal as described on pages 38–39.

2. Spread the flour on a small plate. Put the oil and 1 tablespoon of the butter in a large skillet and place over medium-high heat. While the oil and butter are heating, coat with the flour as many slices of veal as will comfortably fit in the pan, shaking off the excess. Do not coat all the veal at once or it will become soggy.

3. When the oil and butter are hot and the butter is just beginning to turn color, put in as many scaloppine as will comfortably fit. When they have lightly browned on both sides and lost their pink raw color, less than 1 minute per side, remove them, letting the excess oil drip back into the skillet. Set them aside on a platter. Flour and cook the remaining veal in the same manner. If the pan becomes too dry, add a little more oil when the pan is empty and let it get hot before continuing. When all the scaloppine are done, season them with salt and pepper.

4. If there is more than a coating of oil left in the pan, pour it out. Raise the heat to high and add the Marsala. Pour in any juices that the meat on the platter has released. Use a wooden spoon to loosen the browned bits on the bottom of the skillet and let the Marsala bubble away until it is reduced and thickened, 1 to 2 minutes. Add the remaining 1 tablespoon butter and remove the pan from the heat. Stir the butter into the sauce. Return the scaloppine to the pan and turn them in the sauce to heat them through. Serve at once.

VEAL SCALOPPINE
WITH MUSHROOMS

Scaloppine ai Funghi

In Italy this dish would probably be made with chanterelles, and if they are available by all means use them. Shiitake mushrooms, however, are more commonly available here, even in supermarkets, and are also delicious with veal.

Total time: 35 minutes

Serves 4 as a main course or 6 as part of a multicourse Italian meal

> ½ small yellow onion
> 4 ounces shiitake mushrooms

4 ounces white mushrooms
1 pound veal scaloppine
2 tablespoons butter
1 tablespoon vegetable oil
Salt
Freshly ground black pepper
5 or 6 fresh sage leaves
½ cup heavy cream

1. Peel and finely chop the onion. Thinly slice the mushrooms.

2. Pound the veal as described on pages 38–39.

3. Put ½ tablespoon of the butter and the vegetable oil in a large skillet and place over medium-high heat. When the oil and butter are hot and the butter is just beginning to turn color, put in as many scaloppine as will comfortably fit. Lightly brown them on each side, 1 minute or less per side, then place them on a platter. Cook the remaining veal in the same manner, then season with salt and pepper.

4. Put the remaining 1½ tablespoons butter in the pan and add the onion. Sauté, stirring occasionally, until the onion turns a rich golden color, 3 to 5 minutes. Finely shred the sage and add it to the pan. After about 30 seconds, add the sliced mushrooms and season with salt and pepper. Lower the heat to medium and cook until the liquid the mushrooms release is evaporated and the mushrooms begin to brown, about 10 minutes.

5. Add the cream and cook until it is reduced enough to coat the mushrooms. Return the scaloppine to the pan and turn them in the sauce to heat through. Serve at once.

VEAL MARINATED IN TUNA SAUCE

Vitello Tonnato

This classic dish is found predominantly in northern Italy. It is essential to use premium canned tuna packed in olive oil and homemade mayonnaise. Because it is served at room temperature, this is an ideal dish for a buffet. The original and most prized version is with veal, but it also is sometimes prepared with pork or even chicken. To make it with pork, follow this recipe and substitute pork loin for the veal. To make it with chicken, substitute boneless, skinless chicken breasts and decrease the cooking time to 10 to 15 minutes.

Preparation time: 1 hour 25 minutes
Total time from start to finish: 14 hours

Serves 4 as a main course or 6 as part of a multicourse Italian meal

> 1 carrot
> 1 rib celery
> Salt
> 2 to 3 sprigs flat-leaf Italian parsley
> 1½ pounds top round of veal in one piece
> ½ recipe homemade mayonnaise (page 44)
> 4 ounces premium canned tuna packed in olive oil
> 1 tablespoon capers, plus extra for serving
> 3 anchovy fillets

1. Fill a pot with about 3 quarts water, place over high heat, and bring to a boil.

2. While the water is coming to a boil, peel the carrot and celery.

3. Add 1 tablespoon salt, the celery, carrot, parsley, and veal to the boiling water. Lower the heat so that the water simmers and cook for 1 hour. Remove from the heat and let the meat cool in the water it cooked in.

4. While the veal is cooking, make the mayonnaise.

5. Open the can of tuna and drain the oil. Put the tuna, capers, and anchovies in a food processor and run until finely chopped. Add the tuna mixture to the mayonnaise and mix well.

6. When the veal has cooled to at least lukewarm, remove it from the cooking liquid and cut into ¼-inch-thick slices. Choose a serving dish that will hold the veal slices in 2 layers. Spread a thin coating of the tuna sauce over the bottom of the serving dish, then cover with a layer of veal. Spread half of the remaining tuna sauce over the veal. Put the rest of the veal in the dish and spread the remaining tuna sauce on top. Cover with plastic wrap and refrigerate for 12 to 24 hours. Take it out of the refrigerator and allow it to come to room temperature before serving.

Note: For an attractive presentation, decorate the top with capers.

PAN-ROASTED VEAL
WITH PANCETTA AND SAGE

Arrosto di Vitello con Pancetta e Salvia

One of the staples of northern Italian cooking is a pan roast of veal. I make this dish often, and it is always a success at dinner parties. Do not use too lean a cut, such as the top round. The shoulder or breast produces a much moister and more succulent roast. The breast may require some trimming, and if you use the shoulder, you should butterfly it (or ask the meat department if they'll do it for you), so you have a wide thin piece that can be rolled with the pancetta.

Preparation time: 25 minutes
Total time from start to finish: about 2 hours

Serves 4 as a main course or 6 as part of a multicourse Italian meal

2 pounds boneless veal breast or shoulder
4 ounces pancetta, thinly sliced
8 to 10 fresh sage leaves
4 medium cloves garlic
1 tablespoon vegetable oil
2 tablespoons butter
Salt
Freshly ground black pepper
½ cup dry white wine

1. Trim any excess fat from the veal. Lay the meat on a flat surface with the fat side down. Place the pancetta and sage leaves on the meat, then roll the meat tightly. Tie with kitchen string at 1-inch intervals.

2. Lightly crush and peel the garlic cloves. Put the oil, butter, and garlic in a heavy-bottomed braising pan and place it over medium-high heat. When the garlic cloves are lightly browned on all sides, remove and discard them.

3. Put the meat in and brown it well on all sides. Season with salt and pepper. Add the wine and let it bubble rapidly for about 30 seconds to evaporate the alcohol, while stirring with a wooden spoon to loosen the browned bits on the bottom of the pan. Reduce the heat so that the wine simmers gently, cover the pot with the lid slightly askew, and cook until the meat is tender when pierced with a fork, 1½ to 2 hours. Turn the roast about every 20 minutes and, if all the liquid evaporates before the meat is tender, add a little water.

4. Remove the veal from the pot, place it on a cutting board, and remove the string. Cut the roast into ¼-inch slices. If there is a lot of liquid left in the pan, turn the heat to high and let it boil until it is reduced and forms a sauce. If there is no liquid left, add a few tablespoons of water. Return the veal to the pan and turn the slices to coat with the sauce. Serve at once.

Note: The roast can be made 2 to 3 days ahead of time. When ready to serve, slice it and reheat it in its sauce.

PAN-ROASTED VEAL
WITH VEGETABLES

Arrosto di Vitello alle Verdure

Do not be afraid of cooking the vegetables too long here. In typical Italian fashion, the vegetables in this dish cook together with the veal from the beginning, which turns them into a sweet, rich sauce for the meat.

Preparation time: 35 minutes
Total time from start to finish: 2 to 2½ hours

Serves 4 as a main course or 6 as part of a multicourse Italian meal

> 1 green bell pepper
> 1 yellow bell pepper
> 2 medium leeks
> 1 rib celery
> 2 pounds boneless veal shoulder or breast
> 8 to 10 fresh sage leaves
> 2 medium cloves garlic
> 2 tablespoons butter
> 1 tablespoon vegetable oil
> Salt
> Freshly ground black pepper
> ½ cup dry white wine
> 12 grape or cherry tomatoes

1. Core, seed, and peel the peppers (pages 31–32). Cut away any white pith inside the peppers and cut into approximately ¾-inch squares.

2. Trim the root ends and dark green tops from the leeks (page 35). Cut the leeks in half lengthwise (or in quarters if they are more than 1 inch thick), then slice them crosswise into ½-inch pieces. Place the cut leeks in a large bowl of cold water and swish them around to loosen any dirt that is clinging to them.

3. Peel the celery, then cut into ½-inch dice.

4. Trim any excess fat from the veal. Lay the meat on a flat surface with the fat side down. Roll the meat with the sage leaves inside it and tie securely with kitchen twine at 1-inch intervals.

5. Lightly crush and peel the garlic cloves. Put them with the butter and vegetable oil in a heavy-bottomed braising pan over medium-high heat. When the garlic is lightly browned on all sides, remove and discard it. Put the veal in the pan and brown it nicely on all sides. Remove the veal and season the meat with salt and pepper.

6. Add the wine to the pan and let it bubble rapidly for about 30 seconds to evaporate the alcohol, while stirring with a wooden spoon to loosen the browned bits on the bottom of the pan. Reduce the heat so that the wine simmers gently. Add the peppers, leeks, celery, and tomatoes. Season with salt and pepper and stir for about 1 minute. Return the veal to the pan and cover with the lid slightly askew. Cook until the veal is tender when pierced with a fork, 1½ to 2 hours. Periodically turn the veal. If all the liquid evaporates before it is done, add a little water. If the veal is close to being done and there is still liquid in the pan, raise the heat, remove the cover, and allow the excess liquid to evaporate.

7. When the meat is done, take it out of the pan and slice it about ¼ inch thick. Return the veal to the pan and turn the slices to coat them with the sauce. Serve hot, pouring the sauce over the veal.

Note: The roast can be made 2 to 3 days ahead of time. When ready to serve, slice it and reheat it in its sauce.

BRAISED VEAL SHANKS, MILANESE STYLE

Ossobuchi alla Milanese

As is the case with many classic recipes, apart from certain undisputed essential elements, there are often several interpretations. For example, tomatoes were not introduced in this recipe until the end of the eighteenth century. Some people still make it without tomatoes, but I like the richer, rounder flavor tomatoes give, particularly when accompanied in the classic style with saffron risotto (page 222). This recipe is similar to the one my mother makes. Traditionally, a mixture of garlic, lemon, and parsley, called *gremolada,* is added at the end. It adds a distinctive flavor and is optional.

Preparation time: 25 minutes
Total time from start to finish: 2½ hours

Serves 4

>½ small yellow onion
>1 medium carrot
>2 tablespoons butter
>1 tablespoon vegetable oil
>¼ cup all-purpose flour
>4 veal shank slices, about 1 pound each
>Salt
>Freshly ground black pepper
>1 small clove garlic, plus ½ for the optional *gremolada*
>1 to 2 sprigs fresh thyme
>¼ cup dry white wine
>1 cup canned whole peeled tomatoes with their juice
>2 bay leaves
>2 sprigs flat-leaf Italian parsley, plus 3 to 4 sprigs for the
>   optional *gremolada*
>1 teaspoon grated lemon zest for the optional *gremolada*

1. Peel and finely chop the onion. Peel the carrot and cut into ¼-inch dice.

2. Put the butter and vegetable oil in a braising pan large enough to accommodate the veal shanks in a single layer. Place the pan over medium-high heat.

3. Put the flour on a small plate. Pat the veal shanks dry with a paper towel, then coat them on both sides with the flour, shaking off the excess. When the oil in the pan is hot, put in the veal shanks and brown them on both sides. Remove them from the pan and season with salt and pepper.

4. Pour off any oil remaining in the pan. Lower the heat to medium-low and add the onion and carrot. Sauté, stirring, until they begin to brown, about 5 minutes.

5. While the vegetables are sautéing, peel and finely chop the small clove of garlic and remove enough thyme leaves from the stem to measure ½ teaspoon. When the onion and carrot are ready, add the garlic and thyme. Sauté for 30 seconds, then add the wine. Let the wine boil for about 30 seconds to let the alcohol evaporate. Add the tomatoes, season with salt and pepper, and break up the tomatoes with a wooden spoon. Once the tomatoes begin bubbling, lower the heat so that they simmer gently. Add the bay leaves and 2 parsley sprigs and return the veal to the pan. Cover with the lid slightly askew and cook, turning the veal about every 20 minutes, until the meat is very tender, about 2 hours. If all the liquid evaporates before the meat is done, add a little water. If the meat is tender and the sauce is still rather liquidy, uncover the pan, raise the heat, and cook until the sauce reduces and coats the meat. Serve at once.

6. For the optional *gremolada,* finely chop enough of the parsley leaves to measure 1 tablespoon. Finely chop the ½ clove of garlic. Mix the parsley, garlic, and lemon zest together in a small bowl, then add to the pot with the shanks. Cook for another 2 minutes, turning the shanks to distribute the *gremolada,* and serve.

> **Note:** Like most braised meat dishes, the veal shanks will keep well for 2 to 3 days in the refrigerator. To reheat, add a couple tablespoons water, cover, and place over medium-low heat.

VEAL SHANKS BRAISED WITH TOMATOES AND PEAS

Ossobuchi ai Piselli

When braised gently and patiently, veal shanks become fork tender and wonderfully rich in flavor. It's almost impossible to go wrong. This is one of the many variations on the classic recipe (page 283). Peas and veal go very well together.

Preparation time: 20 minutes (30 if using fresh peas)
Total time from start to finish: 2½ hours (2 hours 40 minutes if using fresh peas)

Serves 4

½ medium yellow onion
1 tablespoon vegetable oil
2 tablespoons butter
¼ cup all-purpose flour
4 veal shank slices, about 1 pound each
Salt
Freshly ground black pepper
1½ cups canned whole peeled tomatoes with their juice
1 large beef bouillon cube
10 ounces frozen peas *or* 2 pounds fresh peas in the pod

1. Peel and finely chop the onion.

2. Put the vegetable oil and butter in a braising pan large enough to accommodate the veal shanks in a single layer. Place the pan over medium-high heat.

3. Put the flour on a small plate. Pat the veal shanks dry with a paper towel and coat them on both sides with the flour, shaking off the excess. When the oil and butter in the pan are hot and the butter is just beginning to turn color, put in the veal shanks and brown them on both sides. Remove them from the pan and season with salt and pepper.

4. Lower the heat to medium-low and add the onion. Sauté, stirring occasionally, until it turns a rich golden color, 3 to 5 minutes. Add the tomatoes, season with salt and pepper, and break up the tomatoes with a wooden spoon. Return the veal shanks to the pan. Add the bouillon cube and enough water to come just below the top surface of the meat. Cover with the lid slightly askew and cook, turning the veal about every 20 minutes, until the meat is very tender, about 2 hours. If all the liquid evaporates before the meat is done, add a little water.

5. While the veal is cooking, shell the fresh peas if using. When the veal is tender, add the peas and cook for 10 minutes if using frozen peas, and about 20 minutes if using fresh. If the sauce is still rather liquidy, uncover the pan, raise the heat, and cook until the sauce reduces and coats the meat. Serve at once.

Note: Like most braised meat dishes, the veal shanks will keep well for 2 to 3 days in the refrigerator. To reheat, add a couple tablespoons water, cover, and place over medium-low heat.

MILANESE VEAL CHOPS

Costolette alla Milanese

This is undoubtedly one of the classics of Italian cuisine. Crisp on the outside and moist inside, *alla Milanese* is one of my favorite ways to prepare a veal chop.

Total time: 20 minutes

Serves 4

> 4 veal rib chops
> 2 eggs
> 1 cup fine dry bread crumbs
> 3 tablespoons butter
> 2 tablespoons vegetable oil
> Salt

1. Preheat the oven to 200°.

2. Make 2 or 3 incisions in the ribbon of fat surrounding the veal chops, then pound as described on pages 38–39 until about ½ inch thick.

3. Put the eggs in a shallow bowl and beat lightly until the yolks and whites are well mixed together. Spread the bread crumbs on a small plate.

4. Put the butter and vegetable oil in a large skillet and place over medium-high heat.

5. Dip a chop in the eggs and let the excess drip back into the bowl. Press the bread crumbs onto the meat to coat. Once both sides are completely covered, shake off the excess.

6. When the oil and butter are hot and a corner of the chop sizzles when dipped in, carefully slide in the breaded chop. Bread another chop and add

it to the pan. (Do not coat the meat with the egg and bread crumbs before you are ready to put them in the pan or they will become soggy.) The veal should cook for 3 to 5 minutes on each side for medium. Make a small incision with a knife near the bone to test. When the chops are done, transfer to an ovenproof platter and keep warm in the oven while you bread and cook the remaining chops. Sprinkle generously with salt and serve at once.

VEAL CHOPS WITH PROSCIUTTO AND FONTINA

Costolette di Vitello alla Valdostana

Valdostana refers to the Val d'Aosta region of northern Italy that is famous for Fontina cheese. Here, breaded chops are browned in a pan, then topped with prosciutto and Fontina and finished in the oven, so the cheese melts and the chops remain moist.

Preparation time: 20 minutes
Total time from start to finish: 30 minutes

Serves 4

> 4 veal rib chops
> 1 egg
> 2 tablespoons all-purpose flour
> ¼ cup fine dry bread crumbs
> 2 tablespoons butter
> 1 tablespoon vegetable oil
> Salt
> 4 thin slices prosciutto
> 4 ounces Fontina, sliced

1. Preheat the oven to 400°.

2. Make 2 or 3 incisions in the ribbon of fat surrounding the veal chops, then pound as described on pages 38–39 until about ½ inch thick.

3. Put the egg in a small bowl and whisk until the white and yolk are thoroughly mixed together. Spread the flour on a small plate and the bread crumbs on another.

4. Put the butter and vegetable oil in a 10-inch skillet and place over medium-high heat. Coat 2 of the veal chops with flour, shaking off the excess. Dip each first in the egg, letting the excess drip back into the bowl, then coat with the bread crumbs. When the oil and butter are hot and a corner of the chop sizzles when dipped in, carefully slide in the 2 chops and cook until they are browned on both sides. While the first chops are cooking, bread the remaining 2 chops. When the first chops are done, transfer to a baking sheet and brown the second batch. When all the chops are done, season them with salt.

5. Cover each chop with a slice of prosciutto and one-quarter of the Fontina. Bake until the cheese is melted and the chops are cooked to medium, 8 to 10 minutes. They should still be a little pink in the center. Remove from the oven and serve at once.

VEAL STEW
WITH WILD MUSHROOMS

Spezzatino di Vitello ai Funghi

An Italian *spezzatino* (stew) is cooked much like a braised meat dish or a pan roast. The meat is browned first, then cooked slowly in liquid. In this case, don't take the instructions to brown the meat too literally. Often veal cubes release moisture in the pan, and if you wait until the meat is finally brown, it can become tough. Remove the veal once it loses its raw color, even if it is not brown. Wait until the liquid in the pan evaporates before adding more veal. This stew is delicious served with mashed potatoes (page 369).

Preparation time: 25 minutes
Total time from start to finish: 2 hours

Serves 4 as a main course or 6 as part of a multicourse Italian meal

> 1 ounce dried porcini mushrooms
> ½ small yellow onion
> 1 tablespoon butter
> 1 tablespoon vegetable oil
> 2 pounds veal stew meat, cut into 1-inch cubes
> Salt
> Freshly ground black pepper
> 4 ounces shiitake mushrooms
> 4 ounces cremini or white mushrooms

1. Put the dried porcini in a bowl, cover with water, and soak for at least 15 minutes.

2. Peel and finely chop the onion.

3. Put the butter and vegetable oil in a sauté pan large enough to hold all the veal snugly and place over high heat. When the oil and butter are hot and the butter is just beginning to brown, put in half the veal cubes and brown lightly

on both sides (see introductory note). Transfer to a platter and repeat with the remaining veal. When all the veal is done, season with salt and pepper.

4. Add the onion to the pan and reduce the heat to medium-low. Sauté, stirring occasionally, until the onion is softened and turns a rich golden color, 2 to 3 minutes.

5. While the onion is sautéing, trim the bottom of the shiitake mushroom stems and thinly slice the mushrooms. When the onion is ready, add the shiitake mushrooms and sauté for 2 to 3 minutes.

6. Thickly slice the cremini mushrooms. Add to the pan and season with salt and pepper. Continue sautéing for 2 to 3 minutes.

7. Lift the porcini out of the water and squeeze the excess back into the bowl; do not discard the water. Rinse the mushrooms under running water, then coarsely chop them. Add the porcini to the pan and stir well, then add all of the veal. Add the soaking water. Be aware that there may be some sand at the bottom of the bowl, so pour carefully or strain through a paper towel. Cover with the lid slightly askew and simmer, stirring about every 20 minutes, until the meat is tender, 1 to 1½ hours. If all the liquid in the pan evaporates before the meat is tender, add a little water. If the stew is almost done and there is still liquid in the pan, raise the heat, remove the cover, and allow the excess liquid to evaporate. Serve hot.

Note: This stew can easily be made a couple of days ahead of time and kept in the refrigerator. To reheat, add a little water and place over medium-low heat.

CALF'S LIVER SAUTÉED WITH ONIONS

Fegato alla Veneziana

This is the dish made famous by Harry's Bar in Venice. To ensure the liver is tender, remove any tough membranes and gristle and take care not to over-cook it. I slice one of the onions lengthwise, so that it holds its shape better, and one crosswise, which becomes almost creamy in the end, making a luscious sauce.

Total time: 35 minutes

Serves 4 as a main course or 6 as part of a multicourse Italian meal

> 2 medium sweet onions
> 2 tablespoons extra virgin olive oil
> 3 tablespoons butter
> Salt
> Freshly ground black pepper
> 6 to 8 sprigs flat-leaf Italian parsley
> 1 pound veal liver (a bit more if there is gristle to be removed),
>   sliced no more than ½ inch thick

1. Peel and halve the onions. Thinly slice one onion crosswise and the other lengthwise.

2. Put the olive oil and 1 tablespoon of the butter in a 10-inch skillet. Place over medium-high heat and add the onions. Season with salt and pepper and sauté, stirring occasionally, until the onions begin to brown, about 5 minutes. Lower the heat to medium and cook until the onions are very soft and some almost creamy in consistency, about 15 minutes. Scoop up the onions with a slotted spoon, leaving as much of the oil in the pan as possible, and set aside in a bowl.

3. While the onions are cooking, finely chop enough of the parsley leaves to measure 2 tablespoons. Trim the liver of any membranes and gristle and slice it into 2 x 1-inch strips.

4. After you have removed the onions, put the remaining 2 tablespoons butter in the pan and place over medium-high heat. When the butter is hot and the foam begins to subside, put in half of the liver. Cook for about 1 minute on each side, then transfer to a platter and repeat with the remaining liver. Return all the liver to the pan, season with salt and pepper, and add the onions and parsley. Lower the heat to medium and cook, stirring almost constantly, until the liver is just barely pink in the center, about 2 minutes. Serve at once.

PORK CHOPS
WITH BALSAMIC VINEGAR

Braciola di Maiale all' Aceto Balsamico

The proliferation of cheap balsamic vinegar has prompted its excessive use. I have seen recipes that instruct one to "reduce ½ cup balsamic vinegar." For one thing, a half cup of real balsamic vinegar would have been considered a young girl's dowry in the aristocratic families of Modena. Furthermore, no reduction of balsamic vinegar should ever be necessary. I am not suggesting that only the $150 perfume-sized bottle of balsamic vinegar should be used in this recipe (or any other), but there is no point in using something that costs $3.99 for a half liter either. Look for something in the medium price range, perhaps $25 to $40 for an 8-ounce bottle. You do not need to use much, and it should always be added at the end, off the heat, so as not to lose its precious aroma.

Total time: 35 minutes

Serves 4

> ½ medium yellow onion
> 3 tablespoons extra virgin olive oil
> ¼ cup all-purpose flour
> 4 pork chops, about 8 ounces each
> Salt
> Freshly ground black pepper
> 1 tablespoon red wine vinegar
> ¼ cup water
> 1 tablespoon balsamic vinegar

1. Peel, halve, and thinly slice the onion crosswise.

2. Put the olive oil in a 12-inch skillet and place over medium-high heat.

3. While the oil is heating, spread the flour on a small plate. When the oil is hot and a little flour sprinkled into the pan sizzles, coat both sides of one of the pork chops with flour, shaking off the excess. Place the chop in the pan and repeat until all the chops are in the pan. Brown the chops on both sides, transfer to a plate, and season with salt and pepper.

4. Add the onion to the pan, season with salt, and lower the heat to medium. Sauté, stirring occasionally, until the onion softens and turns a golden color, 8 to 10 minutes.

5. Add the red wine vinegar and let it bubble for 30 seconds. Add ¼ cup water, return the chops to the pan, and cover with the lid slightly askew. Cook until the chops are just barely pink at the center, about 5 minutes.

6. Transfer the chops to a serving platter. The sauce in the pan should be thick enough to coat the meat. If it is too liquidy, raise the heat and cook until it thickens. Remove from the heat and stir in the balsamic vinegar. Pour the sauce over the chops and serve at once.

OVEN-ROASTED PORK SHOULDER WITH FENNEL TOPS

Arrosto di Maiale al Finocchio

Fennel tops, often thrown away, are used here to give a wonderful flavor to this moist and juicy pork roast. Serve it with vegetables sautéed in olive oil, such as Yellow Squash with Grape Tomatoes (page 358), Carrots Sautéed with Garlic and Parsley (page 348), or Broccoli Rabe Sautéed with Olive Oil and Garlic (page 361).

Preparation time: 5 minutes
Total time from start to finish: 1¾ hours

Serves 4 as a main course or 6 as part of a multicourse Italian meal

> ½ cup green feathery fennel tops
> 1 tablespoon extra virgin olive oil
> 1 teaspoon salt
> Freshly ground black pepper
> 2 pounds boneless pork shoulder roast

1. Preheat the oven to 325° on convection heat, or 350° on regular bake.

2. Coarsely chop enough of the fennel tops to measure ½ cup and mix together with the olive oil, salt, and a few turns of the pepper mill in a small bowl. Rub the mixture over the entire surface of the pork and place the pork in a roasting pan.

3. Put the pan in the oven and roast the pork until it reaches an internal temperature of about 170° as measured on an instant-read thermometer, approximately 1½ hours. Remove from the oven and let rest for about 10 minutes during which time the internal temperature will rise another 5 to 10°. Cut into thin slices and serve hot.

PORK LOIN BRAISED IN MILK

Arrosto di Maiale al Latte

Pan roasting meat with milk produces a delectable nutty brown sauce and a very tender and moist roast. I have seen many variations of this recipe but I think this simple version, which I learned from my mother, is still the best.

Preparation time: 15 minutes
Total time from start to finish: 2 hours

Serves 4 as a main course or 6 as part of a multicourse Italian meal

> 1 tablespoon butter
> 2 tablespoons vegetable oil
> 2 pounds boneless pork loin
> Salt
> Freshly ground black pepper
> About 2½ cups whole milk

1. Put the butter and oil in a heavy-bottomed braising pan that will accommodate the pork and place it over medium-high heat. When the butter and oil are hot and the butter is just beginning to turn color, put in the meat with the fat side down. Brown the meat evenly on all sides.

2. Season the pork with salt and pepper and add 1 cup of the milk. When the milk comes to a simmer, lower the heat to medium-low and cover the pot with the lid slightly askew. Cook, turning the meat occasionally, until the milk is reduced and forms a thick brown sauce, about 20 minutes. Add the remaining milk and continue cooking at a gentle but steady simmer with the lid slightly askew, turning the meat every 15 to 20 minutes. The roast is done when it is tender when pierced with a fork, after cooking a total of 1½ to 2 hours, depending on the thickness of the pork loin. If the pan is dry before the meat is tender, add a little more milk.

3. When the pork is done, transfer the meat to a cutting board. The milk should have formed a thick brown sauce. If it hasn't, raise the heat and cook until the

sauce is reduced and turns nut brown. Tip the pot and skim off most of the fat from the surface. Cut the pork into thin slices, return them to the pan, and turn to coat with the sauce. Transfer the meat to a serving platter, pour the sauce over it, and serve at once.

Note: This pork roast can easily be prepared a day or two ahead of time and kept refrigerated. When you are ready to serve, slice the meat and reheat it in the sauce.

PAN-ROASTED PORK LOIN WITH FRESH LEEKS

Lombo di Maiale coi Porri

In this recipe, leeks, a mild and sweet member of the onion family, are cooked slowly along with pork loin until they form a delectable, rich, creamy sauce.

Preparation time: 20 minutes
Total time from start to finish: 2 hours

Serves 4 as a main course or 6 as part of a multicourse Italian meal

> 3 or 4 medium leeks
> 2 tablespoons butter
> ½ cup water
> Salt
> Freshly ground black pepper
> 1 tablespoon vegetable oil
> 2 pounds boneless pork loin
> ½ cup dry white wine

1. Trim the root ends and dark green tops from the leeks (page 35). Cut the leeks lengthwise in half (or in quarters if they are more than 1 inch thick), then slice them crosswise into ½-inch chunks. Place the leeks in a large bowl of cold water and swish them around to loosen any dirt that is clinging to them.

2. Lift the leeks out of the water and put them in a braising pan large enough to accommodate the pork. Add 1 tablespoon of the butter and ½ cup water and season lightly with salt and pepper. Cover the pan and place over medium heat. Cook until the leeks are wilted, about 10 minutes. Pour the leeks and any remaining liquid into a bowl and set aside.

3. Raise the heat under the pan to high and put in the remaining 1 tablespoon butter and the vegetable oil. When the oil and butter are hot and the butter is just beginning to turn color, put in the pork. Brown the meat well on all sides, then season with salt and pepper.

4. Add the wine and let it bubble for about 30 seconds to allow the alcohol to evaporate. Return the leeks with their liquid to the pan, turn the heat down to low, and cover with the lid slightly askew. Cook, turning the meat about every 20 minutes, until the meat is very tender when pierced with a fork, 1½ to 2 hours. If all of the liquid in the pan evaporates before the roast is tender, add a little water.

5. When the pork is done, uncover the pan and transfer the meat to a cutting board. If there is any excess liquid in the pan, raise the heat and cook until the sauce is reduced. If there no liquid at all left in the pan, add a little water, raise the heat, and scrape the cooking residues from the bottom of the pan with a wooden spoon to make a sauce.

Note: This pork roast can easily be prepared a day or two ahead of time and kept refrigerated. When you are ready to serve, slice the meat and reheat it in the sauce.

PORK LOIN
WITH APPLES AND PLUMS

Arrosto di Maiale alle Mele e Susine

Preparation time: 20 minutes
Total time from start to finish: 2 hours

Serves 4 as a main course or 6 as part of a multicourse Italian meal

2 tablespoons butter
1 tablespoon vegetable oil
2 pounds boneless pork loin
Salt
Freshly ground black pepper
1 medium yellow onion
2 medium plums
¾ Gala, Fuji, or other sweet red apple
⅓ cup full-bodied dry red wine

1. Put the butter and vegetable oil in a braising pan large enough to accommodate the pork and place over high heat. When the oil and butter are hot and the butter is just beginning to turn color, put in the pork. Brown the pork on all sides, then transfer it to a plate and season with salt and pepper.

2. While the meat is browning, peel, halve, and thinly slice the onion crosswise. When the meat is out of the pan, lower the heat to medium, put in the onion, and sauté, stirring occasionally, until the onion softens and becomes translucent, about 5 minutes.

3. While the onion is sautéing, peel the plums (see tomato peeling instructions on pages 30–31), halve, and remove the pits. Peel, quarter, and core the apple. Cut the plums and apple into ½-inch chunks. When the onion is ready, add the fruit, season with salt and pepper, and sauté for about 1 minute. Raise the heat to medium-high and add the wine. Let the wine boil for about 30 seconds to let the alcohol evaporate. Adjust the heat so that the liquid in the pan simmers.

Return the pork to the pan and cover with the lid slightly askew. Cook, turning the pork about every 20 minutes, until the meat is tender, 1½ to 2 hours. If all the liquid in the pan evaporates before the meat is done, add a little water. If the pork is almost done and there is still a lot of liquid in the pan, raise the heat and finish cooking uncovered to allow the excess liquid to evaporate.

4. Transfer the pork to a cutting board and cut into thin slices. Put the slices back in the pan and coat them with the sauce. Arrange the slices on a platter and pour the sauce over them. Serve hot.

Note: This pork roast can easily be prepared a day or two ahead of time and kept refrigerated. When you are ready to serve, slice the meat and reheat it in the sauce.

PAN-ROASTED PORK LOIN
WITH RADICCHIO

Arrosto di Maiale al Radicchio

Ideally, you would use the elongated Treviso radicchio, now starting to become available in the States, but this recipe is also excellent with the more common round radicchio.

Preparation time: 20 minutes
Total time from start to finish: 2 hours

Serves 4 as a main course or 6 as part of a multicourse Italian meal

> ½ small yellow onion
> 2 tablespoons extra virgin olive oil
> 2 pounds boneless pork loin
> Salt
> Freshly ground black pepper
> 1 pound radicchio
> ¼ cup dry white wine

1. Peel and finely chop the onion.

2. Put the olive oil in a heavy-bottomed braising pan and place over medium-high heat. When the oil is hot, put in the pork. Brown the pork on all sides, then transfer to a platter and season with salt and pepper.

3. Turn the heat down to medium and put in the onion. Sauté, stirring occasionally, until it turns a rich golden color, 3 to 5 minutes.

4. While the onion is sautéing, trim away the root of the radicchio and finely shred the radicchio crosswise with a knife.

5. Add the wine to the pan and let it bubble for about 30 seconds to allow the alcohol to evaporate. Add the radicchio and season with salt and pepper.

Cover the pan and cook until the radicchio is wilted, about 5 minutes. Return the pork to the pan and adjust the heat so that the liquid in the pan simmers. Cover the pan with the lid slightly askew and cook, turning the pork about every 20 minutes, until the meat is quite tender, 1½ to 2 hours. If all the liquid in the pan evaporates before the meat is done, add a little water. If the pork is almost done and there is still a lot of liquid in the pan, raise the heat and finish cooking uncovered to allow the excess liquid to evaporate.

6. Transfer the pork to a cutting board and cut into thin slices. Put the slices back in the pan and coat them with the sauce. Arrange the slices on a platter and pour the sauce over them. Serve hot.

Note: This pork roast can easily be prepared a day or two ahead of time and kept refrigerated. When you are ready to serve, slice the meat and reheat it in the sauce.

SWEET-AND-SOUR PORK STEW

Spezzatino di Maiale in Agrodolce

This recipe was inspired by a delicious wild boar stew I had at La Cesoia, a restaurant in Bologna. Since the pig is a descendant of wild boar, I decided to try it with pork and was very pleased with the results. Red wine vinegar, balsamic vinegar, and red wine may seem like a surprising combination, but they make a wonderfully rich, luscious sauce. Serve with good crusty bread or Nonna Mary's rice (page 232).

Preparation time: 20 minutes
Total time from start to finish: 1¾ hours

Serves 4 people as a main course or 6 as part of a multicourse Italian meal

> ¼ cup golden raisins
> 3 tablespoons extra virgin olive oil
> 1½ pounds pork stew meat, preferably shoulder, cut into
>   1-inch pieces
> Salt
> Freshly ground black pepper
> 2 medium yellow onions
> 2 tablespoons red wine vinegar
> ¼ cup dry red wine
> 1 tablespoon balsamic vinegar

1. Put the raisins in a small bowl, cover with water, and soak for at least 15 minutes.

2. Put the olive oil in a braising pan or deep sauté pan over high heat. When the oil is hot, put in half the pork cubes and lightly brown on all sides. Transfer to a platter and repeat with the remaining pork. When all the pork is browned, season it with salt and pepper.

3. While the meat is browning, peel, halve, and thinly slice the onion cross-wise. Put the onion in the pan and season lightly with salt. Sauté, stirring occasionally, over medium heat until the onion turns a rich golden color, 8 to 10 minutes.

4. Raise the heat to medium-high. Add the red wine vinegar and let it bubble for about 10 seconds. Add the wine and let it bubble away for about 30 seconds to allow the alcohol to evaporate. Lower the heat to medium, return the pork to the pan, and add the drained raisins. Cover the pan with the lid askew and cook, stirring about every 15 minutes, until the meat is very tender, about 1½ hours. If all the liquid evaporates before the pork is done, add a little water. If the pork is close to being done and there is still liquid in the pan, raise the heat, remove the cover, and allow the excess liquid to evaporate. Remove the pan from the heat and stir in the balsamic vinegar. Serve hot.

Note: The stew can be made 2 to 3 days ahead of time and kept in the refrigerator. When ready to serve, add a little water and reheat over medium-low heat.

PORK AND PORCINI "BURGERS"

Polpette di Maiale e Porcini

Porcini, pine nuts, garlic, and parsley give these tasty pork patties a distinctly Italian flavor. As an alternative to breading and sautéing, omit the last two ingredients and cook on a hot grill. Serve either American style on a bun, or Italian style with crusty bread on the side.

Total time: 45 minutes

Serves 4

> 1 ounce dried porcini mushrooms
> ½ small clove garlic
> 6 to 8 sprigs flat-leaf Italian parsley
> 3 tablespoons pine nuts
> 2½ tablespoons butter
> Salt
> 1 ounce pancetta, thinly sliced
> 1½ pounds ground pork
> 1 large egg
> Freshly ground black pepper
> ¼ cup fine dry bread crumbs
> 1 tablespoon vegetable oil

1. Preheat the oven to 325° on convection heat, or 350° on regular bake.

2. Put the dried porcini in a medium bowl, cover with water, and soak for 15 minutes.

3. While the porcini are soaking, peel and finely chop the garlic. Finely chop enough of the parsley leaves to measure 2 tablespoons.

4. Put the pine nuts on a baking sheet and toast in the oven until lightly browned, about 5 minutes.

5. Lift the porcini out of the water and squeeze the excess back into the bowl; do not discard the water. Rinse the mushrooms under running water, then coarsely chop them. Put ½ tablespoon of the butter in a small skillet and place over medium-high heat. When the butter is hot, add the porcini. Season lightly with salt and stir until they are well coated with butter. Add the soaking water. Be aware that there may be some sand at the bottom of the bowl, so pour carefully or strain through a paper towel. Cook until all the water is evaporated.

6. While the porcini are cooking, finely chop the pancetta and put it in a medium bowl with the pork, garlic, parsley, and egg. Season with salt and pepper and mix thoroughly with your hands. When the porcini are done, add them to the bowl. Mix at first with a spoon, so you will not burn yourself, then with your hands until the mixture is homogeneous. Form the meat into 6 patties about 1 inch thick. Put the bread crumbs on a small plate and coat each patty on all sides with bread crumbs.

7. Put the vegetable oil and the remaining 2 tablespoons butter in a 12-inch skillet and place over medium-high heat. When the oil and butter are hot and the butter is just beginning to turn color, put in the pork patties. Cook about 2 minutes on each side, then lower the heat to medium and cover the pan. Cook until just barely pink inside, about another 2 minutes on each side. Remove them from the pan and serve hot.

FAVA BEANS WITH SAUSAGE

Salsicce e Fave

Fava beans pair well with pork, such as pancetta, prosciutto, and, in this case, sausage. The sausage that is used in Italy is milder than the "Italian sausage" that is available in the States. Use either the homemade sausage on page 45 or a mild sausage, such as breakfast links.

Preparation time: 35 minutes
Total time from start to finish: 1 hour

Serves 4 as a main course or 6 as part of a multicourse Italian meal

> 1 pound fava beans in the pod
> 1¼ pounds homemade sausage (page 45) or mild breakfast
>   sausage links
> 1 small yellow onion
> 2 tablespoons extra virgin olive oil
> 2 cups canned whole peeled tomatoes with their juice
> Salt

1. Shell and peel the fava beans.

2. If using store-bought sausage, cut it into ½-inch pieces. Put the sausage in a large sauté pan with enough water to come about ¼ inch up the side of the pan and place over medium-high heat. If using homemade sausage, break it up with a wooden spoon. Cook until all the water is evaporated and the sausage begins to brown, 5 to 8 minutes.

3. While the sausage is cooking, peel and finely chop the onion. Drain any fat the sausage has released and add the olive oil to the pan. Add the onion and sauté, stirring occasionally, until it turns a rich golden color, 3 to 5 minutes.

4. Add the tomatoes and break them up with a spoon. Add the fava beans, season with salt, and cook until the beans are tender, 20 to 30 minutes. Serve hot with good crusty bread.

> **Note:** You can make this dish up to 2 days ahead and keep it in the refrigerator.

OVEN-ROASTED LAMB
WITH FRESH MINT

Agnello Arrosto con la Mentuccia

Preparation time: 10 minutes
Total time from start to finish: 40 minutes

Serves 4 as a main course or 6 as part of a multicourse Italian meal

1 medium clove garlic
½ small bunch fresh mint
1 teaspoon salt
Freshly ground black pepper
2 teaspoons extra virgin olive oil
3 pounds lamb loin rack *or* 2 pounds boneless loin

1. Preheat the oven to 400° on convection heat, or 425° on regular bake.

2. Peel and finely chop the garlic and chop enough of the mint leaves to measure 3 tablespoons. Mix the garlic, mint, salt, pepper, and olive oil in a small bowl. Rub the mixture all over the lamb with a small spoon or your fingers.

3. Place the meat in a roasting pan and roast in the oven until it reaches an internal temperature of about 135° as measured by an instant-read thermometer for medium-rare, 20 to 25 minutes. Remove from the oven and let rest for about 5 minutes. Cut into ¼-inch-thick slices and serve hot.

Note: Reheating leftovers tends to overcook the meat, but leftover slices at room temperature are delicious in a sandwich.

PAN-ROASTED LAMB
WITH ARTICHOKES

Agnello in Tegame ai Carciofi

Preparation time: 30 minutes
Total time from start to finish: 1¾ hours

Serves 4 as a main course or 6 as part of a multicourse Italian meal

> 2 tablespoons extra virgin olive oil
> 3 pounds bone-in lamb shoulder chops, about 1 inch thick
> Salt
> Freshly ground black pepper
> 1 small clove garlic
> 2 sprigs fresh thyme
> ½ cup dry white wine
> 3 medium artichokes
> 2 lemons

1. Put the olive oil in a braising pan large enough to hold the lamb snugly with minimal overlap. Place the pan over high heat. When the oil is hot, put in half the lamb and brown lightly on both sides. Transfer to a platter and repeat with the remaining lamb. When all the meat is done, season it with salt and pepper.

2. While the lamb is browning, peel and finely chop the garlic and chop enough of the thyme leaves to measure 1 teaspoon. After the lamb is out of the pan, lower the heat to medium-high. Put the garlic and thyme in the pan and stir well. Add the wine and let it bubble away for 30 seconds to let the alcohol evaporate. Return the meat to the pan. Adjust the heat so that the liquid in the pan simmers and cover with the lid askew. Cook, turning the meat every 15 to 20 minutes, until the lamb is almost fully tender, about 1 hour. If all the liquid evaporates before the lamb is done, add a little water.

3. While the meat is cooking, trim the artichokes as described on pages 34–35 and cut them into wedges about ¼ inch thick. Use half of one of the

lemons to rub the cut parts of the artichokes as you are trimming them and squeeze the other half into a large bowl of water. Put the artichoke wedges in the bowl of lemon water.

4. After the lamb has cooked for about 1 hour, drain the artichokes and add them to the pan. Season with salt, cover the pan, and cook until the artichokes are quite tender, at least 30 minutes more. If all the liquid dries up before they are done, add some water. If there is still a lot of liquid in the pan when the artichokes are done, remove the lid, raise the heat, and let it evaporate until the sauce is thick enough to coat a spoon. Squeeze the remaining lemon and add about 2 tablespoons juice to the pan.

Note: This dish can be prepared 1 to 2 days ahead. When ready to serve, gently reheat it with the lid on and add the lemon juice just before serving.

BRAISED LAMB SHANKS

Stinchi di Agnello

The shank is one of the most succulent cuts of meat and is ideally suited to long, slow braising.

Preparation time: 35 minutes
Total time from start to finish: 2 hours 35 minutes

Serves 4 as a main course or 6 as part of a multicourse Italian meal

> 2 medium carrots
> 2 ribs celery
> 1 medium yellow onion
> 3 medium cloves garlic
> 2 tablespoons extra virgin olive oil
> 4 lamb shanks
> Salt
> Freshly ground black pepper
> 3 to 4 sprigs fresh sage
> 1 sprig fresh rosemary
> 6 ounces ripe tomato
> ⅓ cup dry white wine

1. Peel the carrots and celery and cut into ½-inch dice. Peel the onion and cut into 1-inch chunks.

2. Lightly crush and peel the garlic cloves and put them in a heavy-bottomed braising pan with the olive oil. Place over medium-high heat. When the garlic is lightly browned on all sides, remove and discard it. Add the lamb shanks to the oil and brown them on all sides. Transfer to a platter and season with salt and pepper.

3. While the lamb is browning, coarsely chop enough of the sage to measure 2 teaspoons and enough of the rosemary leaves to measure 1 teaspoon.

After the lamb is out of the pan, add the herbs, carrots, celery, and onion. Sauté, stirring occasionally, until the vegetables begin to color, 5 to 8 minutes.

4. While the vegetables are browning, peel the tomato (pages 30–31) and coarsely chop.

5. Add the wine to the pan and let it boil for about 30 seconds to let the alcohol evaporate. Add the tomato and season lightly with salt and pepper. Return the lamb shanks to the pan and adjust the heat so the liquid in the pan simmers. Cook, covered with the lid slightly askew, turning the shanks every 15 to 20 minutes, until tender, about 2 hours. If all the liquid evaporates before the lamb is tender, add a little water. If the lamb is almost done and there is still liquid in the pan, raise the heat and finish cooking uncovered to allow the excess liquid to evaporate. Serve hot with good crusty bread.

> **Note:** This dish can easily be made 1 to 2 days ahead of time and kept in the refrigerator. Gently reheat, adding a little water if necessary.

LAMB STEW WITH OLIVES

Spezzatino di Agnello alle Olive

This savory stew is wonderful served with Nonna Mary's White Rice (page 232) or simply with good crusty bread.

Preparation time: 30 minutes
Total time from start to finish: 2 hours

Serves 4 as a main course or 6 as part of a multicourse Italian meal

> 1 small clove garlic
> 1 sprig fresh rosemary
> 2 tablespoons extra virgin olive oil
> 2 pounds boneless lamb shoulder, cut into 1-inch cubes
> Salt
> Freshly ground black pepper
> ⅓ cup dry white wine
> 1½ cups canned whole peeled tomatoes with their juice
> 6 to 8 sprigs flat-leaf Italian parsley
> 12 Kalamata olives

1. Peel and finely chop the garlic. Chop enough of the rosemary leaves to measure 1 teaspoon.

2. Put the olive oil in a heavy-bottomed braising pan and place over high heat. When the oil is hot enough to make the lamb sizzle, put in half the meat and lightly brown it on all sides. Transfer to a platter and repeat with the remaining lamb. When all of the lamb is done, season the meat with salt and pepper.

3. Add the garlic and rosemary to the pan and lower the heat to medium-high. Add the wine and let it bubble for about 30 seconds to let the alcohol evaporate. Add the tomatoes and break them up with a wooden spoon. Lightly season the tomatoes with salt and, once they begin bubbling, return the meat to the pan. Adjust the heat so that the tomatoes simmer and cover with the lid

slightly askew. Cook, stirring every 15 to 20 minutes, until the meat is tender, about 1½ hours. If all the liquid evaporates before the lamb is tender, add a little water.

4. While the meat is cooking, chop enough of the parsley leaves to measure 2 tablespoons. Slice the flesh of the olives away from the pits.

5. When the meat is tender, add the parsley and olives and continue cooking for about 5 minutes. If there is a lot of liquid in the pan, raise the heat and finish cooking uncovered to let the excess liquid evaporate. Serve hot.

Note: This dish can easily be made 1 to 2 days ahead of time and kept in the refrigerator. Wait to add the olives and parsley until you are ready to reheat the stew and serve it.

LAMB RIB CHOPS GRILLED ITALIAN STYLE

Costolette di Agnello Scottadito

Use New Zealand lamb, which more closely resembles Italian lamb; it is smaller and younger than lamb raised in America. Larger American lamb chops of course will also be quite delicious prepared this way. In Italy lamb chops are trimmed so that you can pick them up by the bone, hence the name *scottadito,* which means "burn your finger." You can apply this basic grilling recipe to steaks, pork chops, and boneless chicken breasts as well.

Total time: 25 minutes

Serves 4 people as a single-course meal or 6 people as part of a multi-course meal

> 3 pounds lamb rib chops
> Salt
> Freshly ground black pepper
> 2 tablespoons extra virgin olive oil

1. Preheat a charcoal or gas grill.

2. Season the lamb chops on both sides with salt and pepper.

3. When the grill is very hot, put on the lamb chops. Grill until browned but still red, or at least pink, in the center. Small New Zealand chops will need 2 to 3 minutes on each side; larger chops, 3 to 4 minutes each side.

4. Transfer the chops to a platter, drizzle the olive oil over them, and serve at once.

BEEF TENDERLOIN WITH BALSAMIC, ARUGULA, AND PARMIGIANO

Filetto di Bue all'Aceto Balsamico

Lorella, our friend from Italy, loves to cook and prepared this delicious dish for us one day. Three contrasting flavors, the saltiness of Parmigiano-Reggiano, the spiciness of arugula, and the sweet acidity of balsamic vinegar, together enhance the mild flavor of tenderloin.

Total time: 15 minutes

Serves 4

> ¼ cup extra virgin olive oil
> 1½ pounds beef tenderloin, in one piece
> Salt
> Freshly ground black pepper
> 2 tablespoons balsamic vinegar
> 1 medium bunch arugula, about 2 ounces, leaves washed and
>   stems removed
> ¼ cup shaved Parmigiano-Reggiano

1. Put the olive oil in a 10-inch skillet and place over medium-high heat. Season the beef tenderloin with salt and pepper. When the oil is very hot, put the beef in and brown it on all sides. Transfer the beef to a platter and set aside. Remove the pan from the heat.

2. Cut the beef into 1½- to 2-inch chunks. Put the pan back over medium-high heat and, when it is hot again, add the balsamic vinegar. Let it bubble away for about 15 seconds, while loosening the browning residue on the bottom of the pan with a wooden spoon. Return the meat to the pan and cook to your preferred degree of doneness, 1 to 2 minutes for medium-rare.

3. Remove the beef from the pan and divide it among individual dinner plates. Distribute the arugula and Parmigiano shavings over the meat, then pour some of the hot sauce from the pan over each serving. Serve at once.

BEEF TENDERLOIN
WITH CHERRIES

Filetto di Bue alle Ciliege

Italians use fruit in savory dishes with surprisingly delicious results. Cherries make a sauce that is a perfect accompaniment for filet mignon. Use red Bing cherries or, for a sweeter, more delicate, flavor, try Rainier cherries. Grappa (page 410) also gives this dish a distinct flavor.

Total time: 25 minutes

Serves 4

> 12 ounces cherries
> 1 tablespoon vegetable oil
> 2 tablespoons butter
> 4 beef tenderloin steaks, about 6 ounces each
> Salt
> Freshly ground black pepper
> 2 tablespoons grappa
> 1 tablespoon fresh lemon juice
> 1 teaspoon tomato paste

1. Rinse and stem the cherries. Cut each one crosswise around the pit, twist the halves apart, and remove the pit. Or use a cherry pitter if you have one and halve crosswise.

2. Put the vegetable oil and 1 tablespoon of the butter in a skillet large enough to accommodate the steaks comfortably and place over medium-high heat. When the oil and butter are hot and the butter is just beginning to turn color, put the steaks in and cook, without moving them for 4 minutes. Turn them over and cook another 3 to 4 minutes for medium-rare. Remove them from the pan and set aside on a platter. Season with salt and pepper.

3. Remove the pan from the heat and pour in the grappa. Stir with a wooden spoon to loosen the browned bits from the bottom of the pan. Return the pan

to medium heat and add the cherries. Season with salt and generously with pepper and cook, stirring periodically, until the cherries become soft and begin forming a syrupy sauce, 7 to 8 minutes. Add the lemon juice and tomato paste. Stir and cook for another minute. Turn the heat down to low and swirl in the remaining 1 tablespoon of butter. When the butter is melted, return the steaks to the pan and turn them in the sauce. Cover the pan for about 1 minute to allow the meat to heat through. Serve at once.

BEEF TENDERLOIN WITH TOMATO, PANCETTA, AND THYME

Filetto di Bue al Pomodoro e Pancetta

Total time: 25 minutes

Serves 4

> 2 tablespoons extra virgin olive oil
> 4 beef tenderloin steaks, about 6 ounces each
> Salt
> Freshly ground black pepper
> ½ small yellow onion
> 12 ounces ripe tomatoes
> 1 sprig fresh thyme
> 8 thin slices pancetta

1. Put 1 tablespoon of the olive oil in a skillet large enough to accommodate the steaks comfortably and place over medium-high heat. When the oil is hot, put the steaks in and cook, without moving them for 4 minutes. Turn them over and cook another 3 to 4 minutes for medium-rare. Remove them from the pan and set aside on a platter. Season with salt and pepper.

2. While the steaks are cooking, peel and finely chop the onion. Peel the tomatoes (pages 30–31) and coarsely chop.

3. After removing the steaks, lower the heat to medium and add the remaining 1 tablespoon olive oil. Add the onion and sauté, stirring occasionally, until it softens and turns a rich golden color, 3 to 5 minutes.

4. While the onion is sautéing, chop enough of the thyme leaves to measure ½ teaspoon. When the onion is done, add the thyme and tomatoes and season lightly with salt. Add the pancetta, raise the heat to medium-high, and cook until the tomatoes are reduced and no longer watery, 10 to 15 minutes.

5. Return the steaks to the pan and turn them in the sauce. Cover the pan for about 1 minute to allow the meat to heat through. Serve at once, topping each steak with 2 slices pancetta and some sauce.

SLICED STEAK WITH OLIVE OIL, GARLIC, AND ROSEMARY

Tagliata all'Olio, Aglio, e Rosmarino

Tagliata, a favorite Italian way to serve grilled steak, is a thick steak served sliced and seasoned or topped in a variety of ways. Italians do not eat as large portions of meat as Americans do, and this is a perfect way to serve thick steak without going overboard on the portion size. Use a 1¼-inch-thick piece of your favorite cut (mine is the boneless rib-eye).

Total time: 20 minutes

Serves 4 as a main course or 6 as part of a multicourse Italian meal

> **4 garlic cloves**
> **¼ cup extra virgin olive oil**

2 sprigs fresh rosemary
Coarse sea salt
Freshly ground black pepper
2 boneless rib-eye steaks, about 1½ pounds each, at least
1¼ inches thick

1. Preheat a charcoal or gas grill.

2. Lightly crush and peel the garlic cloves. Put them in a large skillet with the olive oil and rosemary sprigs and place over medium-high heat. When the garlic is lightly browned on all sides, remove and discard it and the rosemary. Remove the pan from the heat.

3. Generously sprinkle coarse sea salt and black pepper on both sides of the steaks. Grill for about 5 minutes on each side for rare steak. Bear in mind that after it is sliced, the meat will be briefly exposed to heat in the skillet.

4. Transfer the steaks to a cutting board and cut on a bias into ¼-inch-thick slices. Heat the olive oil in the skillet over medium-high heat. As soon as it is hot, add the sliced steak and toss until it is well coated. Serve at once.

SLICED STEAK WITH ARUGULA AND PECORINO

Tagliata alla Rucola e Pecorino

Total time: 20 minutes

Serves 4 as a main course or 6 as part of a multicourse Italian meal

4 ounces arugula
2 tablespoons extra virgin olive oil, plus extra for drizzling
Salt
2 boneless rib-eye steaks, about 1½ pounds each, at least
    1¼ inches thick
Coarse sea salt
Freshly ground black pepper
½ cup freshly grated medium-aged pecorino cheese
Balsamic vinegar for drizzling

1. Preheat a charcoal or gas grill.

2. Cut off the arugula stems and wash the leaves. Put the olive oil in a medium skillet and place over medium-high heat. When the oil is hot, put in the arugula leaves and sprinkle with salt. Cook, stirring occasionally, until the arugula is wilted and any liquid is evaporated, 3 to 4 minutes. Remove from the heat.

3. Generously sprinkle coarse sea salt and black pepper on both sides of the steaks. Grill for about 6 minutes on each side for rare steak.

4. Transfer the steaks to a cutting board and cut on a bias into ¼-inch-thick slices. Put the skillet with the arugula back over high heat just long enough to heat it through. Arrange the sliced steak on a serving platter and distribute the wilted arugula over it. Sprinkle the grated pecorino on top and drizzle sparingly with olive oil and balsamic vinegar. Serve at once.

SAVORY BEEF STEAKS
WITH TOMATOES AND OLIVES

Bistecche Saporite

This recipe works well with either tenderloin steaks or thinly cut rib-eye steaks. The combination of tomatoes, olives, and oregano give this dish a distinctively Italian flavor. Serve with good crusty bread to soak up the sauce.

Preparation time: 25 minutes
Total time from start to finish: 40 minutes

Serves 4

> 1 medium yellow onion
> 3 tablespoons extra virgin olive oil
> 1 medium clove garlic
> 1 pound ripe tomatoes
> Salt
> Freshly ground black pepper
> 6 Kalamata olives
> 1 to 2 sprigs fresh oregano
> 4 beef rib-eye steaks, 6 to 8 ounces each, about ½ inch thick, or
>   6-ounce tenderloin steaks, about 1 inch thick

1. Peel, halve, and thinly slice the onion crosswise. Put it with 2 tablespoons of the olive oil in a 10-inch skillet and place over medium heat. Sauté, stirring occasionally, until the onion turns a rich golden color, about 10 minutes.

2. While the onion is sautéing, peel and thinly slice the garlic. Peel the tomatoes (pages 30–31) and coarsely chop. When the onion is done, add the garlic and sauté for 1 minute. Add the tomatoes, season with salt and pepper, and cook until the tomatoes are reduced and no longer watery, 15 to 20 minutes.

3. While the tomatoes are cooking, slice the flesh of the olives from the pits. Chop enough of the oregano leaves to measure 1½ teaspoons. Once the

tomatoes are reduced, add the olives and oregano and cook for another minute. Remove from the heat and set aside.

4. Put the remaining 1 tablespoon olive oil in a large skillet and place over medium-high heat. When the oil is hot, put in as many steaks as will fit. Cook for 3 to 4 minutes on each side for medium-rare tenderloin or 2 to 3 minutes for rib-eye. When all the steaks are done, season them with salt and pepper and put them in the pan with the sauce. Place over high heat to reheat the sauce. Turn the steaks in the sauce and serve at once.

BEEF ROLLS FILLED WITH CHEESE, CAPERS, AND OLIVES

Braciole Napoletane

Braciole are a specialty of southern Italy from Naples to Sicily. They are thin slices of beef rolled with a variety of fillings. I had this version in Caserta, near Naples.

Total time: 30 minutes

Serves 4 as a main course or 6 as part of a multicourse Italian meal

1½ pounds thinly sliced beef bottom round
Salt
6 ounces fresh whole-milk mozzarella
12 Kalamata olives
½ cup freshly grated medium-aged pecorino cheese
2 tablespoons capers
2 tablespoons fine dry bread crumbs
2 tablespoons extra virgin olive oil

1. Preheat a charcoal or gas grill.

2. Pound the beef slices as described on pages 38–39, until no more than ¼ inch thick. Cut the slices in half if necessary so that you end up with pieces 3 to 4 inches wide and 5 to 6 inches long. Lightly season with salt.

3. Slice the mozzarella ¼ inch thick and place 2 or 3 slices on each piece of beef. Slice the olive flesh away from the pits and distribute over the mozzarella. Sprinkle the pecorino on top, then sprinkle with the capers and bread crumbs. Drizzle a little of the olive oil over each slice. Roll up the beef loosely so that the ends just overlap and secure with toothpicks.

4. Place the rolls on a hot grill and brown on all sides. Cover the grill and cook for about 5 minutes until the meat is cooked through. Serve hot.

Note: You can assemble the rolls up to 1 hour ahead without refrigerating. If you hold them any longer, they will become soggy.

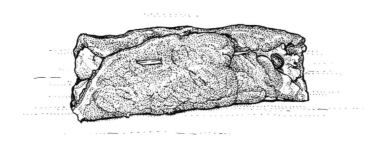

BEEF BRAISED
WITH ANCHOVIES

Stracotto di Manzo alle Acciughe

By the time the meat is done, the anchovies are undetectable but give this dish a distinctively rich flavor. *Stracotto* in Italian means "overcooked," and it's the long, slow cooking process that makes this beef so tender and succulent.

Preparation time: 20 minutes
Total time from start to finish: 3¼ hours

Serves 4 as a main course or 6 as part of a multicourse Italian meal

> 2 ounces pancetta, thinly sliced
> 4 anchovy fillets
> 2 tablespoons extra virgin olive oil
> 2 pounds beef brisket or chuck
> Salt
> Freshly ground black pepper
> Pinch freshly grated nutmeg
> ½ cup white wine
> 6 to 8 sprigs flat-leaf Italian parsley

1. Finely chop the pancetta and anchovy fillets.

2. Put the olive oil in a heavy-bottomed braising pan and place over medium-high heat. When the oil is hot, put in the meat and brown it on all sides. Remove it from the pan and season with salt and pepper.

3. Put the pancetta, anchovies, and nutmeg in the pan and stir until the anchovies dissolve and the pancetta starts to brown, 1 to 2 minutes. Add the wine and let it bubble away for about 30 seconds to let the alcohol evaporate. Adjust the heat so that the wine simmers and return the meat to the pan. Cover and cook, turning the meat every 15 to 20 minutes, until the beef is very tender, about 3 hours. If all the liquid evaporates before it is done, add a little

water. If the beef is almost done and there is still liquid in the pan, raise the heat and finish cooking uncovered to allow the excess liquid to evaporate.

4. While the meat is cooking, finely chop enough of the parsley leaves to measure 2 tablespoons.

5. When the beef is done, transfer it to a cutting board. Add the parsley to the sauce, stir for about 30 seconds, and remove the pan from the heat. Cut the meat into ½-inch slices, put it back in the pan, and turn to coat the meat with the sauce. Serve at once.

Note: This dish can be made 2 to 3 days ahead of time. When ready to serve, slice the meat and reheat it in the sauce with 2 tablespoons water.

BEEF BRAISED WITH LEMON

Brasato al Limone

The lemon flavor in this dish is subtle, yet makes the beef wonderfully fragrant and light.

Preparation time: 20 minutes
Total time from start to finish: 2 hours

Serves 4 as a main course or 6 as part of a multicourse Italian meal

> 3 tablespoons extra virgin olive oil
> 2 pounds beef chuck
> Salt
> Freshly ground black pepper
> 1 large yellow onion
> ¼ cup dry white wine
> ½ cup water
> 1 large beef bouillon cube
> ¼ cup fresh lemon juice

1. Put the olive oil in a braising pan large enough to accommodate the beef and place over high heat. When the oil is hot, put in the beef and brown it on all sides. Transfer to a platter and season with salt and pepper.

2. While the beef is browning, peel, halve, and thinly slice the onion cross-wise. After the meat has browned, put the onion in the pan and place it over medium heat. Sauté, stirring occasionally, until the onion softens and becomes translucent, 5 to 8 minutes.

3. Raise the heat to high and add the wine. Let the wine bubble for about 30 seconds to let the alcohol evaporate, then add the water and bouillon cube. Stir to dissolve the bouillon cube. Adjust the heat so that the liquid in the pan simmers and return the beef to the pan. Cook, covered with the lid slightly askew, turning the meat every 15 to 20 minutes, for 1¼ hours. If all the liquid evaporates, add a little water.

4. Add the lemon juice and continue cooking until the meat is very tender, about 30 minutes more. If there is still a lot of liquid in the pan when the beef is done, raise the heat and finish cooking uncovered until the sauce is thick enough to coat a spoon. Transfer the beef to a cutting board and cut into ¼-inch slices. Put the slices in the pan and coat them with the sauce. Serve hot.

Note: The beef can be prepared 1 to 2 days ahead of time through step 3. Store, covered, in the refrigerator.

SLOW-COOKED BEEF, "PASTISADA" STYLE

Pastisada di Manzo

Pastisada is a thousand-year-old specialty of Verona. It is traditionally prepared with horse meat, but I have found the recipe works fabulously with beef as well. Do not be dissuaded by the rather long ingredient list; the dish is actually simple to prepare. You just have to be patient enough to let the meat cook for 6 hours. Traditionally, the wine used is Amarone, a rich jammy Veronese wine made from dried grapes, which can be somewhat pricey. A possible and more economical alternative is a good, rich Zinfandel. Serve with polenta (page 372), the traditional pairing, or mashed potatoes (page 369).

Preparation time: 20 minutes
Total time from start to finish: 6½ hours

Serves 4 as a main course or 6 as part of a multicourse Italian meal

> 1 large yellow onion
> 1 large carrot
> 2 ribs celery
> 2½ pounds beef chuck
> 1 tablespoon butter
> 2 tablespoons extra virgin olive oil
> Salt
> Freshly ground black pepper
> 1 tablespoon tomato paste
> 2 sprigs fresh rosemary
> 3 to 4 sprigs fresh sage leaves
> ⅛ teaspoon ground cinnamon
> ⅛ teaspoon freshly grated nutmeg
> 2 bay leaves
> 8 cloves
> 1 cup Amarone or Zinfandel wine

1. Peel and finely chop the onion. Peel the carrot and celery and cut into ¼-inch dice. Cut the meat into approximately 2-inch pieces.

2. Put the butter and olive oil in a heavy-bottomed braising pan and place over medium-high heat. When the oil and butter are hot and the butter is just beginning to turn color, put in the meat and brown it on all sides. Transfer the meat to a platter and season with salt and pepper.

3. While the meat is browning, dissolve the tomato paste in the wine. Chop enough of the sage and rosemary leaves to measure 2 teaspoons each. After browning the meat, put the onion, carrot, and celery in the pan and sauté, stirring occasionally, until the vegetables begin to brown, 8 to 10 minutes. Add the rosemary, sage, cinnamon, nutmeg, bay leaves, and cloves. Stir for a few seconds, then add the wine. Season with a little salt and return the meat to the pan. When the wine begins to bubble, lower the heat so that it simmers gently. Cover the pan and cook, stirring every 25 to 30 minutes, for 6 hours. If all the liquid evaporates before the time is up, add some water. If there is still liquid in the pan when the meat is done, raise the heat, remove the cover, and allow the excess liquid to evaporate until the sauce is thick enough to coat a spoon. Discard the bay leaves and serve hot.

Note: This dish can be made 1 to 2 days ahead of time and kept in the refrigerator.

BEEF SHORT RIBS BRAISED WITH TOMATOES AND POTATOES

Costicine di Manzo al Pomodoro e Patate

These fork-tender, succulent short ribs are the perfect antidote to a cold winter's day. By the end the potatoes become partly mashed and together with the tomatoes form a wonderful thick sauce.

Preparation time: 20 minutes
Total time from start to finish: about 2 hours

Serves 4 as a main course or 6 as part of a multicourse Italian meal

> 3 tablespoons extra virgin olive oil
> 3 pounds beef short ribs
> Salt
> Freshly ground black pepper
> 1 medium yellow onion
> 1 pound ripe tomatoes
> 6 to 8 sprigs fresh sage
> 1 pound Yukon Gold potatoes

1. Put the olive oil in a braising pan large enough to accommodate the ribs snugly over medium-high heat. When the oil is hot, add half of the short ribs and brown them on all sides. Transfer to a platter and repeat with the remaining short ribs. After all the meat is browned, season with salt and pepper.

2. While the meat is browning, peel, halve, and slice the onion. When the meat is done, add the onion to the pan and reduce the heat to medium-low. Season lightly with salt and sauté, stirring occasionally, until it begins to brown, about 10 minutes.

3. While the onion is sautéing, peel the tomatoes (pages 30–31) and cut into ½-inch dice. Chop enough of the sage to measure 1 tablespoon and add it to the onion when it is done. Stir and cook for 2 minutes, then add the tomatoes.

Season the tomatoes lightly with salt, then return the short ribs to the pan. Cover with the lid slightly askew and cook for 1 hour, turning the ribs every 15 to 20 minutes. If all the liquid evaporates before 1 hour has elapsed, add some water to the pan.

4. While the meat is cooking, peel the potatoes and cut them into ¾-inch cubes. Place them in a bowl and cover with cold water to prevent them from discoloring. After the meat has cooked for 1 hour, add the drained potatoes to the pan and stir well. Season lightly with salt and add about ½ cup water. Cover the pan completely and cook until the potatoes and the meat are very tender, 30 to 45 minutes; add more water if needed. Serve hot.

   Note: This dish can be made 1 to 2 days ahead of time and kept in the refrigerator.

MEATBALLS WITH TOMATOES
AND PEAS

Polpettine al Pomodoro e Piselli

These tender, delicate meatballs are comfort food at its best. This recipe, with minor variations, has passed from generation to generation in my family. I learned it from my mother, who learned it from her mother, and it is a favorite of my five-year-old daughter, who is already learning how to make it. The meatballs are particularly delicious with Nonna Mary's White Rice (page 232).

Preparation time: 35 minutes
Total time from start to finish: 1 hour

Serves 4 (makes about 20 meatballs)

>   1 slice white sandwich bread
>   2 tablespoons whole milk
>   ¼ medium yellow onion
>   1 pound ground beef chuck
>   1 large egg
>   ¼ cup freshly grated Parmigiano-Reggiano
>   Pinch freshly grated nutmeg
>   Salt
>   Freshly ground black pepper
>   ¼ cup fine dry bread crumbs
>   ½ cup or more vegetable oil
>   1 cup canned whole peeled tomatoes with their juice
>   1¼ pounds fresh peas in the pod *or* 7 ounces frozen peas

1. Trim the crust from the bread, and put the bread and milk in a small bowl.

2. Peel and finely chop enough of the onion to measure 1 tablespoon. Mash the bread and milk to a pulp with your fingers. Put it in a large bowl with the ground meat, onion, egg, Parmigiano, and nutmeg. Season with salt and pepper. Mix everything together thoroughly with your hands. Form the mixture into small compact meatballs, about 1½ inches in diameter.

3. Put the bread crumbs in a small shallow bowl and roll each meatball in them until coated on all sides.

4. Put enough oil to come ¼ inch up the sides in a large skillet or sauté pan that will accommodate all the meatballs snugly and place over medium-high heat. When the oil is hot, carefully slide in about half of the meatballs using a large spoon. Lightly brown them on all sides and set aside. Repeat with the remaining meatballs.

5. Pour off most of the oil in the pan, leaving just enough to coat the bottom. Return the pan to medium heat, add the tomatoes, and break them into small pieces with a spoon. Lightly season the tomatoes with salt, then return all of the meatballs to the pan. Adjust the heat so that the tomatoes simmer and cover the pan with the lid slightly askew. Cook for about 10 minutes, turning the meatballs once after about 5 minutes.

6. If using fresh peas, shell them. Add the peas and cook, stirring occasionally, until tender, about 15 minutes for frozen peas or 20 to 25 minutes for fresh. Serve hot with good crusty bread or rice.

> *Note:* These meatballs can be made ahead of time and kept in the refrigerator for 1 to 2 days or in the freezer for up to 2 months. If reheating on the stove, add a couple tablespoons of water to prevent them from drying out.

MEATLOAF WITH MUSHROOMS

Polpettone ai Funghi

In typical Italian fashion, this meatloaf is cooked on top of the stove instead of in the oven.

Preparation time: 30 minutes
Total time from start to finish: 1 hour 20 minutes

Serves 4 as a main course or 6 as part of a multicourse Italian meal

> ½ medium yellow onion
> 4 ounces shiitake mushrooms
> 4 ounces white mushrooms
> 1½ slices white sandwich bread
> 3 tablespoons whole milk
> 1½ pounds ground beef chuck
> 1 large egg
> ⅛ teaspoon freshly grated nutmeg
> ⅓ cup freshly grated Parmigiano-Reggiano
> Salt
> Freshly ground black pepper
> 1 tablespoon butter
> 1 tablespoon vegetable oil
> 3 tablespoons fine dry bread crumbs
> 3 to 4 sprigs fresh sage leaves
> ⅓ cup dry white wine
> 12 ounces ripe tomatoes

1. Peel and finely chop the onion. Trim the stems of the shiitake mushrooms and thinly slice them. Thinly slice the white mushrooms.

2. Trim the crusts from the bread and put the bread and milk in a small bowl. Mash the bread with your fingers until you have a smooth pulp. Put it in a mixing bowl with the ground beef, egg, nutmeg, and Parmigiano. Season with salt and pepper and mix everything together thoroughly with your hands.

3. Put the butter and vegetable oil in a heavy-bottomed braising pan and place over medium-high heat.

4. Spread the bread crumbs on a plate. Shape the meat into a loaf 3½ to 4 inches thick. Roll the loaf in the bread crumbs to coat it all around.

5. When the oil and butter are hot and the butter is just beginning to turn color, gently slide the meatloaf into the pan. Once it has browned on the bottom, carefully turn it, using 2 spatulas, to brown the other side. Use the spatulas to lift the meatloaf out of the pan and set it aside on a plate. Be aware that the loaf can easily come apart if you are not careful.

6. Turn the heat down to medium and add the onion. Sauté, stirring occasionally, until it turns a rich golden color, 3 to 5 minutes. Chop enough of the sage to measure 2 teaspoons and stir it in. Raise the heat to medium-high, add the wine, and let it bubble away until it is completely evaporated. Add the mushrooms, season with salt and pepper, and cook, stirring occasionally, for 5 minutes.

7. While the mushrooms are cooking, peel the tomatoes (pages 30–31) and coarsely chop them. Add the tomatoes to the pan, season lightly with salt, and put the meatloaf back in. The easiest way to do this is to hold the plate over the pan and slide the meatloaf into the pan. Once the tomatoes have started bubbling, lower the heat so that they simmer. Cover the pan and cook, turning the meatloaf every 15 to 20 minutes, until it is cooked through, about 45 minutes. Remove the cover. If the sauce is still somewhat watery, raise the heat to medium-high and cook, stirring often, until the sauce is thick enough to coat a spoon. Take the meatloaf out of the pan and cut into ½-inch slices. Place the slices on a serving platter and pour the sauce over them. Serve hot with some good crusty bread.

Note: This is a dish that will be still very good 2 to 3 days after it's made. Slice the meat loaf when you are ready to serve, then reheat it in its sauce on top of the stove, in a 350° oven, or in a microwave.

MIXED BOILED MEATS
(AND HOMEMADE MEAT BROTH)

Bollito Misto

Mixed boiled meats may not sound particularly appetizing to the uninitiated, but it is one of Italy's most refined and delectable dishes, one whose successful execution can be a determining factor in a restaurant's reputation. At its most ambitious, *bollito misto* may include close to a dozen different meats, such as beef, veal, chicken, pork, turkey, pheasant, calf's head, tongue, and *cotechino* and *zampone* (two types of boiled sausage). Such a *bollito misto* is no small feat, requiring many different pots, and is best left to a restaurant kitchen.

The following recipe requires only one pot and has the additional benefit of producing a wonderful Italian meat broth. It has three meats: beef, veal, and chicken, but if you wish, you can make it with only beef and veal or beef and chicken. Italian broth is quite different from dark French meat stock. It is a delicate, light broth made with raw meats and vegetables, not the oven-roasted bones and vegetables that give French stock its intense, concentrated flavor. The meats of a *bollito misto* are very good served just with a drizzle of extra virgin olive oil and a sprinkling of coarse sea salt, with Smothered Red and Yellow Peppers (page 356), or Salsa Verde (page 238). The marrow from the bones is delicious with a few drops of lemon juice and a sprinkling of salt.

Preparation time: 15 minutes
Total time from start to finish: 3½ hours

Serves 8 and makes at least 2 quarts broth

> 2 medium carrots
> 1 medium ripe tomato *or* 1 canned whole peeled tomato
> 1 medium yellow onion
> 2 or 3 ribs celery
> 1 sprig flat-leaf Italian parsley
> 1 chicken, about 3½ pounds

1½ to 2 pounds veal neck or rib bones
1 pound veal breast or shoulder
1 pound beef chuck
8 beef marrow bones
1 tablespoon salt
1 tablespoon whole black peppercorns

1. Peel the carrots and the fresh tomato (pages 30–31). Peel the onion and cut it in half.

2. Put all of the ingredients in a large stockpot and add enough cold water to cover by 2 inches. Cover the pot, place over high heat, and bring to a boil. Turn the heat down to very low, uncover, and use a skimmer or ladle to remove the scum that rises to the surface. Cover the pot and cook at a very gentle simmer for at least 3 hours.

3. If you will be serving the meats right away, lift them out of the pot, carve the chicken, slice the meats, and serve on a platter with a little of the broth to keep them moist.

4. Strain the broth into a large container and set aside to cool. Refrigerate for up to 2 days. The broth can also be frozen for up to 2 months. As soon as the broth has chilled and a layer of fat has solidified on the surface, take the broth out of the refrigerator and lift the fat off with a slotted spatula or spoon. Freeze in ice cube trays. Pop the cubes out of the trays and store them in resealable freezer bags in the freezer. The cubes are easier to thaw than broth frozen in larger containers, and they are convenient when you only need a small amount of broth.

Note: If you are not going to serve the meats right away or if you have leftovers, place the cooled meats in a container with enough broth to cover and refrigerate for up to 2 days. When you are ready to serve, reheat the meat in the broth.

VEGETABLES
AND SIDE DISHES

- **Artichokes Braised with Olive Oil and Garlic**
- **Whole Artichokes Braised Roman Style**
- **Vegetable Stew**
- **Gratinéed Cardoons**
- **Carrots Sautéed with Garlic and Parsley**
- **Eggplant Parmigiana**
- **Grilled Eggplant**
- **Eggplant Sautéed with Garlic and Parsley**
- **Fried Portobello Mushrooms**
- **Baked Stuffed Red and Yellow Peppers**
- **Smothered Red and Yellow Peppers**
- **Yellow Squash with Grape Tomatoes**
- **Zucchini Casserole**
- **Broccoli Rabe Sautéed with Olive Oil and Garlic**
- **Sautéed Swiss Chard with Olive Oil and Garlic**
- **Sautéed Mixed Greens**
- **Green Beans with Parmigiano**
- **Cannellini Beans with Savoy Cabbage and Fennel**
- **Fresh Cranberry Beans with Garlic and Sage**
- **Italian Mashed Potatoes**
- **Oven-Roasted Potatoes**
- **Savory Stewed Potatoes**
- **Polenta**

A vegetable dish is called *il contorno* in Italian, which means "that which contours or surrounds," because it is often served on the same plate with meat or fish. Although it may seem that vegetables play a supporting role, they never are an afterthought or simply plate decoration. Italians are masterful at preparing delectable vegetables, extracting more flavor than you ever thought possible. In choosing a vegetable to accompany a meat or fish dish, pair olive-oil–based vegetable dishes with meats and fish that are cooked with olive oil, and match butter-based dishes similarly. Also avoid serving a vegetable that is cooked with tomatoes with tomato-based meat and fish dishes.

ARTICHOKES BRAISED WITH OLIVE OIL AND GARLIC

Carciofi all'Olio e Aglio

Preparation time: 30 minutes
Total time from start to finish: 50 minutes

Serves 6

> 1 lemon
> 4 medium artichokes
> ½ small yellow onion
> 1 small clove garlic
> 3 to 4 sprigs flat-leaf Italian parsley
> 3 tablespoons extra virgin olive oil
> ¼ cup water
> Salt
> Freshly ground black pepper

1. Halve the lemon. Squeeze the juice from half the lemon into a medium bowl and fill the bowl halfway with cold water. Trim the artichokes as described on pages 34–35. Cut them into wedges about ½ inch thick and put them in the bowl of lemon water to prevent them from discoloring.

2. Peel and finely chop the onion and garlic. Finely chop enough of the parsley leaves to measure 1 tablespoon. Put the olive oil and onion in a medium braising pan over medium heat. Sauté, stirring occasionally, until the onion turns a rich golden color, about 5 minutes.

3. Add the garlic and parsley and stir for about 20 seconds. Drain the artichokes and add them to the pan along with ¼ cup water. Season with salt and pepper and cover the pan. Cook until the artichokes are tender, about 20 minutes. If all the water evaporates before the artichokes are done, add a little more water, a couple tablespoons at a time.

4. When the artichokes are tender, uncover the pan and simmer until any remaining water evaporates. Serve at once.

Note: The artichokes can be prepared several hours ahead of time and kept in the pan. Once refrigerated, they will not taste as fresh.

WHOLE ARTICHOKES BRAISED ROMAN STYLE

Carciofi alla Romana

These artichokes are striking. Cooked and served whole, stems still attached, they are entirely edible as all the tough parts have been removed. The technique for trimming them, which is described and illustrated on pages 34–35, is simple and should take 5 minutes per artichoke. Serve these artichokes either as a vegetable side dish or an appetizer.

Preparation time: 30 minutes
Total time from start to finish: 1 hour

Serves 4

> 1 lemon
> 4 large artichokes
> 1 small clove garlic
> 6 to 8 sprigs flat-leaf Italian parsley
> 6 to 8 fresh mint leaves
> Salt
> Freshly ground black pepper
> ¼ cup extra virgin olive oil

1. Halve the lemon. Squeeze the juice from half the lemon into a medium bowl and fill the bowl halfway with cold water. Trim the artichokes as described on pages 34–35 but do not cut off the stems. Leave each artichoke whole, trimming the stem while it is still attached. Put the artichokes in the bowl of lemon water to prevent them from discoloring.

2. Peel and finely chop the garlic. Finely chop enough of the parsley leaves to measure 2 tablespoons. Finely chop the mint. Mix the herbs and garlic in a small bowl. Season with salt and pepper. Drain the artichokes. Rub each artichoke with the herb mixture, both inside and out.

3. Pour the olive oil into a heavy-bottomed braising pan and add enough water to come ½ inch up the side of the pan. Place the artichokes in the pan with the stems pointing up. If the stems are taller than the sides of the pan, trim them so that the lid will fit snugly. Place the pan over medium heat, cover, and cook until the artichokes are tender, 15 to 20 minutes once the water begins simmering.

4. Uncover the pan, raise the heat to medium-high, and cook until all the water is evaporated and the tops of the leaves are lightly browned, 2 to 3 minutes. Some people serve the artichokes warm, but I prefer them at room temperature.

Note: The artichokes can be prepared several hours ahead of time and kept in the pan. Once refrigerated, they will not taste as fresh.

VEGETABLE STEW

Caponatina

In this classic Italian dish, vegetables are slowly stewed together to bring out the flavor of each ingredient to its fullest. Salt is added in stages, as described in Basic Techniques (pages 26–27), which helps bring out the flavor of each vegetable. *Caponatina* can be served as a side dish, an appetizer, or on toasted canapés as an hors d'oeuvre.

Preparation time: 25 minutes
Total time from start to finish: 1½ hours

Serves 6

> 1 medium yellow onion
> 3 tablespoons extra virgin olive oil
> Pinch crushed red pepper flakes
> Salt
> 1 small clove garlic
> 1 pound eggplant
> 1 yellow bell pepper
> 1 pound zucchini
> 1 pound ripe tomatoes *or* 2 cups canned whole peeled
>   tomatoes with their juice
> 12 basil leaves

1. Peel, halve, and thinly slice the onion crosswise. Put the onion, olive oil, and crushed red pepper in a 12-inch skillet over medium heat. Season lightly with salt and sauté, stirring occasionally, until the onion turns a rich golden color, about 10 minutes.

2. While the onion is sautéing, finely chop the garlic. Peel the eggplant and cut into 1-inch cubes. When the onion is ready, add the garlic and stir for a few seconds. Add the eggplant, season lightly with salt, and cover the pan. Cook until the eggplant starts to become tender but is not completely cooked through, about 10 minutes.

3. While the eggplant is cooking, core, seed, and peel the pepper (pages 31–32). Cut away any white pith inside the pepper and cut into 1 x ½-inch strips. Cut off the ends of the zucchini and cut into ½-inch dice. Put the pepper and zucchini in the pan, season with salt, and cook, covered, for about 5 minutes.

4. Peel the ripe tomatoes (pages 30–31) if using. Cut the fresh or canned tomatoes into ½-inch dice. Coarsely chop the basil. Add the tomatoes and basil to the pan and cook, uncovered, until all of the liquid is evaporated and the vegetables are tender, 15 to 20 minutes. Transfer to a serving bowl or platter and set aside to cool. Serve at room temperature.

Note: This dish can be made 1 to 2 days ahead and refrigerated. Remove from the refrigerator 1 to 2 hours before serving to bring the vegetables to room temperature.

GRATINÉED CARDOONS

Cardi Gratinati al Parmigiano

Although cardoons look like a head of celery, they are part of the artichoke family and their flavor is evocative of an artichoke heart. Cardoons are available in late fall and early winter; they show up at my local supermarket every year around the middle of November.

Preparation time: 15 minutes
Total time from start to finish: 45 minutes

Serves 6

> 1 cardoon
> Salt
> 1½ tablespoons butter
> ¼ cup freshly grated Parmigiano-Reggiano

1. Fill a pot with at least 6 quarts of water, place over high heat, and bring to a boil.

2. Separate the stalks of the cardoon from the heart and trim away any leaves. Cut a sliver from the top and bottom of each stalk. Use a vegetable peeler to peel the backs of the stalks to remove the outer layer of skin and any tough strings. Trim the heart so only the white inner part remains. Cut the stalks into 6-inch-long pieces and rinse in cold water.

3. Add 1 tablespoon salt to the boiling water and put in the cardoon. Cover the pot and boil until tender, 30 to 35 minutes.

4. Preheat the oven to 425° on convection heat, or 450° on regular bake.

5. Drain the cardoon and place it in a baking dish in a single layer. Season with salt, dot with the butter, and sprinkle the Parmigiano on top. Bake until the cheese melts and just begins to brown, 10 to 15 minutes. Serve hot.

Note: You can prepare the cardoon up until it is ready to bake a day ahead of time and keep it in the refrigerator. Let it warm to room temperature before baking.

CARROTS SAUTÉED WITH GARLIC AND PARSLEY

Carote all'Aglio e Prezzemolo

The classic combination of olive oil, garlic, and parsley, as well as patient, watchful cooking, produces these delectable carrots. The key is to cook the carrots longer than usual until they begin to shrivel up and become sweet.

Preparation time: 15 minutes
Total time from start to finish: 45 minutes

Serves 6

1½ pounds carrots
1 small clove garlic
10 to 12 sprigs flat-leaf Italian parsley
3 tablespoons extra virgin olive oil
Salt
Freshly ground black pepper

1. Peel the carrots and cut into 1½ x ¼-inch sticks.

2. Peel and finely chop the garlic. Finely chop enough of the parsley leaves to measure 3 tablespoons. Put the olive oil, garlic, and parsley in a large skillet and place over medium-high heat. Let the garlic and parsley sizzle briefly without letting the garlic brown, 1 to 2 minutes. Add the carrot sticks, season with salt and pepper, and stir to coat the carrots.

3. Add enough water to come about ¼ inch up the side of the pan and cook until all of the water is evaporated. Sauté the carrots for about 1 minute before adding a little more water. Continue this routine until the carrots are tender, 15 to 20 minutes total. Lower the heat to medium-low and sauté the carrots, stirring occasionally, until they start to shrivel and brown, about 10 minutes. Serve at once.

Note: The carrots can be made 1 to 2 days ahead of time and kept in the refrigerator.

EGGPLANT PARMIGIANA

Melanzane alla Parmigiana

One of the problems I've always had with this dish is that the fried eggplant was too oily, but I did not like to bake or grill the eggplant either because the flavor wasn't right. Although eggplant soaks up oil easily, ironically the more oil you fry it in, the less it absorbs. Also, once cooked, it usually releases most of the absorbed oil. So the trick, I discovered, is frying the eggplant in *a lot* of oil, at least 1 inch deep in the pan, and simply removing the excess oil after baking. Salting the eggplant before frying draws the bitterness out.

Preparation time: 40 minutes
Total time from start to finish: 2¼ hours

Serves 4 as a main course

> 2¾ pounds eggplants
> Salt
> 3 cups canned whole peeled tomatoes with their juice
> 1 tablespoon olive oil
> 8 ounces fresh whole-milk mozzarella
> 1 quart vegetable oil, or more depending on the size of the pan
> ⅓ cup freshly grated Parmigiano-Reggiano
> 15 basil leaves

1. Peel the eggplants and cut them lengthwise into ¼-inch slices. Place a layer of eggplant on the bottom and sides of a colander and sprinkle with salt. Top with another layer of eggplant and sprinkle with salt again. Continue until all of the eggplant is in the colander. Place a bowl on top of the eggplant with something in it to weight it down. Leave the colander in the sink for an hour while the salt draws out the eggplant's bitterness.

2. Coarsely chop the tomatoes and put them in a 10-inch skillet with the olive oil. Place over medium heat and season with salt. Cook until the tomatoes are reduced and no longer watery, 20 to 30 minutes. Remove from the heat and set aside.

3. Thinly slice the mozzarella.

4. Choose a deep sauté pan that will fit no more than 2 slices of eggplant and pour in the oil. If the pan is wider, you'll need more oil to come 1 inch up the side of the pan. Place over medium-high heat. Set a wire rack over a baking sheet or line a plate with paper towels.

5. While the oil is heating, begin patting the eggplant slices dry with paper towels. When the oil is hot enough to make the corner of an eggplant slice sizzle, carefully slip in 2 eggplant slices and fry until golden brown on one side, 1 to 2 minutes. Turn the slices over and brown on the other side. Lift the eggplant out of the pan, letting as much oil as possible drip back into the pan, then place on the wire rack or paper-towel-lined plate. Continue until all the eggplant is fried.

6. Preheat the oven to 400° on convection heat, or 425° on regular bake.

7. Put a layer of eggplant on the bottom of an 11 x 8-inch baking dish but not all the way to the edges to make it easier to remove the excess oil later. Spread one-fifth of the tomatoes over the eggplant, then place one-fifth of the mozzarella slices over the tomatoes. Sprinkle one-fifth of the Parmigiano on top. Tear 3 of the basil leaves into small pieces and sprinkle over the cheese. Repeat until you have 5 layers.

8. Bake for 20 minutes, then remove the dish from the oven. Tip the dish to the side and use a small ladle to scoop out as much oil as possible. Put the dish back in the oven and bake until golden brown on top, about 5 minutes. Take the dish out of the oven and scoop out any remaining oil in the pan. Let rest for 5 minutes before serving.

Note: You can prepare this dish 2 to 3 days ahead of time. Reheat in the oven at 350° or in a microwave.

GRILLED EGGPLANT

Melanzane alla Griglia

Not only is eggplant easy to prepare on the grill, but it is also a delicious accompaniment to grilled meat. Serve the eggplant half in one piece. Usually the skin is too tough to eat, so you scrape the flesh out with your knife and fork.

Total time: 30 minutes

Serves 6

>1 medium clove garlic
>6 to 8 sprigs flat-leaf Italian parsley
>Salt
>4 tablespoons extra virgin olive oil
>3 medium eggplants

1. Preheat a charcoal or gas grill.

2. Peel and finely chop the garlic. Finely chop enough of the parsley leaves to measure 2 tablespoons. Put the garlic and parsley in a small bowl. Season with salt, add 2 tablespoons of the olive oil, and mix well with a spoon.

3. Cut off the tops of the eggplants and cut them lengthwise in half. Score the cut side with a half dozen diagonal slashes about ½ inch deep (do not cut all the way down to the skin). Sprinkle with salt and drizzle with the remaining 2 tablespoons olive oil.

4. Grill the eggplants cut side down until they have grill marks, 1 to 2 minutes. Turn them over and spread the parsley mixture over each eggplant half. Grill, covered, until the flesh of the eggplant is tender, about 15 minutes. Serve hot or lukewarm.

EGGPLANT SAUTÉED WITH GARLIC AND PARSLEY

Melanzane al Funghetto

The classic Italian preparation for fresh porcini mushrooms is to sauté them with olive oil, garlic, and parsley. When other vegetables are prepared that way, they are often called *al funghetto,* meaning "mushroom style." To avoid using too much oil, cook the eggplant in a covered skillet so that the steam provides enough moisture to cook the eggplant.

Total time: 25 minutes

Serves 6

> 1½ pounds eggplants
> 1 medium clove garlic
> 6 to 8 sprigs flat-leaf Italian parsley
> ¼ cup extra virgin olive oil
> Salt

1. Peel the eggplants and cut into ¾-inch cubes.

2. Peel and finely chop the garlic. Finely chop enough of the parsley leaves to measure 2 tablespoons. Put the garlic, parsley, and olive oil in a 12-inch skillet and place over medium-high heat. When the garlic sizzles, after 1 to 2 minutes, add the eggplant and season with salt. Lower the heat to medium-low and cover the pan. Cook, stirring occasionally, until the eggplant is tender and lightly browned, 10 to 15 minutes.

3. Uncover the pan and cook for 1 to 2 minutes to evaporate any liquid in the pan. Serve hot.

FRIED PORTOBELLO MUSHROOMS

Funghi Fritti

Fried foods need not be heavy or oily. When done well, fried foods have a wonderful crispy outside with the flavor and moisture sealed inside. For a discussion on frying techniques, see pages 24–25. In Italy, fresh porcini mushrooms are sometimes prepared this way. Since fresh porcini are not easily available in the States, I use portobello mushrooms instead, with excellent results.

Total time: 20 minutes

Serves 6

> 1 pound portobello mushrooms
> About 3 cups vegetable oil
> 1 large egg
> ½ cup fine dry bread crumbs
> Salt

1. Trim the mushroom stems and brush away any soil. Cut the mushrooms into ½-inch-thick slices.

2. Put enough vegetable oil in a medium skillet to come at least ½ inch up the side of the pan. Place over medium-high heat. Set a wire rack over a baking sheet or line a plate with paper towels.

3. Put the egg in a bowl wide enough to hold a mushroom slice and whisk until the white and the yolk are well mixed together. Put the bread crumbs on a plate. Dip one mushroom slice at a time in the egg, then coat it with the bread crumbs.

4. When the oil is hot enough to make a corner of the mushroom slice sizzle, carefully slide in as many breaded pieces as will comfortably fit in the pan. When the bottom is lightly browned, after about 1 minute, turn the slices over and brown the other side. Lift the mushrooms out of the pan, letting as

much oil as possible drip back into the pan, then lay them on the wire rack or paper-towel-lined plate. Sprinkle with salt and serve at once.

BAKED STUFFED RED AND YELLOW PEPPERS

Peperoni Ripieni al Forno

These savory stuffed peppers make a great side dish or vegetarian meal. Because they are served at room temperature, they are also perfect for a buffet.

Preparation time: 25 minutes
Total time from start to finish: 1 hour 25 minutes

Serves 4

> 1 slice white sandwich bread
> 2 tablespoons whole milk
> 1 red bell pepper
> 1 yellow bell pepper
> 8 ounces ripe tomatoes
> 10 Niçoise olives
> 4 ounces medium-aged pecorino cheese
> 8 basil leaves
> 1 tablespoon extra virgin olive oil, plus a little for the baking dish
> Salt

1. Preheat the oven to 350° on the regular bake setting.

2. Trim the crust from the bread and put the bread in a small bowl with the milk.

3. Cut the peppers lengthwise in half, then core, seed, and peel them (pages 31–32).

4. Peel the tomatoes (pages 30–31), remove the seeds, cut into ¼-inch dice, and put them in a medium bowl. Cut the flesh of the olives away from the pits, chop, and add to the tomatoes. Cut half of the pecorino cheese into ¼-inch dice and add to the bowl. Chop the basil and put it in the bowl. Squeeze the bread in your hand to get a smooth pulp and add it to the bowl. Add the olive oil, season with salt, and thoroughly mix all the ingredients.

5. Coat the bottom of a baking pan with olive oil and place the pepper halves in the pan. Divide the filling among the 4 pepper halves. Thinly slice the remaining pecorino cheese and top the stuffed peppers with it. Bake until the cheese begins to brown and the peppers are quite tender, about 1 hour. Serve warm or at room temperature.

Note: You can make the peppers 1 to 2 days ahead and keep them in the refrigerator. Bring them to room temperature or reheat them in the oven or microwave before serving.

SMOTHERED RED AND YELLOW PEPPERS

La Peperonata

More of a sauce than a vegetable dish, *peperonata* is the classic accompaniment to *bollito misto* (page 338). It is also great with grilled steaks, lamb chops, or pork chops, especially with some good crusty bread. Do not be concerned about overcooking the peppers. When the *peperonata* is done, the peppers should be so tender they almost melt in your mouth. The pinch of crushed red pepper is meant to give the dish a little liveliness. If you'd like it spicier, increase the amount.

Preparation time: 25 minutes
Total time from start to finish: 45 minutes

Serves 6

> 1 medium yellow onion
> 3 tablespoons extra virgin olive oil
> Pinch crushed red pepper flakes
> Salt
> 2 red bell peppers
> 2 yellow bell peppers
> 1 pound ripe tomatoes

1. Peel, halve, and thinly slice the onion crosswise. Put the onion in a 12-inch skillet with the olive oil and crushed red pepper. Season lightly with salt and place over medium-high heat. Sauté, stirring occasionally, until the onion begins to brown, about 5 minutes. Reduce the heat to medium-low and cook until the onion is softened completely, 10 to 15 minutes.

2. While the onion is sautéing, core, seed, and peel the peppers (pages 31–32). Cut away any white pith inside the peppers and cut into narrow strips about 1½ inches long.

3. Raise the heat under the onion to medium high and add the peppers. Season lightly with salt and sauté, without stirring too often, until the peppers are tender and begin to brown, 8 to 10 minutes.

4. While the peppers are cooking, peel the tomatoes (pages 30–31) and coarsely chop. Once the peppers are tender and lightly browned, lower the heat to medium and add the tomatoes. Sprinkle lightly with salt. Cook until all the liquid the tomatoes release evaporates, 15 to 20 minutes. Serve hot.

   Note: This dish can be made 1 to 2 days ahead and kept in the refrigerator. Gently reheat with a couple tablespoons water.

YELLOW SQUASH
WITH GRAPE TOMATOES

Zucchine Gialle con i Ciliegini

While shopping together one day, my then four-year-old daughter, Gabriella, presented me with a package of yellow squash and a box of Florida grape tomatoes saying, "I want this for dinner, Papa." The simplicity of using only onions and marjoram, and patient sautéing to bring out the sweetness of the squash and grape tomatoes, makes this recipe distinctively Italian. This dish has become a family favorite.

Preparation time: 15 minutes
Total time from start to finish: 45 minutes

Serves 4

> 1 medium yellow onion
> 2 tablespoons extra virgin olive oil
> 2 to 3 sprigs fresh marjoram
> 1½ pounds yellow squash
> 8 ounces grape or sweet cherry tomatoes
> Salt
> Freshly ground black pepper

1. Peel, halve, and thinly slice the onion lengthwise. Place the onion and olive oil in a large skillet over medium-high heat. Chop enough of the marjoram leaves to measure 2 teaspoons and add it to the pan. Sauté, stirring occasionally, until the onion turns a rich golden color, 8 to 10 minutes.

2. While the onion is sautéing, trim the ends of the yellow squash. Slice each squash lengthwise in half, then crosswise into ¼-inch-thick half-moons. When the onion is ready, add the squash to the pan and sauté, stirring occasionally, until it is tender and begins to brown, 15 to 20 minutes.

3. While the squash is cooking, cut the tomatoes in half. When the squash is done, add the tomatoes, season with salt and pepper, and cook until the tomatoes begin to break down, 5 to 10 minutes. Serve at once.

Note: You can make this dish several hours ahead of time and keep it in the pan. When ready to serve, warm it over low heat. It will lose its freshness if kept longer or if refrigerated.

ZUCCHINI CASSEROLE

Teglia di Zucchine al Forno

This dish can be served warm or at room temperature, which makes it well suited for a buffet.

Preparation time: 30 minutes
Total time from start to finish: 50 minutes

Serves 6

>2 pounds small zucchini
>2 tablespoons butter, plus extra for greasing the baking dish
>Salt
>Freshly ground black pepper
>1 medium clove garlic
>3 to 4 sprigs flat-leaf Italian parsley
>2 large eggs
>2 tablespoons freshly grated Parmigiano-Reggiano
>1 tablespoon heavy cream
>1 tablespoon fine dry bread crumbs
>6 ounces Fontina cheese

1. Trim the ends of the zucchini and slice into ¼-inch rounds. Put the butter in a 12-inch skillet and place over medium heat. When the butter is hot and just beginning to turn color, add the zucchini, season with salt and pepper, and sauté, stirring occasionally, until lightly browned and tender, about 15 minutes.

2. While the zucchini are sautéing, peel and finely chop the garlic. Finely chop enough of the parsley leaves to measure 1 tablespoon. Beat the eggs in a medium bowl. Add the garlic, parsley, Parmigiano, and cream to the eggs. Season lightly with salt and pepper and mix thoroughly.

3. Preheat the oven to 350° on the regular bake setting. Smear the bottom and sides of an 8 x 6-inch baking dish with butter and dust it with the bread crumbs.

4. Add the zucchini to the bowl with the eggs and mix thoroughly. Put a layer of the zucchini mixture on the bottom of the dish. Thinly slice the Fontina cheese and place a layer over the zucchini. Continue alternating layers of zucchini and cheese, ending with zucchini on the top layer. Bake until the top is golden brown and the egg no longer looks runny, about 20 minutes. Serve hot, warm, or even at room temperature.

> **Note:** This dish can be made 1 day ahead and kept in the refrigerator. Reheat in a 350° oven before serving, even if serving warm or at room temperature, so that the casserole won't be chilled in the center.

BROCCOLI RABE SAUTÉED WITH OLIVE OIL AND GARLIC

Broccoletti all'Aglio e Olio

This classic Italian recipe for broccoli rabe (also known as rapini) can be made with broccoli or broccolini as well. When using broccoli, you'll need to peel the tough outer part of the stalk. Broccolini needs only to have its stems trimmed.

Preparation time: 25 minutes
Total time from start to finish: 45 minutes

Serves 6

> 1 bunch broccoli rabe, about 1 pound
> 1 medium clove garlic
> Salt
> 3 tablespoons extra virgin olive oil
> Freshly ground black pepper

1. Fill a pot with at least 4 quarts water, place over high heat, and bring to a boil.

2. Trim the bottom of the broccoli rabe stems and rinse in cold water. Peel and finely chop the garlic.

3. Add 1 tablespoon salt to the boiling water and put in the broccoli rabe. Cook until the stems are tender, usually no more than 5 minutes. Drain well in a colander.

4. Put the olive oil and garlic in a 12-inch skillet and place over medium-high heat. When the garlic begins to sizzle, add the broccoli rabe. Season with salt and pepper and sauté, stirring occasionally, until the broccoli rabe is fully flavored with the olive oil and garlic, about 10 minutes. Serve at once.

SAUTÉED SWISS CHARD
WITH OLIVE OIL AND GARLIC

Biete all'Aglio e Olio

Students in my cooking classes often ask why I boil greens before sautéing them. The reason is that if you put raw greens, such as Swiss chard or spinach, directly in a skillet with the olive oil and garlic, they release liquid and simmer in their juices rather than sauté. As that liquid cooks down, it gives the greens a strong and somewhat bitter flavor. Italians sauté already cooked greens so they simply take on the flavor of the oil and garlic. You end up with a much sweeter-tasting vegetable.

Total time: 35 minutes

Serves 6

> 2 pounds Swiss chard
> Salt
> 3 medium cloves garlic
> 3 tablespoons extra virgin olive oil
> Freshly ground black pepper

1. Put 1 quart water in a large pot, place over high heat, and bring to a boil.

2. Separate the leaves from the stalks of the Swiss chard. Cut the stalks into 1½ x ¼-inch strips and cut the leaves crosswise into 2 or 3 pieces. Rinse the leaves and stalks separately in cold water.

3. Add 1 tablespoon salt to the boiling water and put in the Swiss chard stalks. Cook for 1 minute, then add the leaves. Cook until the Swiss chard is tender, 4 to 5 minutes. Drain in a colander and squeeze out as much water as possible by pressing on the leaves with a spoon.

4. Lightly crush and peel the garlic. Put the garlic and olive oil in a large skillet over medium-high heat. Brown the garlic on all sides, being careful not to

burn it, then remove and discard it. Slide the Swiss chard into the pan carefully so as not to splatter the hot oil. Season with salt and pepper and sauté, stirring occasionally, until the chard is well flavored with the oil and garlic, about 6 minutes. Serve at once.

SAUTÉED MIXED GREENS

Verdure Saltate all'Olio e Aglio

Using an assortment of greens ranging from sweet to slightly bitter makes for a delicious vegetable dish. Experiment with different combinations. The recipe below uses Savoy cabbage for sweetness and mustard greens for their slight bitterness. To tip the scale a little more on the bitter side, you could use broccoli rabe instead. Use a fresh batch of water for each green, so that each vegetable maintains its individual flavor.

Total time: 40 minutes

Serves 6

> 1 pound Swiss chard
> 8 ounces mustard greens
> 1 pound Savoy cabbage
> Salt
> 1 large clove garlic
> 5 tablespoons extra virgin olive oil
> Freshly ground black pepper

1. Put 1 quart water in a large pot, place over high heat, and bring to a boil.

2. Separate the Swiss chard leaves from the stalks and rinse separately in cold water. Rinse the mustard greens. Cut the Savoy cabbage into quarters.

3. Add 1 tablespoon salt to the boiling water and put in the Swiss chard stalks. Cook for 1 minute, then add the leaves. Cook until the Swiss chard is tender, 4 to 5 minutes. Drain in a colander and squeeze out as much water as possible by pressing on the leaves with a spoon.

4. Refill the pot with at least 4 quarts water, bring to a boil, add salt, and cook the mustard greens until tender, 5 to 6 minutes. Drain well and repeat the process to cook the cabbage.

5. Coarsely chop all of the vegetables together.

6. Peel and finely chop the garlic and put it with the olive oil in a 12-inch skillet over medium heat. Let the garlic sizzle for a few seconds but do not brown. Add the greens, season with salt and pepper, and sauté, stirring often, for about 15 minutes. Serve at once.

Note: You can reduce the preparation time to 40 minutes by using 3 separate pots and cooking the vegetables simultaneously.

GREEN BEANS WITH PARMIGIAN

Fagiolini al Burro e Formaggio

Total time: 20 minutes

Serves 6

    1 pound green beans
    Salt
    2 tablespoons butter
    ¼ cup freshly grated Parmigiano-Reggiano

1. Fill a pot with at least 4 quarts water, place over high heat, and bring to a boil.

2. Rinse the green beans, then snap or cut both ends off. Add 1 tablespoon salt to the boiling water and put in the beans. Cook until the beans are tender, 6 to 8 minutes. Drain and set aside.

3. Put the butter in a 10-inch skillet and place over medium-high heat. When the butter is hot and just beginning to turn color, add the green beans. Season with salt and sauté, stirring occasionally, for 5 minutes.

4. Sprinkle the grated cheese over the beans and remove the pan from the heat. Leave the beans in the pan for 1 to 2 minutes, without stirring, to allow the cheese to partially melt. Serve hot.

CANNELLINI BEANS
WITH SAVOY CABBAGE AND FENNEL

Fagioli con la Verza e Finocchi

This dish is substantial enough for a meal and is entirely vegetarian.

Preparation time: 20 minutes
Total time from start to finish: 50 minutes

Serves 4 as a main course or 6 to 8 as a side dish

> ½ medium yellow onion
> 1 small garlic clove
> 2 tablespoons extra virgin olive oil
> ½ small Savoy cabbage
> Salt
> ½ medium fennel bulb
> 1 cup canned whole peeled tomatoes with their juice
> 1½ cups drained canned cannellini beans
> Freshly ground black pepper

1. Peel and finely chop the onion and garlic. Put the onion in a 4-quart saucepan with the olive oil. Place over medium-high heat and sauté, stirring occasionally, until the onion turns a rich golden color, about 5 minutes.

2. While the onion is sautéing, cut the core from the Savoy cabbage and finely shred the leaves. When the onion is done, add the garlic and stir for about 1 minute. Add the cabbage and season lightly with salt. Lower the heat to medium and cook until the cabbage wilts, 5 to 10 minutes.

3. While the cabbage is cooking, cut the fennel lengthwise into 2 quarters, then thinly slice crosswise. Once the cabbage is wilted, add the fennel. Coarsely chop the tomatoes and add them to the pan. Add the beans and season with salt and pepper. Cook until the tomatoes are reduced and no longer watery and the cabbage and fennel are tender, 25 to 30 minutes. Serve hot with good crusty bread.

Note: This dish can be made 1 to 2 days ahead and kept in the refrigerator.

FRESH CRANBERRY BEANS WITH GARLIC AND SAGE

Borlotti all'Olio, Salvia, e Aglio

Now that fresh cranberry beans are more widely available in the States, even in supermarkets, you can enjoy one of the delicacies of central Italy: the rich, satisfying full flavor of fresh beans braised with olive oil, garlic, and sage. Canned beans are not a viable substitute here, because they do not cook long enough to fully absorb the flavor of the garlic and sage.

Preparation time: 15 minutes
Total time from start to finish: 1¼ hours

Serves 6

> 2 pounds fresh cranberry beans in the pod
> 3 medium cloves garlic
> 4 tablespoons extra virgin olive oil
> 12 fresh sage leaves
> Salt
> Freshly ground black pepper

1. Shell the beans.

2. Lightly crush and peel the garlic cloves and put them in a large saucepan. Add 2 tablespoons of the olive oil and place over medium-high heat. When the garlic just begins to brown, add the sage and the beans. Season lightly with salt and stir until they are well coated. Add enough water to come about 1 inch above the beans and bring to a boil. Adjust the heat so that the

water simmers gently, cover the pan, and cook until tender, about 1 hour. If all the water evaporates before the beans are done, add just enough water to cover as often as necessary. If the beans are almost done and there is a lot of liquid left in the pan, raise the heat to medium-high and finish cooking uncovered to allow the excess liquid to evaporate.

3. Discard the garlic cloves and transfer the beans to a serving platter. They are best served warm but are also good at room temperature. Just before serving, add the remaining 2 tablespoons olive oil, season with salt and pepper, and toss well.

> **Note:** The beans can be prepared 1 to 2 days ahead and kept in the refrigerator. Gently reheat, adding 1 to 2 tablespoons water if necessary.

ITALIAN MASHED POTATOES

Puré di Patate

The key to smooth, silky mashed potatoes is using a food mill rather than a potato ricer. Parmigiano-Reggiano gives these mashed potatoes a distinctively Italian flavor.

Preparation time: 15 minutes
Total time from start to finish: 40 minutes

Serves 6

> 1½ pounds Yukon Gold or white boiling potatoes
> 3 tablespoons butter
> 1 cup whole milk
> Salt
> ¼ cup freshly grated Parmigiano-Reggiano

1. Scrub the potatoes and put them in a medium saucepan. Add enough water to cover the potatoes by 1 inch and place over high heat. Cover the pan and bring to a boil, then adjust the heat so that the water simmers. Cook until the potatoes are tender when pierced, about 30 minutes. Try not to pierce them too often or they may become waterlogged.

2. When the potatoes are almost done, melt the butter in a saucepan large enough to accommodate the potatoes over low heat. Remove from the heat. Put the milk in a small saucepan over medium-low heat and heat to just under a boil. When the milk releases steam when stirred, remove it from the heat.

3. Drain the potatoes and peel them as soon as possible. Mash them through the medium disk of a food mill into the pot with the melted butter. Place the pot over low heat and stir vigorously with a wooden spoon to incorporate the butter. Season with salt, add half of the milk, and mix thoroughly. Add the Parmigiano, mix well, and add the rest of the milk. Stir vigorously until the potatoes are smooth and silky, 1 to 2 minutes. Serve at once.

OVEN-ROASTED POTATOES

Patate Arrosto

Preparation time: 15 minutes
Total time from start to finish: 1 hour

Serves 6

> 2 pounds red or white creamer potatoes
> 3 medium cloves garlic
> 1 tablespoon fresh rosemary leaves
> 3 tablespoons extra virgin olive oil
> Salt
> Freshly ground black pepper

1. Preheat the oven to 425° on convection heat or 450° on regular bake.

2. Scrub the potatoes with a vegetable brush under cold water. Cut the potatoes into approximately ¾-inch cubes, place in a bowl, and cover with cold water to prevent the potatoes from turning brown.

3. Drain the potatoes and pat them with a cloth towel to dry them as much as possible. Place the potatoes in a baking pan large enough to accommodate them snugly in a single layer (some overlap is fine). Lightly crush and peel the garlic cloves and add them to the potatoes with the rosemary and olive oil. Season generously with salt and pepper. Stir to coat the potatoes with the olive oil.

4. Bake until the potatoes are tender and have formed a nice brown crust, 40 to 45 minutes. You can check on the potatoes periodically but it is not necessary to turn them. Serve hot.

> *Note:* You can prepare the potatoes a few hours ahead of time, set aside at room temperature, and reheat them in the oven for about 10 minutes when ready to serve.

SAVORY STEWED POTATOES

Patate Saporite

Total time: 35 minutes

Serves 4

> 1½ pounds Yukon Gold or large red potatoes
> 3 medium cloves garlic
> 2 tablespoons extra virgin olive oil
> 4 anchovy fillets
> Salt
> Freshly ground black pepper
> 1 cup canned whole peeled tomatoes with their juice
> 1 tablespoon capers

1. Peel the potatoes and cut into 1-inch cubes. Put them in a bowl and cover with cold water to prevent the potatoes from turning brown.

2. Lightly crush and peel the garlic cloves and put them in a 10-inch skillet with the olive oil. Place over medium-high heat and sauté until the garlic is lightly browned on all sides, then remove and discard the garlic cloves.

3. Coarsely chop the anchovies and add them to the pan. Cook, stirring, for 1 minute or less until they are mostly dissolved. Drain the potatoes and add them to the pan. Season with salt and pepper and sauté for about 2 minutes, stirring occasionally.

4. While the potatoes are sautéing, coarsely chop the canned tomatoes. Add them to the potatoes, lower the heat to medium-low, and cover the pan. Cook until the potatoes are tender, 15 to 20 minutes, turning the potatoes approximately every 5 minutes.

5. Coarsely chop the capers, add to the potatoes, and stir for about 30 seconds. Serve hot.

Note: This dish can be made 1 to 2 days ahead and kept in the refrigerator. Wait to add the capers until ready to serve. Reheat over low heat with a couple tablespoons water.

POLENTA

In the Veneto and adjoining Friuli regions polenta is as essential to a meal as pasta or bread in other regions. It is a perfect accompaniment to the savory sauces of the regions' many meat and seafood stews. Polenta is also delicious on its own with Gorgonzola, or butter and Parmigiano-Reggiano. It can be served either soft and steamy as soon as it is done, or in rectangular or triangular slabs that are cooled and then grilled or sometimes fried.

Polenta has a reputation for being labor intensive, demanding constant stirring for at least 40 minutes. Actually it's possible to make excellent polenta that is far superior to "instant" polenta with only occasional stirring. Although it still needs to cook for 35 to 40 minutes, you are free to attend to other things. Use cornmeal imported from Italy, not because the corn is necessarily better but because the grind is coarser, which is best suited to polenta.

Total time: 45 minutes

Serves 6

  8 cups water
  1 tablespoon salt
  2 cups coarse yellow cornmeal, preferably imported from Italy

1. Put the water in a 4-quart heavy-bottomed sauce pan, cover, and bring to a boil over high heat.

2. Add the salt to the boiling water and lower the heat to medium. Pour in the cornmeal in a thin, steady stream, while stirring constantly with a wooden

spoon. Continue stirring steadily for 2 minutes after all the cornmeal has been added, then cover and cook for 10 minutes. Stir again for 2 minutes, then cover and cook for another 10 minutes. Repeat a third time. Do not be concerned if a thin layer of cornmeal sticks to the bottom of the pan. After the third time, stir for 3 to 4 minutes. The polenta is done when it forms a mass that separates easily from the sides of the pot when stirred. Serve hot.

GRILLED OR FRIED POLENTA

Coat an 11 x 9-inch baking dish with cold water and pour the polenta into it. Let the polenta chill completely in the refrigerator. Place a cutting board over the baking dish, then flip it over, letting the polenta settle onto the cutting board. Cut the polenta into 2-inch rectangles or triangles. Grill over a hot fire until the polenta has grill marks on both sides, or fry in plenty of vegetable oil until golden brown (see pages 24–25 for how to fry). Serve hot.

SALADS

- **Arugula, Fennel, and Avocado Salad**
- **Asparagus Salad**
- **Green Beans with Olive Oil and Vinegar**
- **Swiss Chard with Olive Oil and Lemon**
- **Fresh Beet Salad**
- **Very Simple Potato Salad**
- **Savory Tomato Salad**
- **Tuna and Bean Salad**
- **Bottarga Salad**
- **Sardinian Bread Salad**

A simple Italian salad generally consists of one or more varieties of lettuce to which one or more of the following can be added: arugula, radicchio, grated carrots, sliced cucumber, sliced fennel, and tomatoes. I personally like to include red or yellow peppers and avocado as well. The salad course is normally served after the meat or fish course and is meant to refresh and cleanse the palate.

Italian salads are dressed just before serving, not with a premixed dressing, but simply by seasoning with a few basic ingredients. The recipe for dressing an Italian salad comes in the form of a proverb which says you need four people to dress a salad: a wise person for the salt, a generous person for the extra virgin olive oil, a stingy person for the red wine vinegar, and a patient person to toss it until every leaf is evenly coated. Sometimes we substitute lemon for the red wine vinegar, and for special occasions we might call on a fifth, wealthy person for some balsamic vinegar. Sometimes cooked vegetables are dressed "salad style" with oil and vinegar and are served either alongside the meat course or after it. Some of the salads in this chapter are a bit more substantial and are well suited for a buffet, as an antipasto, or as a light lunch.

ARUGULA, FENNEL, AND AVOCADO SALAD

Insalata di Rucola, Finocchio, e Avocado

Arugula and fennel are typical Italian ingredients, and avocado is becoming more and more popular in Italy. I particularly like this contrast of flavors and textures. The spicy arugula, the crunchy, refreshing fennel, and the creamy sweet avocado complement each other perfectly.

Total time: 15 minutes

Serves 4

> 4 ounces arugula
> 1 large or 2 small fennel bulbs
> 1 ripe avocado
> Salt
> 4 to 5 tablespoons extra virgin olive oil
> 3 tablespoons fresh lemon juice
> 2 ounces Parmigiano-Reggiano

1. Rinse and dry the arugula and remove any thick stems. Place it in a salad bowl.

2. Cut off the tops of the fennel where they meet the bulb and discard them. Pare any bruised parts from the bulb and remove a thin slice from the bottom. Cut the bulb in half lengthwise, then very thinly slice crosswise. Add to the arugula.

3. Cut the avocado lengthwise in half and twist it to separate it from the pit. Remove the peel, then cut the flesh into half-moon slices. Add to the bowl.

4. Season with salt, enough olive oil to coat all the ingredients, and the lemon juice. Toss gently but thoroughly. Shave the Parmigiano using a vegetable peeler and sprinkle the shavings over the salad. Serve at once.

ASPARAGUS SALAD

Asparagi in Insalata

A vegetable served *in insalata* means it is dressed with oil and vinegar like a basic salad and served usually at room temperature. Many people are convinced of the superiority of thin asparagus. I prefer the thicker, meatier stalks, especially when prepared simply as in this recipe. Trimming and peeling the asparagus makes the entire stalk tender and edible.

Preparation time: 20 minutes
Total time from start to finish: 45 minutes

Serves 6

> 2 pounds asparagus
> Salt
> 2 tablespoons red wine vinegar
> 3 to 4 tablespoons extra virgin olive oil

1. Fill a deep 10-inch skillet halfway with water, place it over high heat, and bring to a boil.

2. Cut off the woody bottom of the asparagus, then peel the bottom third of the stalks.

3. Add 1 tablespoon salt to the boiling water and slide in the asparagus. Cook until tender, 5 to 7 minutes. The asparagus is done when it bends easily when waved back and forth but remains fairly straight when held still. Transfer the asparagus to a platter and set aside to cool to room temperature.

4. Drain off any water on the platter. Season the asparagus lightly with salt and add the vinegar and enough olive oil to coat the asparagus. Gently turn the asparagus in the dressing and serve.

> *Note:* You can prepare the asparagus several hours ahead of time but do not refrigerate.

GREEN BEANS WITH OLIVE OIL AND VINEGAR

Fagiolini in Insalata

Preparation time: 15 minutes
Total time from start to finish: 45 minutes

Serves 6

> 1 pound green beans
> Salt
> 3 to 4 tablespoons extra virgin olive oil
> 1 tablespoon red wine vinegar

1. Fill a pot with at least 4 quarts water, place over high heat, and bring to a boil.

2. Rinse the green beans in cold water, then snap or cut both ends off. Add 1 tablespoon salt to the boiling water and put the green beans in. Cook until the beans are tender, 6 to 8 minutes. Drain the beans and set aside on a platter to cool to room temperature.

3. Season lightly with salt, enough olive oil to coat the beans well, and the vinegar. Toss thoroughly and serve.

Note: You can prepare the green beans several hours ahead of time but do not refrigerate.

SWISS CHARD
WITH OLIVE OIL AND LEMON

Biete all'Olio e Limone

Since the chard stalks take a little longer to cook than the leaves, I hold the leaves back and add them after the stalks have cooked a bit by themselves.

Total time: 20 minutes

Serves 6

> **2 pounds Swiss chard**
> **Salt**
> **3 tablespoons extra virgin olive oil**
> **1 tablespoon fresh lemon juice**

1. Put 1 quart water in a large pot, place over high heat, and bring to a boil.

2. Separate the leaves from the stalks of the Swiss chard. Cut the stalks into 1½ x ¼-inch strips and cut the leaves crosswise in two or three pieces. Rinse the leaves and stalks separately in cold water.

3. Add 1 tablespoon salt to the boiling water and put in the Swiss chard stalks. Cook for 1 minute, then add the leaves. Cook until the Swiss chard is tender, 4 to 5 minutes. Drain in a colander and squeeze out as much water as possible by pressing on the leaves with a spoon. Transfer the chard to a shallow serving bowl and set aside to cool to room temperature.

4. Season the chard lightly with salt and toss with the olive oil and lemon juice. Serve at once.

FRESH BEET SALAD

Bietole in Insalata

If you have ever wondered what to do with those bunches of fresh beets at the market, you'll be amazed at how easy they are to prepare and how delicious they are.

Preparation time: 10 minutes
Total time from start to finish: 2¼ hours

Serves 6

> 6 medium beets with greens
> Salt
> 3 tablespoons extra virgin olive oil
> 1 tablespoon red wine vinegar

1. Preheat the oven to 400°.

2. Rinse the beets under cold water, then cut the greens from the beets and set aside. Put the wet root bulbs on a sheet of heavy-duty aluminum foil and seal them in a pouch, allowing enough space inside for the steam to circulate. Place the pouch on a baking sheet and bake until the beets are tender when pierced with a toothpick, about 1½ hours.

3. While the beets are baking, fill a pot that will comfortably hold the beet tops with water, place over high heat, and bring to a boil.

4. When the water in the pot is boiling, add 1 tablespoon salt and put the greens in. Cook until tender, 10 to 15 minutes. Drain in a colander and squeeze out as much water as possible by pressing on the leaves with a spoon.

5. When the beets are cool enough to handle, trim the tops and bottoms and peel them. The skin should come off easily using your fingers. Cut the beets lengthwise in half, then slice into half-moons. Put the beets on a serving platter.

6. Cut the greens into bite-sized pieces and add them to the platter. Sprinkle generously with salt, add the oil and vinegar, and toss gently. The beets are best served lukewarm or at room temperature.

Note: The beets can be baked 1 to 2 days ahead and kept in the refrigerator. Take them out of the refrigerator at least 1 hour before serving to let them warm to room temperature. The greens are best served within a few hours of being cooked.

VERY SIMPLE POTATO SALAD

Patate Lesse in Insalata

This is called a salad because the potatoes are seasoned the same way Italians dress a green salad. I use red potatoes because of their smooth creamy texture, and since I peel them, I prefer the large red ones. With so few ingredients, it is essential that they all be very good. Make sure you use an excellent extra virgin olive oil, a rich red wine vinegar, and even the salt should ideally be a premium coarse sea salt, such as *fleur de sel.*

Preparation time: 5 minutes
Total time from start to finish: about 45 minutes

Serves 6

> 6 large red potatoes, about 2 pounds
> Premium coarse sea salt
> 5 to 6 tablespoons extra virgin olive oil
> 2 tablespoons red wine vinegar

1. Scrub the potatoes, put them in a pot, and add enough water to cover by 1 inch. Place over high heat and bring to a boil. Lower the heat so that the water simmers and cook until the potatoes are tender when pierced with a fork or cake tester, 30 to 35 minutes. Try not to pierce them too often or they may become waterlogged.

2. Drain the potatoes and peel them as soon as possible; the hotter the potatoes are the easier they are to peel. Slice the potatoes into ¼-inch-thick rounds and lay them out on a serving platter so they are just slightly overlapping. Drizzle with the vinegar. Just before serving, sprinkle generously with salt, then drizzle with enough olive oil to coat the potatoes. Serve either warm or at room temperature.

Note: You can prepare the potatoes several hours ahead but do not refrigerate.

SAVORY TOMATO SALAD

Insalata di Pomodori Saporita

Assemble the salad just before serving or the liquid tomatoes release when salted will turn this into a soup.

Preparation time: 25 minutes
Total time from start to finish: 45 minutes

Serves 6

> 1½ pounds ripe tomatoes
> 6 Kalamata olives
> 4 Sicilian-style green olives
> 3 anchovy fillets
> 1 tablespoon capers
> Salt
> ¼ cup extra virgin olive oil
> 1 tablespoon red wine vinegar

1. Halve the tomatoes lengthwise, remove the core, and cut into bite-size wedges. Put the tomatoes in a serving bowl.

2. Slice the flesh of the olives from the pits. Chop the anchovies.

3. Add the olives, anchovies, and capers to the tomatoes and season with salt. Add the oil and vinegar, toss well, and serve at once.

TUNA AND BEAN SALAD

Insalata di Tonno e Fagioli

Fresh or canned cranberry beans (*borlotti* in Italian) are the ideal bean to use here. Look for a premium canned tuna packed in olive oil, ideally *ventresca* (pages 14–15), not the flavorless tuna packed in water. This salad is substantial enough to be a light lunch.

Preparation time: 20 minutes if using fresh beans, 10 minutes if using
       canned
Total time from start to finish: 45 minutes if using fresh beans,
       20 minutes if using canned

Serves 4

> 3 pounds fresh cranberry beans in the pod *or* 2 cups drained
>   canned cranberry or cannellini beans
> Salt
> ½ small red onion
> 7 ounces canned tuna packed in olive oil
> Freshly ground black pepper
> ¼ cup extra virgin olive oil
> 1 tablespoon red wine vinegar

1. If using fresh beans, fill a pot with at least 4 quarts of water, place over high heat, and bring to a boil. Shell the beans. Add 1 tablespoon salt to the boiling water and put in the beans. Cook until tender, 25 to 30 minutes. Drain the beans and transfer to a serving bowl. Set aside to cool. If using canned beans, place them in a serving bowl.

2. Peel and thinly slice the red onion crosswise, put it in a separate bowl, and cover with cold water. Soak for 10 to 15 minutes.

3. Lift the tuna out of the can, break up the chunks into large flakes with a fork, and add to the beans. Drain the red onion and add it to the serving bowl. Sea-

son with salt and pepper. Add the olive oil and vinegar and toss thoroughly but gently so as not to mash the beans. Serve at room temperature.

Note: You can assemble the salad up to 1 day ahead and keep it in the refrigerator. Wait to add the onion and to season it until just before serving.

BOTTARGA SALAD

Insalata di Bottarga

Bottarga (page 20), pressed and salted dried mullet or tuna roe, is a Sardinian specialty and is found in many dishes including pastas, appetizers, and salads. Here its rich aroma contrasts wonderfully with the spiciness of red radishes and arugula and the fragrance of citrus. Raw artichokes provide a delightful crunch.

Total time: 20 minutes

Serves 4

> 1 lemon
> 1 medium to large artichoke
> 3 ounces arugula
> 6 red radishes
> 1 orange
> ½ small red onion
> 1 ounce *bottarga*
> Salt
> 3 to 4 tablespoons extra virgin olive oil

1. Cut the lemon in half and squeeze the juice into a medium bowl. Measure 1 tablespoon and set it aside. Add about 2 cups water to the lemon juice in the bowl. Trim the artichoke as described on pages 34–35, halve lengthwise, and thinly slice lengthwise. Soak the artichoke slices in the lemon water.

2. Cut off the arugula stems, then rinse and dry the leaves. Tear into bite-sized pieces and place in a serving bowl.

3. Trim the tips and roots from the radishes. Thinly slice the radishes and add them to the arugula.

4. Use a sharp knife to cut the rind from the orange with some of the fruit attached. Finely dice until you have about 3 tablespoons and add to the salad.

5. Peel and thinly slice the red onion crosswise. Slice the *bottarga* as thinly as you can and add it to the bowl along with the onion. Drain the artichoke slices and add to the salad. Season with salt. Add the lemon juice and enough olive oil to coat the ingredients. Toss well and serve at once.

SARDINIAN BREAD SALAD

Panzanella Sarda

This bread salad differs from the traditional Tuscan *panzanella* by using pecorino cheese (not surprisingly, Sardinia being the land of sheep's milk cheese) and no cucumbers or onions.

Total time: 15 minutes

Serves 4

> 3 cups cubed crustless day-old bread
> 1½ pounds ripe tomatoes
> 2 ounces medium-aged pecorino cheese
> Salt
> 1 tablespoon red wine vinegar
> 4 to 5 tablespoons extra virgin olive oil

1. Place the bread in a bowl and cover it with cold water.

2. While the bread is soaking, cut the tomatoes into ¾-inch chunks. Place them in a serving bowl.

3. Lift the bread from the water and use your hands to squeeze out as much of the water out as possible. Add it to the tomatoes.

4. Using a peeler, slice thin shavings of the pecorino over the bread and tomatoes. Season with salt and add the vinegar and enough olive oil to coat the ingredients. Toss well and serve at once.

DESSERTS

- **Italian Almond Cake**
- **Flourless Chocolate Cake**
- **Ricotta Pie**
- **Lorella's Ricotta and Amaretti Cake**
- **Grandma's Custard Pie**
- **Neapolitan Lemon Trifle**
- **Tiramisù**
- **Zuppa Inglese**
- **Rum-and-Coffee–Flavored Chocolate Mousse Cake**
- **Raisin, Pine Nut, and Cornmeal Cookies**
- **Berry Salad**
- **Mandarin Orange Sorbet**
- **Cantaloupe Ice Cream**
- **White Nectarine Ice Cream**

Ending an Italian meal with dessert is more the exception than the rule, at least at home. More often, we'll have cheese, dried fruits, and nuts in winter, or just fresh fruit when it's in season. Of course, we don't always abstain from sweets, and there are several desserts here that should satisfy your sweet tooth. They are all simple, easy-to-make, homestyle desserts.

ITALIAN ALMOND CAKE

Torta di Mandorle

This moist, easy-to-make cake is great for breakfast or afternoon tea. Of course, it is also a delicious dessert at the end of a meal, particularly if topped with some whipped cream. Simply whip 1 cup heavy cream with 1 teaspoon sugar just before serving.

Preparation time: 20 minutes
Total time from start to finish: 3 hours

Serves 12

> 12 tablespoons (1½ sticks) unsalted butter, at room
>   temperature, plus extra for greasing the cake pan
> 1½ cups all-purpose flour, plus extra for dusting the cake pan
> 8 ounces unblanched almonds
> 2 teaspoons baking powder
> Pinch salt
> ¾ cup sugar
> 4 large eggs

1. Preheat the oven to 350° on the bake setting. Smear the bottom and sides of a 9-inch springform pan with butter and dust with flour.

2. Put the almonds, 1½ cups flour, baking powder, and salt in a food processor and chop the almonds to a medium-fine consistency. Transfer the almond mixture to a large bowl and set aside.

3. Cut the 12 tablespoons butter into 12 pieces and put it in the bowl of an electric mixer with the sugar. Beat on medium-high speed, preferably with the paddle attachment if you have one, until the mixture is light and fluffy, 2 to 3 minutes.

4. Separate the eggs, adding the yolks to the butter mixture and putting the whites in a separate bowl. Mix until the yolks are thoroughly incorporated. If

you've been using the paddle, add the almond mixture to the bowl with the butter mixture and mix until homogeneous; transfer to a medium bowl. If you have been using a whisk, transfer the butter mixture to a medium bowl, add the almond mixture, and mix thoroughly by hand with a wooden spoon.

5. Wash and dry the bowl and whisk of the electric mixer. Take care that no traces of the butter mixture are left in the bowl or the whites will not whip properly. Whip the egg whites in the electric mixer on high speed until they form firm peaks. Carefully fold the egg whites into the cake batter with a rubber spatula. Pour the batter into the prepared cake pan, shake it gently to even it out, and lightly smooth the surface using the rubber spatula. Bake until a cake tester inserted into the center comes out dry, about 45 minutes.

6. Remove from the oven and cool on a wire rack. Serve at room temperature.

Note: This almond cake will keep for 3 to 4 days in the refrigerator.

FLOURLESS CHOCOLATE CAKE

Torta al Cioccolato

Many cuisines have a flourless chocolate cake in their repertoire and Italy is no exception. A slight variation here is the addition of rum. Also, many recipes require baking in a water bath, which is a somewhat cumbersome procedure. This recipe makes it possible to bake the cake without putting it in water. It is served chilled, and although quite delicious by itself, this cake is fantastic with whipped cream or a sauce made of berries puréed with sugar (or both).

Preparation time: 20 minutes
Total time from start to finish: 12 hours

Serves 12

>   1 pound premium semisweet chocolate
>   16 tablespoons (2 sticks) unsalted butter
>   5 large eggs
>   ½ cup sugar
>   1 tablespoon rum

1. Preheat the oven to 350° on the regular bake setting.

2. Place a saucepan half filled with water over medium heat. Put the chocolate and the butter in a metal bowl and put it over the saucepan. When the chocolate and butter are melted, mix together well with a rubber spatula.

3. In an electric mixer, whip the eggs and the sugar together on high speed until the mixture is smooth and pale yellow, about 3 minutes. Stir in the rum and chocolate mixture.

4. Pour the batter into a 9-inch springform pan and bake for 10 minutes. Cover with aluminum foil and bake for another 15 minutes. Remove the cake from the oven and set aside to cool. Refrigerate the cake overnight.

5. When ready to serve, run a paring knife around the sides, then remove the outer ring of the springform pan. Serve chilled.

Note: The cake will keep refrigerated for 2 to 3 days.

RICOTTA PIE

Torta di Ricotta

I must confess I have never been fond of ricotta pies because they are often too dry for me. I love this ricotta pie, however, because the milk used in the filling makes it lusciously creamy and almost custardlike.

Preparation time: 35 minutes
Total time from start to finish: 6 hours

Serves 8 to 10

> FOR THE PASTRY CRUST
> 2 cups all-purpose flour, plus extra for rolling the crust
> ½ cup sugar
> 8 tablespoons (1 stick) unsalted butter, at room temperature
> 3 large egg yolks
> Grated zest of 1 lemon
> Pinch of salt

1. Preheat the oven to 350° on the regular bake setting.

2. Put the 2 cups flour, sugar, butter, egg yolks, lemon zest, and salt in a food processor and run the processor until mixed well together. If the mixture is too dry, add cold water 1 tablespoon at a time until the mixture forms a smooth dough when you roll it between your fingers.

3. Transfer the dough to a counter and form into a smooth ball. Remove the bottom of a 2-inch-deep, 9-inch-diameter tart pan or a 9-inch springform pan and put it in the center of your work counter. Sprinkle a little flour on the counter around the edges of the pan bottom and place the dough in the middle of the pan bottom. Flatten the dough a bit with your hands, then use a rolling pin to roll it out ⅛ inch thick. Loosen the edges that extend past the pan bottom with a pastry scraper, then use the scraper to lift the pan bottom and the dough. Carefully lower into the ring of the tart or springform pan. Patch any

tears or holes, making sure the dough comes all the way up the sides. Cut off any excess dough at the top. Lightly press a sheet of aluminum foil over the dough and cover with pie weights or dried beans. Put the pan on a baking sheet and bake for 10 minutes. Remove the foil and weights, return the crust to the oven, and bake until very lightly browned, about 10 minutes.

FOR THE FILLING
1 large egg
1 large egg yolk
⅓ cup granulated sugar
⅓ cup all-purpose flour
3 tablespoons 10X confectioner's sugar
1 teaspoon pure vanilla extract
2 cups whole milk
2 cups (1 pound) whole-milk ricotta
2 tablespoons chopped candied citron

4. While the pie crust is baking, make the ricotta filling. Whip the egg, egg yolk, and granulated sugar in an electric mixer on high speed until the mixture is smooth and pale yellow. Add the flour, confectioner's sugar, and vanilla and mix until homogeneous. Slowly pour in the milk while whisking on medium-low speed. Add the ricotta and mix thoroughly. Stir in the candied citron by hand with a rubber spatula.

5. After the crust is done, raise the oven temperature to 375°.

6. Pour the ricotta filling into the pie crust and bake until the filling is firm and begins to brown on top, about 1¼ hours. Test by jiggling the pan gently. Remove from the oven and cool on a wire rack. Refrigerate for at least 3 hours or overnight before serving. Serve chilled.

Note: The pie will keep in the refrigerator for 1 to 2 days.

LORELLA'S RICOTTA AND AMARETTI CAKE

Torta di Ricotta e Amaretti

Lorella, our children's Italian babysitter, has quite a sweet tooth and periodically feels the irresistible urge to make a dessert, an urge we, of course, enthusiastically encourage. This is one of her particularly well-received creations. Amaretti cookies give this ricotta cake a distinctive flavor and texture. It is also quick and simple to prepare.

Preparation time: 25 minutes
Total time from start to finish: 2¾ hours

Serves 8

FOR THE DOUGH
8 tablespoons (1 stick) unsalted butter, at room temperature, plus
    extra for greasing the cake pan
2 cups all-purpose flour, plus extra for dusting the cake pan
⅔ cup sugar
1 tablespoon baking powder
1 teaspoon pure vanilla extract
1 large egg

1. Preheat the oven to 375° on the bake setting. Smear the sides and bottom of a 9-inch springform pan with butter. Add a little flour and shake it around until the butter is coated with flour. Tap out any excess flour.

2. Cut the 8 tablespoons butter into 16 pieces and place it in a medium bowl. Add the 2 cups flour, sugar, baking powder, vanilla, and egg and mix thoroughly with your hands, rubbing the ingredients between your fingers, until the mixture is crumbly and homogeneous.

FOR THE FILLING
1 ounce (⅛ cup) unblanched almonds
⅓ cup granulated sugar
7 ounces amaretti cookies
10 ounces (1¼ cups) whole-milk ricotta
1 large egg
1 tablespoon 10X confectioner's sugar

3. Put the almonds and granulated sugar in a food processor and chop very fine. Transfer to a medium bowl. Coarsely crush the cookies into the bowl with your hands. Add the ricotta and egg. Use a wooden spoon to mix the ingredients very thoroughly.

4. Use your fingers to crumble half of the dough into the springform pan. Pour the ricotta filling on top. Crumble the remaining half of the dough over the filling.

5. Bake until the top turns golden brown, about 45 minutes. Remove from the oven and cool on a wire rack.

6. Dust the top of the cake with the confectioner's sugar. Serve at room temperature or chilled.

Note: The cake will keep 1 to 2 days in the refrigerator.

GRANDMA'S CUSTARD PIE

Torta della Nonna

This deliciously sweet and comforting pie is a favorite in many homes and restaurants throughout northern Italy. The recipe below was given to me by my good friends the talented Simili sisters, award-winning bakers and cookbook authors from Bologna.

Preparation time: 45 minutes
Total time from start to finish: 6½ hours

Serves 8

FOR THE PASTRY CRUST
8 tablespoons (1 stick) unsalted butter, at room temperature
2 cups all-purpose flour, plus extra for rolling the crust
½ cup sugar
1 large egg
1 large egg yolk
Pinch salt

1. Cut the butter into 12 pieces and put it in a food processor with the 2 cups flour, sugar, egg, egg yolk, and salt. Run the machine until the dough comes together and is homogeneous. Remove the dough and place it on a counter. Briefly knead it with your hands to form a smooth ball. Wrap it in plastic and refrigerate for at least 2 hours or overnight.

2. Preheat the oven to 350° on the regular bake setting.

3. Cut the dough into two pieces, one slightly larger than the other. Wrap the smaller piece with plastic and set it aside. Remove the bottom of a 9½-inch tart pan and put it in the center of your work counter. Sprinkle a little flour on the counter around the edge of the pan and place the larger piece of dough in the middle of the pan bottom. Flatten the dough a bit with your hands, then use a rolling pin to roll it out ⅛ inch thick. Loosen the edges that extend past the pan bottom with a pastry scraper, then use the scraper to lift the pan bottom

and the dough. Carefully lower into the ring of the tart pan. Patch any tears or holes, making sure the dough comes all the way up the sides. Cut off any excess dough at the top. Put the pan on a baking sheet and bake until very lightly browned, about 10 minutes. Remove from the oven and set aside.

FOR THE FILLING
1 cup whole milk
1 cup heavy cream
7 tablespoons all-purpose flour
6 tablespoons sugar
3 large eggs
1 large egg yolk
Pinch salt
2 tablespoons unsalted butter, at room temperature
¼ cup pine nuts

4. While the pastry crust is baking, make the filling. Put the milk and heavy cream in a saucepan and place over medium heat. When the mixture releases steam when stirred, but before it comes to a boil, remove the pan from the heat.

5. While the milk and cream are heating, put the flour, sugar, 2 of the eggs, the egg yolk, and salt in the bowl of an electric mixer. Cut the butter into 4 pieces and add to the bowl. Whisk on medium speed until the mixture is smooth, pale, and forms ribbons, 2 to 3 minutes. Transfer the milk and cream to a pitcher. With the mixer on low speed, slowly add the hot milk and cream. Once all the milk and cream have been added, pour the mixture back into the saucepan and place over medium-low heat. Cook, whisking constantly, until the custard thickens, about 10 minutes.

6. Pour the custard into the baked pastry crust. Unwrap the remaining dough and roll it out ⅛ inch thick on a counter sprinkled with flour. Roll the dough onto the rolling pin and unroll over the custard filling. Pinch the edges together, cutting off any excess dough. Lightly beat the remaining egg and brush it over the top of the pie. Sprinkle the pine nuts on top. Bake until the top is golden brown, about 45 minutes. Remove from the oven and cool on a wire rack. Refrigerate for at least 3 hours before serving. Serve chilled.

Note: The pie will keep in the refrigerator for 1 to 2 days.

NEAPOLITAN LEMON TRIFLE

Delizia al Limone

Preparation time: 30 minutes
Total time from start to finish: 12 hours

Serves 6

> 2 lemons
> 4 cups whole milk
> 4 large egg yolks
> ¼ cup granulated sugar
> ¼ cup 10X confectioner's sugar
> ½ cup all-purpose flour
> 2 tablespoons clear cherry brandy, such as kirsch
> 1 tablespoon rum
> 2 tablespoons water
> 8 ounces soft ladyfingers

1. Using a swivel motion with a peeler, as described for peeling tomatoes on pages 30–31, peel the yellow zest of one of the lemons in long strips. Juice the lemon and set the juice aside in a small bowl. Put the lemon zest and milk in a medium saucepan and place over medium heat. When the milk releases steam when stirred, but before it comes to a boil, remove the pan from the heat.

2. Put the egg yolks with both sugars in the bowl of an electric mixer. Whisk at high speed until the mixture is smooth, pale yellow, and forms ribbons, 2 to 3 minutes. Add the flour and mix it in on low speed.

3. Remove the lemon zest from the milk and transfer the milk to a pitcher. With the mixer on low speed, slowly pour in the milk. Once all the milk has been added, return the mixture to the saucepan and place over medium-low heat. Cook, whisking constantly, until the custard thickens, about 10 minutes. Do not be discouraged if nothing seems to happen for a while. When the foam

on the surface begins to subside, the custard will start to thicken. Once the custard is done, remove the pan from the heat.

4. Add the cherry brandy, rum, and water to the reserved lemon juice.

5. Line the bottom of a trifle dish, approximately 10 x 7 inches (or the equivalent), with half of the ladyfingers. Using a pastry brush, dab the ladyfingers with half of the liqueur mixture. Pour half of the custard over them, then top with the remaining ladyfingers. Dab the ladyfingers with the remaining liqueur mixture, then pour the rest of the custard on top. Grate the zest of the remaining lemon and sprinkle it on top. Cover and refrigerate overnight before serving.

   Note: If desired, this dessert can be assembled in individual goblets instead.

TIRAMISÙ

No comprehensive Italian cookbook would be complete without a recipe for tiramisù, even though this dessert was born relatively recently, around the mid-twentieth century in Venice. There are innumerable interpretations but two elements are always present. The first is mascarpone, a creamy, sweet, almost buttery cheese now available in most gourmet specialty shops and many grocery stores. The second is coffee; after all in Italian, *tirami sù* means "pick me up." The flavor of Italian coffee is essential here, but you do not need an expensive espresso machine to make good Italian coffee. Most Italians use a stovetop Moka coffeemaker (page 39). Although not all recipes use them, I believe ladyfingers and Strega liqueur are also essential. Strega, a distillate of about seventy herbs and spices, gives this dessert a unique flavor that makes it worth the effort to hunt it down. If you cannot find Strega, use yellow Chartreuse instead. Be aware that this dessert does contain raw eggs.

Preparation time: 45 minutes
Total time from start to finish: 12 hours

Serves 12

2 cups Italian coffee
About 8 ounces dry ladyfingers
4 large egg yolks
5 tablespoons sugar
3 tablespoons Strega or yellow Chartreuse liqueur
2 tablespoons dark rum
1 pound (500 grams) mascarpone cheese
½ cup heavy cream
1 tablespoon unsweetened cocoa powder

1. Make the coffee and pour it into a shallow bowl wide enough to soak 2 ladyfingers at a time. Set aside to cool.

2. Soak half the ladyfingers in the coffee, 2 at a time, allowing the liquid to penetrate them completely but letting the excess drain out of them, and

place them in a single layer on the bottom of a 3-quart serving dish at least 1½ inches deep.

3. Whisk the egg yolks and sugar with an electric mixer, or by hand with a whisk, until the mixture is smooth, pale yellow, and forms ribbons, 2 to 3 minutes. Mix in the Strega and rum, then mix in the mascarpone, about ½ cup at a time, being careful not to overwhip the mixture so it does not separate.

4. In a separate bowl, whip the cream until it forms firm peaks. Carefully fold the cream into the mascarpone mixture with a rubber spatula.

5. Spread half of the mascarpone mixture over the coffee-soaked ladyfingers. Soak the remaining ladyfingers and arrange them over the mascarpone, then spread the remaining mascarpone mixture on top. Use a fine-mesh strainer or sifter to sprinkle the cocoa over the top, covering the mascarpone mixture completely. Cover the dish with plastic wrap and refrigerate for 12 hours or overnight.

6. Serve chilled, cutting the tiramisù into square portions with a serving spatula and placing them on dessert plates.

ZUPPA INGLESE

Zuppa Inglese means "English soup," probably because it somewhat resembles an English trifle and is customarily eaten with a spoon. It originated in Naples in the nineteenth century and is made of liqueur-soaked pound cake layered with custard and chocolate. Traditionally its distinguishing bright red color comes from soaking the pound cake with Alkermes, a syrupy sweet liqueur of Spanish and Arab origin made from an assortment of spices. Its deep red color comes from being steeped with dry cochineals, which are used to make red dyes. It is difficult to find Alkermes, even in Italy, and most people make it with a combination of liqueurs that usually includes rum. I add grenadine syrup to the mix to give it its distinctive red color.

Preparation time: 30 minutes
Total time from start to finish: 12 hours

Serves 8

> 2 ounces semisweet chocolate
> 3 cups whole milk
> 6 large egg yolks
> 1 cup 10X confectioner's sugar
> ⅓ cup all-purpose flour
> Grated zest of 1 lemon
> 1 store-bought pound cake, about 10 ounces
> ¼ cup grenadine syrup
> 2 tablespoons Cognac
> 2 tablespoons Drambuie
> 1 tablespoon rum
> 2 tablespoons coarsely chopped unblanched almonds or shaved
>   semisweet chocolate for the topping

1. Place a saucepan half filled with water over medium heat. Cut the chocolate into small pieces and put it in a small metal bowl. Put the bowl over the saucepan. Once the chocolate is melted, remove the pot from the heat but leave the bowl with the chocolate over it.

2. Put the milk in a saucepan and place over medium heat. When the milk releases steam when stirred, but before it comes to a boil, remove the pan from the heat.

3. While the milk is heating, whisk the egg yolks and sugar with an electric mixer until the mixture is smooth, pale yellow, and forms ribbons, 2 to 3 minutes. Add the flour and mix it in on low speed. Transfer the hot milk to a pitcher. With the mixer on low speed, slowly pour in the milk.

4. Transfer the mixture to the saucepan you used to heat the milk and place over medium-low heat. Cook, whisking constantly, until the custard thickens, about 10 minutes. Do not be discouraged if nothing seems to happen for a while. When the foam on the surface begins to subside, the custard will start to thicken. Once the custard is done, remove the pan from the heat and stir in the lemon zest.

5. Smear the bottom of a 2½-quart flat-bottomed serving dish at least 2 inches deep with about ½ cup of the hot custard.

6. Cut the pound cake lengthwise into ¼-inch slices and place about one-third of the slices over the custard. Mix together the grenadine, Cognac, Drambuie, and rum in a small bowl. Use a pastry brush to generously dab the cake with the liqueur mixture. Spread one-third of the remaining custard over the cake slices. Cover with another layer of pound cake slices and dab again with the liqueur.

7. Divide the remaining custard in half and mix the melted chocolate into one of the halves. Spread the chocolate custard over the cake, then cover with a final layer of cake slices. Dab the cake with liqueur, then spread the remaining custard on top. Top with chopped almonds or shaved chocolate, cover with plastic wrap, and refrigerate overnight. Serve chilled.

Note: Zuppa Inglese will keep in the refrigerator for 1 to 2 days.

RUM-AND-COFFEE–FLAVORED CHOCOLATE MOUSSE CAKE

Il Diplomatico

Whipping the eggs and sugar when my mother made this dessert was one of my first jobs in the kitchen. Incredibly easy, *Il Diplomatico* always elicits oohs and aahs of delight. As with tiramisù, this dessert requires the flavor of Italian coffee. See page 38 for directions on how to make it.

Preparation time: 45 minutes
Total time from start to finish: 12 hours

Serves 8

> ½ cup Italian coffee
> 3 tablespoons plus 1 teaspoon sugar
> ½ cup water
> 2 tablespoons rum
> 8 ounces semisweet chocolate
> 1 store-bought pound cake, about 12 ounces
> 6 large eggs
> 1 cup heavy cream
> About 1 cup assorted berries, such as strawberries, blackberries,
>   blueberries, and raspberries

1. Make the coffee and mix in 1 tablespoon of the sugar, the water, and rum. Set aside to cool.

2. Place a saucepan half filled with water over medium heat. Cut the chocolate into small pieces and put it in a small metal bowl. Put the bowl over the saucepan. Once the chocolate is melted, remove the pot from the heat but leave the bowl with the chocolate over it.

3. Slice the pound cake lengthwise into ¼-inch slices and line the bottom and sides of a 1½-quart loaf pan with the cake. Use a pastry brush to generously

dab the pound cake with the coffee mixture. The cake should be soaked through but not so drenched that it falls apart.

4. Separate the eggs. Put the yolks in the bowl of an electric mixer and the whites in a separate bowl. Add 2 tablespoons of the sugar to the yolks and whisk until the mixture is smooth, pale yellow, and forms ribbons. Add the melted chocolate and mix well. Whip the egg whites on high speed until they form stiff peaks, then carefully fold them into the chocolate mixture. To make folding easier, mix in a spoonful of egg whites first to soften the mixture.

5. Pour the mixture into the lined loaf pan. Cover with a layer of the remaining sliced pound cake and dab with the coffee mixture. Cover with plastic and refrigerate overnight or up to 2 days.

6. When ready to serve, whip the cream with the remaining 1 teaspoon sugar until it forms firm peaks. Unmold the cake onto a flat plate, tapping it gently to loosen it. Frost it with the whipped cream and decorate with the berries. Serve chilled.

RAISIN, PINE NUT, AND CORNMEAL COOKIES

Zalletti

Yellow cornmeal inspired the name of these deliciously crunchy, chewy cookies—"little yellow ones." This recipe is from the Veneto region of Italy.

Total time: 45 minutes

Makes approximately 2 dozen 2-inch cookies

> 1 cup golden raisins
> 4 tablespoons (½ stick) unsalted butter
> ⅔ cup sugar
> 3 large egg yolks
> Grated zest of 1 lemon
> 1 cup pine nuts
> 2 cups yellow cornmeal
> 2 tablespoons all-purpose flour, plus extra for rolling

1. Put the raisins in a bowl and cover with cold water. Soak until the raisins soften, 20 to 30 minutes.

2. Preheat the oven to 400° on the regular bake setting.

3. Cut the butter into 8 pieces and put it in the bowl of an electric mixer with the sugar. Beat on medium-high speed, preferably with the paddle attachment if you have one, until the mixture is light and fluffy, 2 to 3 minutes. Add the egg yolks and mix until they are thoroughly incorporated.

4. Drain the raisins. If you've been using the paddle attachment, add the raisins to the bowl along with the lemon zest and pine nuts; mix well. If you have been using a whisk, transfer the butter mixture to a medium bowl, add the raisins, lemon zest, and pine nuts, and mix thoroughly by hand with a wooden spoon. Add the cornmeal and flour and mix using the paddle or the wooden spoon until the dough is homogeneous.

5. Transfer the dough to a counter, shape it into a ball with your hands, and flatten it into a thick disk. Sprinkle some flour on the counter and roll out the dough ¼ inch thick with a rolling pin. Use cookie cutters to make as many cookies as you can and place them at least 1½ inches apart on a nonstick cookie sheet or a silicone baking mat placed on a cookie sheet. Shape the remaining dough into a ball again and repeat until you have used up all the dough.

6. Bake the cookies until golden, about 12 minutes. Serve warm or at room temperature.

Note: You can make the dough 1 day ahead and keep it in the refrigerator. Once baked, these cookies will keep for 3 to 4 days at room temperature.

BERRY SALAD

Insalata di Bosco

Grappa is made by distilling the grape skins that are discarded after the initial fermentation process in wine making. It is a potent beverage that, when well made, evokes the fragrances of the grapes. Italians drink it straight after a meal, mix a little with their espresso, sometimes use it in cooking, and also steep cherries in it. Fruit with grappa is a wonderful combination with a distinctively Italian flavor. Berries are used here, but almost any fresh, ripe fruit can be substituted.

Preparation time: 10 minutes
Total time from start to finish: 2¼ hours

Serves 6

> 2 pints assorted berries, such as blueberries, blackberries, raspberries, and golden raspberries
> 6 tablespoons sugar
> 1 lemon
> ½ cup fresh orange juice
> 2 tablespoons grappa

Place the berries in a large serving bowl. Add the sugar. Grate the zest from the lemon and juice half the lemon. Add the zest and juice to the bowl along with the orange juice and grappa. Stir gently, being careful not to damage the berries. Cover the bowl and refrigerate for at least 2 hours or up to 24 hours. Stir once again and serve chilled.

MANDARIN ORANGE SORBET

Sorbetto al Mandarino

Making a sorbet still requires an ice cream maker but almost any kind will work fine. A key ingredient here is prosecco, a light, barrel-fermented, dry sparkling white wine from the Veneto. It is inexpensive, easily available, and on its own makes for a wonderfully refreshing drink before dinner.

Preparation time: 15 minutes
Total time from start to finish: 3 hours

Makes about 1 quart

> 6 mandarin oranges
> 1 cup water
> 1 cup sugar
> 1 cup prosecco
> ¼ cup fresh lemon juice

1. Using a swivel motion with a peeler, as described for peeling tomatoes on pages 30–31, peel the zest from 2 mandarin oranges in long strips. Put the zest with the water and sugar in a small saucepan. Cover, place over medium heat, and bring to a boil. Stir until the sugar is completely dissolved, then remove from the heat.

2. Squeeze all the oranges and measure 1½ cups juice.

3. Discard the orange zests and put the sugar water in a medium bowl. Add the prosecco, mandarin orange juice, and lemon juice and mix well. Refrigerate until cold.

4. Transfer the mixture to an ice cream maker and freeze according to the manufacturer's directions. Transfer the sorbet to a container, cover, and freeze for a couple of hours before serving.

Note: The sorbet will keep in the freezer for several days.

CANTALOUPE ICE CREAM

Gelato di Melone

This simple ice cream uses no eggs, requires no cooking, and will reward you with the essence of cantaloupe flavor.

Preparation time: 15 minutes
Total time from start to finish: 40 minutes

Makes 1 quart

> 1 pound cantaloupe, 1 small or ½ large melon
> ¾ cup sugar
> 2 tablespoons fresh lemon juice
> 1 cup cold water
> ¼ cup heavy cream

1. Cut the rind from the cantaloupe, cut the melon in half, and remove the seeds. Cut the melon into 1-inch chunks and put it in a food processor with the sugar and lemon juice. Run the processor until you have a smooth purée. Add the water and run the processor again to mix.

2. In a large bowl, whip the cream by hand until it thickens to the consistency of yogurt. Pour the melon mixture into the bowl and mix well. Transfer to an ice cream maker and freeze according to the manufacturer's directions. Serve right away if you like a soft consistency. For a firmer ice cream, transfer to a container, cover, and freeze for 2 hours.

Note: The ice cream can be frozen for several days before the surface begins to crystallize.

WHITE NECTARINE ICE CREAM

Gelato di Nettarina Bianca

Preparation time: 10 minutes
Total time from start to finish: 30 minutes

Makes about 3 cups

> 3 white nectarines, about 1 pound
> ½ cup sugar
> 2 tablespoons fresh lemon juice
> ¾ cup water
> ¼ cup heavy cream

1. Cut the nectarines lengthwise in half, twist the halves apart to remove the pits, and peel, using the tomato peeling technique described on pages 30–31.

2. Put the nectarines, sugar, and lemon juice in a food processor or blender and run until puréed. Add the water and run the processor until well mixed.

3. In a large bowl, whip the heavy cream by hand until it thickens to the consistency of yogurt. Add the nectarine mixture to the bowl and stir well. Transfer to an ice cream maker and freeze according to the manufacturer's directions. Serve right away if you like a soft consistency. For a firmer ice cream, transfer to a container, cover, and freeze for 2 hours.

Note: The ice cream can be frozen for several days before the surface begins to crystallize.

ACKNOWLEDGMENTS

Beth Wareham, for your vision, and for so enthusiastically embracing this project, thank you.

Rica Allannic, thank you for the thoroughness with which you went through my manuscript. Your attention to detail has unquestionably made this a better book.

Dana Gallagher, thank you once again for capturing the essence of my food with your mouthwatering images.

Jee Levine, you made my food look so inviting while staying true to my recipes. Thank you for all your hard work.

Laura Maestro, thank you for capturing my techniques so skillfully with your illustrations.

Frank DeFalco, thank you for your support, dedication, and generosity.

David Black, you are always there for me. I value your insight and advice. I am grateful to you for believing in me and, most importantly, for your friendship.

My parents, Victor and Marcella, *grazie* for your guidance and inspiration. What you've taught me has made it possible for me to write this book.

My children, Gabriella and Michela, thank you for your patience all the times I had to work on this book and could not be with you, and for the joy you give me when I cook for you.

My wife, Lael, thank you for your love and unwavering support. Your encouragement and discerning palate are invaluable to me. I am so lucky to have you.

INDEX

bay leaves, pan-seared tuna with fresh
    tomatoes and, 244–45
bean(s), 14
    shrimp and, 55
    and tuna salad, 385–86
    see also specific beans
béchamel sauce, 43
beef, 317–39
    braised with anchovies, 326–27
    braised with lemon, 328–29
    meatballs with tomatoes and peas,
        334–35
    meatloaf with mushrooms, 336–37
    mixed boiled meats (and homemade
        meat broth), 338–39
    rolls filled with cheese, capers, and
        olives, 324–25
    short ribs braised with tomatoes and
        potatoes, 332–33
    sliced steak with arugula and
        pecorino, 322
    sliced steak with olive oil, garlic, and
        rosemary, 320–21
    slow-cooked, "pastisada" style,
        330–31
    steaks, savory, with tomatoes and
        olives, 323–24
    in Tuscan ragù, 110–11
beef tenderloin:
    with balsamic, arugula, and Parmi-
        giano, 317
    with cherries, 318–19
    with tomato, pancetta, and thyme,
        319–20
beet, fresh, salad, 381–82
berry salad, 410
Biete all'Aglio e Olio, 362–63
Biete all'Olio e Limone, 380
Bietole in Insalata, 381–82
Bistecche Saporite, 323–24
black-eyed peas, leek and fennel soup
    with, 74–75
boiled lobster with marjoram and
    parsley sauce, 237

bollito misto, 338–39
Bolognese meat sauce, classic,
    108–10
    lasagna with, 194–95
    with porcini mushrooms, 110
Borlotti all'Olio Salvia, e Aglio,
    367–68
bottarga, 20
    and mozzarella canapés, 48
    as pantry staple, 20
    salad, 386–87
bouillon cubes, 21
Braciola di Maiale all'Aceto Balsamico,
    294–95
Braciole Napoletane, 324–25
braised, braising, 25–26
    beef short ribs with tomatoes and
        potatoes, 332–33
    beef with anchovies, 326–27
    beef with lemon, 328–29
    chicken, with porcini mushrooms,
        264–66
    chicken with peppers and eggplant,
        263–64
    chicken with tomato and chickpeas,
        261–62
    lamb shanks, 312–13
    pork loin, in milk, 297–98
    veal shanks, Milanese style, 283–84
    whole artichokes, Roman style,
        344–45
Branzino Mantecato, 49
Brasato al Limone, 328–29
bread, 20
    tomato soup, Tuscan, 69–70
bread crumbs, 14
    homemade, 42
    maccheroni with olives, and
        anchovies, 160–61
    salad, Sardinian, 388
Broccoletti all'Aglio e Olio, 361
broccoli rabe:
    orecchiette with, 168–69
    sautéed with olive oil and garlic, 361

Giuliano Hazan is the author of two previous cookbooks, *The Classic Pasta Cookbook,* nominated for a James Beard Award in 1994, and *Every Night Italian,* winner of the World Cookbook Award for best Italian cookbook in the English language. Hazan teaches students "how to cook Italian" at cooking schools throughout North America and abroad; in Italy, together with their partner, Marilisa Allegrini, Hazan and his wife have a school in Verona's wine country. Visit Hazan's website at www.giulianohazan.com. He lives in Sarasota, Florida, with his wife, Lael, and their two daughters, Gabriella and Michela.